India and West Asia in the Era of Globalisation

India and West Asia in the Era of Globalisation

Edited by
Anwar Alam

New Century Publications
New Delhi, India

NEW CENTURY PUBLICATIONS
4800/24, Bharat Ram Road,
Ansari Road, Daryaganj,
New Delhi - 110 002

Tel.: 23247798, 65396605
Telefax: 011-41017798
E-mail: indiatax@vsnl.com
www.newcenturypublications.com

Editorial office:
34, Gujranwala Town, Part-2,
Delhi - 110 009
Tel.: 27247805, 27464774

First Published - 2008

ISBN 13: 978-81-7708-154-1
ISBN 10: 81-7708-154-3

Published by New Century Publications and printed at Singhal Print Media, New Delhi -110 005

PRINTED IN INDIA

CONTENTS

About the book viii
Editor's Profile ix
Editor's Introduction x
Contributors xxi

Part I: Globalisation, India and WANA: Theoretical Dimensions

1. **Hamid Ansari:** India and West Asia in the Era of Globalisation 3

2. **Achin Vanaik:** National Interest: A Flawed Notion-Explaining the Shift in Indian Foreign Policy in the Age of Neo-liberal Globalisation and its Implications for WANA Region 10

3. **A.K. Ramakrishnan:** Neo-liberal Globalist: Transformations in India's Foreign Policy: Implications for West Asia and North Africa 25

Part II: Globalisation, India and WANA: Energy Security Dimensions

4. **Gulshan Dietl:** Transnational Gas Pipelines: Global Context, Indian Experience 33

5. **Shebonti Ray Dadwal:** Can West Asia Retain its Position in the Oil Market? Implications for India 43

Part III: Globalisation, India and Gulf: Economic Dimensions

6. **Javed Ahmad Khan:** India and Arab Gulf's Look East Policy: Strengthening Economic Relations since 1995 55

7. **N. Janardhan:** GCC-India Relations: What Next? 71

Part IV: Globalisation, India and WANA: Political Dimensions

8. **Chintamani Mahapatra:** American Hegemony in WANA Region: Challenges for India 93

9. **Qamar Agha:** Indo-Arab Relations: The Pakistan Factor 107

Part V: Globalisation, India and WANA: Cultural and Diasporic Dimensions

10. **Aftab Kamal Pasha:** India's Cultural Diplomacy in West Asia and North Africa 127

11. **Prakash C. Jain:** Globalisation and Indian Diaspora in West Asia and North Africa: Some Policy Implications 161

12. **El Sayed Mekkawi:** The Changing Dimensions of India's Image in the Arab World 188

Part VI: Globalisation, India and North Africa: Bilateral Dimensions

13. **Jagdish P. Sharma:** Fostering Ties with the Arab-African World 219

14. **John Cherian:** The Ongoing Struggle for Independence: Saharawi Arab Democratic Republic and Indo-Algerian Ties 227

15. **Sebastian N:** Social Development, State and Globalisation: A Comparative Study of Egypt and India 241

Part VII: Globalisation, India and Israel-Palestine Conflict

16. **P.R. Kumaraswamy:** Contextualising Israel in India's Middle East Policy 273

17. **Bansidhar Pradhan:** Globalisation and the Shift in India's Palestine Policy 286

18. **Sujata Ashwarya Cheema:** Palestinian-Israeli Peace Process in the 'New Middle East': Can India Have a Role to Play? 303

Index 321

ABOUT THE BOOK

India's foreign policy posture in recent years, particularly towards the region of West Asia and North Africa (WANA), has been a subject of intense debate. India's growing relationship with the US and Israel, and its 'lukewarm stand' on Iraqi crisis and Iranian nuclear issue has been seen as a fundamental shift in the Indian foreign policy exercise. Critics have accused the succeeding Indian governments during the past one and half decades of abandoning its 'independent' foreign policy, of deviating from Nehruvian national consensus in foreign policy matters, and towing the pro-American line. Others have argued that the radical shift in the orientation of Indian foreign policy in terms of its pro-American tilt bears the mark of "realism" and "pragmatism" that is dictated by the demand of globalisation. Therefore, at a broader level, this book seeks to capture the emerging orientation of Indian state vis-à-vis the region of WANA in the context of globalisation. In particular, it examines the political, economic, cultural, security and diasporic dimensions of the evolving relationship between India and countries of WANA in the context of globalisation.

EDITOR'S PROFILE

Anwar Alam is Professor and Deputy Director at the Centre for West Asian Studies, Jamia Millia Islamia, New Delhi. He obtained his M.A., M.Phil. and Ph.D. degrees from Jawaharlal Nehru University (JNU), New Delhi. He has served as lecturer in the Department of Political Science, Aligarh Muslim University, Aligarh and Assistant and Associate Professor at the Centre for West Asian and African Studies, JNU, New Delhi. He has been awarded the ICSSR Doctoral Fellowship, International Visitor Programme (Islamic) Scholarship, USA, Indo-French Social Scientist Exchange Programme Fellowship and Alexandor Von Humboldt Post-doctoral Fellowship. He has been a Visiting Fellow at Maison des Sciences de l'Homme (MSH), Paris, Centre for Citizenship and Ethnicity, Department of Sociology, University of Bristol, Bristol, UK and International Institute for the Study of Islam in the Modern World (ISIM), Leiden, Netherlands. He has authored a book, *Religion and State: A Comparative Study of Contemporary Egypt, Iran and Saudi Arabia* (1998) and contributed several articles in national and international referred journals. His areas of research interest include Religion and Politics, Political Islam, Globalisation and Muslim society.

EDITOR'S INTRODUCTION

Globalisation, though a contested term, is a complex and multifaceted phenomenon. While there is no scholarly consensus on the meaning and dimension of globalisation, it is considered as affecting all parts of human life and their institutions viz., social, cultural, economic and political. Perhaps its impact on the notion of nation-state was felt more deeply than in any other area of social science. In this context, the debate has mainly centered on the theme of 'fragmentation' of region/nation or re-assertion of national identity. Its implications for the foreign policy exercise have hardly been explored. Therefore, at a broader level, this book seeks to capture the emerging orientation of Indian foreign policy vis-a vis the region of WANA in the context of globalisation and its implications for the future relationship between the two.

India's foreign policy posture in recent years, particularly towards the region of WANA, has been a subject of intense debate. India's growing relationship with the US and Israel, and its 'lukewarm stand' on Iraqi crisis and Iranian nuclear issue has been seen as a fundamental shift in the Indian foreign policy exercise. Critics have accused the succeeding Indian governments during the past one and half decades of abandoning its 'independent' foreign policy, of deviating from Nehruvian national consensus on foreign policy matters, and towing the pro-American line. Others have argued that the radical shift in the orientation of Indian foreign policy in terms of its pro-American tilt bears the mark of "realism" and "pragmatism" that is dictated by the demand of globalisation.

The significance of WANA for India in terms of oil, gas and labour remittance is too well known to be repeated here. However, most of the works relating to this area either focus on the conventional bilateral relationship between India and the countries of WANA or highlight the economic potential of this region for India. Studies on the bilateral relationship between the countries concerned are by no means an unimportant academic activity and are considered very vital from a foreign policy perspective. However this volume, while highlighting on the various aspects of bilateral relationship between India and the countries of WANA, seeks to understand how globalisation is changing the conception of the region of WANA and how it affects the Indian perception of the region.

Though defining 'globalisation' appears the most problematic part, various papers that have been listed in this volume have tried to capture the 'sense of globalisation' while analyzing their respective themes. The volume unfolds itself with *key note address* delivered by Ambassador Hamid Ansari. In his address titled *India and West Asia in the Era of Globalisation,* he has outlined the complexities surrounding the term globalisation and concluded that in terms of the accepted criteria of globalisation, neither India nor the West Asian countries are considered a success in globalisation. The question of globalisation-induced foreign policy orientation, according to him, therefore, has to be approached more in terms of possible future developments rather than for existing ground realities.

Reflecting on the debate whether India has a regional foreign policy, he showed how Indian strategists have rightly fashioned its foreign policy orientation by dividing WANA into two broad segments: Persian-Gulf littoral and hinterland (GCC, Iraq, Iran, Yemen, Saudi Arabia) and other areas of West Asia and North Africa (Egypt, Jordan, Israel, Palestine, Syria, Libya, Morocco, Sudan, Algeria, etc). As globalisation in this region, particularly in the Persian Gulf states, is likely to increase the business opportunity for India in the field of education, healthcare, information technology, construction services, insurance and banking, business and financial services, and tourism, a long-term political stability and stable security in this region is very vital for India. He cautioned the Indian government from buying the American understanding of globalisation that has an element of Clash of Civilizations. As far as the second group is concerned, the principal challenge to Indian policy, according to him, lies in crafting an approach that would maintain equilibrium between the technology-cum-strategic relationship with Israel and the political relations with the larger Arab states some of whom are in the process of becoming partners in the energy calculus.

This part of the book also reflects on the conceptual and theoretical dimensions of Indian foreign policy exercise vis-à-vis the region of WANA in the context of globalisation. Apart from Ansari's article, the other two articles that have reflected upon this aspect of Indian foreign policy are Achin Vanaik, *National Interest - A Flawed Notion: Explaining the Shift in Indian Foreign Policy in the Age of Neo-liberal Globalisation and its Implications for WANA Region* and A.K. Ramakrishnan, *Neo-liberal Globalist: Transformations in India's Foreign Policy: Implications for West Asia and North Africa.*

Vanaik's paper provides a critique of the notion of "national interest" around which matters concerning foreign policy of any nation is generally understood. He debunks the realist construction of national interest as 'myth'. For him, the notion of national interest is nothing but a principle of legitimation and justification of foreign policy of a nation. It lacks any analytical value to explain the changes in the foreign policy behaviour of a state. According to him, it is the political (and therefore moral) character of the leadership strata that shapes and makes foreign policy decisions. This political and moral character of these important social layers (usually dominant classes and their middle class support base) changes over time. It is itself shaped by the changes in power relations between classes and social groups nationally and internationally as well as between countries. It is reflective of the changes that take place in the dominant forms of thought and values. It is changed by the complex concatenation of processes and events that have taken place over time domestically and globally.

Applying the above theoretical premise of understanding of a foreign policy orientation, he demonstrates how since the end of Cold War, India has been pursuing politics in geo-economic dimension (strengthening neo-liberal economic policies) and geo-political dimension (strengthening of relationship with US and Israel). He, therefore, concludes that one should not expect the

Indian government to do anything positive when it comes to relations with the region of WANA where the United States is the most dominant power.

Ramakrishnan also identifies the shift in India's foreign policy orientation to the context of what he calls 'neo-liberal globalism'. According to him, the shift in India's public policy, particularly foreign policy, is not from ideology to pragmatism as generally described, but from an earlier developmental statist ideology and practice to a neo-liberal ideology and practice.

Since the beginning of 1990s, India has emerged as one of fastest growing economies in the world. This has brought the issue of energy security as a matter of uppermost national concern. The government of India has come out with a comprehensive document of Hydrocarbon Vision 2025 to realize the goal of energy security. There are two papers that have reflected on this dimension. These are Gulshan Dietl, *Transnational Gas Pipelines: Global Context, Indian Experience* and Shebonti Ray Dadwal, *Can West Asia Retain its Position in the Oil Market? Implications for India.*

Dietl highlights strategic importance of pipelines—whether gas or oil—that cut across several regions and countries. According to her, gaining access to or control over energy pipelines in today's globalised world has been the driving force behind much of geopolitics. The politics behind pipelines is full of power play that has a spill-over effect in other areas of co-operation between/among the parties and often kills the most sensible and mutually beneficial constructions. This she has demonstrated by examining three gas pipelines: Turkmenistan-Russia-Ukraine pipeline, El Gran Gasoducto del Sur and the Iran-Pakistan-India pipeline.

Dadwal argues that compared to all available sources of oil and gas, Gulf remains a reliable source of energy supplies. She has noted how the share of consumption pattern of oil and gas resources among the Asian countries including India is rising steadily against the industrialized nations of the US, EU and Japan. Reflecting on this trend and its implications for India's energy security she argues that with the demand for oil in India projected to double over the next two decades, it is in New Delhi's interest to ensure augmentation of international production, for reasons pertaining to supply security as well as prices. She concludes by suggesting that given the several threats that the oil market is facing, ranging from regional conflicts, terrorist threats and domestic political problems, it is only through cooperation—bilateral as well as multilateral—that individual countries can ensure their energy security.

How does globalisation affect the economic cooperation between India and other countries of WANA, particularly the Gulf States where India's stake is considered very high. Should Indian diplomacy be geared to go beyond economic cooperation and develop very strong political and strategic relations with the countries of Gulf region? These are the few questions that have been addressed in two sets of inter-related papers. These are: Javed Ahmad Khan, *India and Arab Gulf's Look East Policy: Strengthening Economic Relations since 1995* and N. Janardhan, *India-GCC Relations: What Next*?

Ahmad tries to capture the emerging trend of economic cooperation between the Gulf and India since 1995. He underlines the reasons for the growing investment of GCC states in the Asian region, particularly India. According to him, the GCC has emerged as India's fastest growing trading partner with two-way trade moving above US$ 16 billion, surpassing China and lagging behind US only. He concludes by suggesting that India must seize this opportunity of mutual goodwill, must be more transparent while enhancing friendship with Arabs and remove unnecessary barriers in order to attract Gulf markets.

Janardhan, while recognising the importance of GCC's Look East Policy, argues that the GCC's new 'Look East' policy has to go beyond preferential trading arrangements and newfound political warmth, and address security strategies as well. Such political and security arrangements must go beyond the US-centric security paradigm that prevails in the Gulf. He concludes that notwithstanding the historic ties between the GCC and India, which have been sustained by the current oil, trade and expatriate dynamics, the way forward for a robust bilateral relationship between the two rests on developing a paradigm that hinges on strategic political, economic and security dimensions.

One of the most important developments that are linked with the aspects of globalisation is the emergence of Pax-Americana. Whereas the cold war period was understood to provide a space for third parties like India to pursue their legitimate interest in various regions including WANA, the over-riding supremacy of America in the Gulf war of 1990-91 leading to occupation of Iraq is considered diminishing the same. How far and in what manner the US hegemony in WANA has affected the capacity of Indian state to play its independent role in the region? How far the involvement of Pakistan in the strategic design of the United States has adversely affected the legitimate interest of India in the region? What are the challenges that Indian foreign policy faces in the light of these developments? These inter-related questions have been explored in the two set of papers. These are: Chintamani Mahapatra, *American Hegemony in WANA Region: Challenges for India* and Qamar Agha, *Indo-Arab Relations: The Pakistan Factor*.

Mahapatra provides a historical background of how US sought to establish its hegemony in the world for over last century. Though he recognizes US as the most dominant power in the world, but argues that the US has not been successful in exercising the complete hegemony, including the WANA region. He cautions the Indian government for building a 'strategic partnership' with the US at a time when there is growing anti-Americanism in the WANA region. The central challenge for India, according to him, lies in its growing stakes in the WANA region but without an adequate clout or power to realize the same. In other words, how to maintain a balancing act that meets the American aspirations as well as concerns and needs of the Arab states in the region is the challenge for Indian diplomacy. Hence, according to the author, developing a viable and long-term strategy is the need of the time.

Agha highlights the significance of 'Pakistan factor' in affecting India's relations with Arab countries in both pre-globalisation and post-globalisation periods. He draws a conclusion that since it is the economics, not political-ideological issues, that matters most in the conduct of foreign policy of any nation in the age of globalisation, Pakistan is unlikely to adversely affect the growing cooperative relations between Arab states and India.

Globalisation has brought the cultural interface and interactions among the human civilizations and societies much closer. As a result 'culture', though always has been a factor in conducting inter-state relationship, is increasingly being recognized as an important ingredient in influencing the discourses about foreign policy. States and nations are now increasingly engaged in using its cultural resources to maximize its external goals. Similarly, globalisation has decisively affected the pace of what is called 'pull' and 'push' factors of the process of migration, making the existing nations relatively more plural. This has led to a re-conceptualization of 'labour-immigrants' as 'diasporic community'. As a result 'diaspora' is fast emerging an important aspect of foreign policy goals. There are three papers that have reflected on these aspects of globalisation and its implications for structuring the relationship between India and the countries of the WANA. These are: Aftab Kamal Pasha, *India's Cultural Diplomacy in West Asia and North Africa*, Prakash C. Jain, *Globalisation and Indian Diaspora in West Asia and North Africa: Some Policy Implications* and El Sayed Mekkawi, *The Changing Dimensions of India's Image in the Arab World.*

Pasha provides a historical account of cultural exchanges that have been taking place between India and the countries of West Asia and North Africa since time immemorial. Globalisation as a process has further resulted in the multiple avenues of cultural interactions and contacts between the two. He highlights the role of films, artists, music, and scholars in the cultural exchanges between the two.

Jain first analyzes the meaning of globalisation and then proceeds to understand its implication for the Indian diasporic community in the Gulf. He concludes how in spite of the variable and at times contradictory effects of globalisation processes—the movement of people, capital and ideas—India has been successful in exploiting them to its economic advantage. According to him, not only an ever-increasing number of Indians are migrating abroad, particularly to the Gulf countries, the quantum of remittances, investment and trade networking has also grown significantly. The bond between India and its diaspora has given a new meaning and form to 'Indianess' that is increasingly global.

Mekkawi reflects upon the changing image of India in the Arab World. He underlines that historically India has enjoyed good image in the Arab world. However since 1990s the image of India has started deteriorating both among the elites and masses of the Arab world. The rise of Hindutava ideology, the demolition of Babri Masjid, Gujarat riots (2002) and growing Indo-Israeli relations are some of the factors that, according to him, have affected the image of India adversely in the Arab World.

Though the Persian Gulf countries often receive disproportionate attention on the subject matters of Indo- West Asia relationship due to the factors that have been mentioned earlier, India's bilateral relations with the countries of North Africa in the context of globalisation have not been adequately explored. There are three set of papers that fill this gap. These are: Jagdish P. Sharma, *Fostering Ties with theArab-African World*, John Cherian, *The Ongoing Struggle for Independence: Saharawi Arab Democratic Republic and Indo-Algerian Ties,* Sebastian N, *Social Development, State and Globalisation: A Comparative Study of Egypt and India.*

Sharma highlights the historical role of India in fostering closer relation with the countries of Arab Africa (i.e. North Africa) that is further strengthened by economic and commercial linkages. He points out a number of joint venture projects that have been concluded between India and Algeria, Morocco, Sudan, Jordan, Tunisia and Libya.

Cherian reflects on the historical relations between India and Algeria. He emphasizes how the de-recognition of SADR by the Indian government in 2002 brought strain between the two countries. As a consequence of this act India also lost moral influence in much of the African continent. Despite the setback, the author has noted that the bilateral trade between the two countries has gone up to US$ 256 million in 2004. India was invited as an observer for the first time during the Arab League summit held in Algiers in 2005. He concludes that India needs to assert the principle of Non-Aligned Movement in foreign policy in order to foster the closer relations with Algeria and other African countries.

Sebastian undertakes a comparative study of the role of state in social development in the age of globalisation with special reference to Egypt and India. He explores how the difference in the political structure in India and Egypt affects the process of globalisation in dealing with their social development goals.

Finally, this book reflects on the problems of the Arab world, i.e. the Israeli-Palestinian conflict. Is globalisation changing the Indian perception about the 'Palestinian Question' and state of Israel? What are the directions of shift in the Indian position via-a vis the issue of Israel-Palestine conflict, if there is any? There are three papers that have reflected on this issue. These are: P.R. Kumaraswamy, *Contextualising Israel in India's Middle East Policy*, Bansidhar Pradhan, *Globalisation and the Shift in India's Palestine Policy* and Sujata Ashwarya Cheema,*Palestinian-Israeli Peace Process in the 'New Middle East': Can India Have a Role to play?*

Kumaraswamy, argues how developments of late 1980s and early 1990s fundamentally altered the status quo and India was presented with the freedom to pursue a foreign policy without any overarching ideological framework or prism. This became the background for the gradual normalisation of relations with Israel. However, he concludes that the real importance of normalization and need for a closer ties with Israel would have to be understood within the larger West Asian context. A mere bilateral approach towards Israel would prevent India from identifying and benefiting from it.

Pradhan in his paper notes the negative shift in India's foreign policy towards Palestine. According to him, compulsions of the current phase of globalisation played key roles in effecting this shift. Further, the paper demonstrates how both the US and Israel played a crucial role in influencing India's Palestine policy. Thus, in the post-Cold War period, the compulsions of globalisation and the predominant role that the US plays in the process have probably forced India to dilute its earlier pro-Palestine policy.

Cheema's paper echoes similar concern as that of Pradhan concerning the role of Indian foreign policy vis-a-vis Israeli-Palestinian conflict. Her essay analyses the future of the peace process in the context of the New Middle East, as understood by the current US administration, and seeks to investigate India's role therein. She argues that given a context where India is seeking a closer relationship with the United States and the Neocons in the American administration working hard to ensure that Israel is not pressurised to negotiate with the Palestinians, the role of India in the peace process in the New Middle East is insignificant. She concludes that despite its consistent support for the Palestinian cause and later normalization of relations with Israel, India has not been able to play any role in the peace process.

Many efforts have gone in making this book a reality, which is an outcome of the two day national seminar on 'India and WANA in the Era of Globalisation' organised by the Centre for West Asian and African Studies, School of International Studies, Jawaharlal Nehru University, New Delhi. The seminar would not have been possible without the financial support of Jawaharlal Nehru University (JNU), New Delhi and Indian Council of Social Science Research (ICSSR), New Delhi. Therefore, I would like to acknowledge the same. Thanks are also due to students, particularly those belonging to the Centre for West Asian and African Studies, School of International Studies (SIS), JNU, for their efforts in organizing and participating in the Seminar. In this regard, my special thanks to Kumar Raka who provided a valuable assistance in editing this volume. A special note of appreciation is also for Rakesh Ranjan, Virushal, Junaid, Abdul Ansari and Nijish who helped me at different stages in organizing the Seminar. I would also like to express my deep sense of gratitude to all paper contributors for taking pains in writing for this volume.

Last but not the least, I would like to thank New Century Publications, New Delhi, for bringing out this book in the academia for larger debates and discussions. All omissions and commissions related to this book would rest with me.

New Delhi

Anwar Alam

CONTRIBUTORS

Hamid Ansari has held many distinguished posts including Permanent Representative of Government of India to the UN, Vice-chancellor, Aligarh Muslim University, Aligarh and Chairman, National Commission of Minorities. He has edited a book and contributed numerous articles in national and international dailies and journals. He is currently the Vice President of the Republic of India.

Achin Vanaik is Professor of International Relations and Global Politics in the Department of Political Science, University of Delhi. He has been a Fellow at the Transnational Institute (TNI), Amsterdam since 1987. He has authored 5 books apart from 4 edited and co-edited volumes. Moreover, he has contributed chapters for various books and articles for numerous national and international academic journals.

A.K. Ramakrishnan is Reader and former Director, School of International Relations and Politics, Mahatma Gandhi University, Kottayam, Kerala. He was a Distinguished International Scholar at Bucknell University, Pennsylvania, USA. His articles and reviews have been published in national and international journals.

Gulshan Dietl is Professor and Director, the Gulf Studies Programme, Centre for West Asian and African Studies, Jawaharlal Nehru University, New Delhi. She has authored many books and contributed articles in various national and international referred journals on different aspects of West Asia. Her latest co-edited publication is *Contemporary Saudi Arabia and the Emerging Indo- Saudi Relations* (2007).

Shebonti Ray Dadwal is a Research Fellow at the Institute of Defence and Strategic Analysis (IDSA), New Delhi.

Javed Ahmad Khan is Reader at the Centre of West Asian Studies, Jamia Millia Islamia, New Delhi. His most recent publication is *India's Energy Security and the Arabian Gulf: Oil and Gas Market in Decontrolled Regime* (2005).

N. Janardhan is the Program Manager of Gulf-Asia Relations, and Editor of 'Gulf in the Media' at the Gulf Research Center in Dubai. He was formerly with the "The Asian Age" (New Delhi) and "The Gulf Today" (UAE) dailies, and was the Gulf correspondent for the Inter Press Service (Bangkok). He has had over 350 analyses published in Indian and Middle East newspapers.

Chintamani Mahapatra is Associate Professor at the School of International Studies, Jawaharlal Nehru University, New Delhi. He was a Fulbright Scholar at the University of Delaware, USA, Commonwealth Scholar at the University of London, Foreign Policy Fellow at University of Maryland, USA, Salzburg Seminar Fellow in Austria and a Visiting Fellow at the Australian Defence Studies Centre, Canberra. He has several academic publications to his credit in India and abroad.

Qamar Agha is Visiting Professor at the Center for West Asian Studies, Jamia Millia Islamia, New Delhi. He was a UGC Fellow for the Gulf Studies programme during 1978-80. He also edited "Arab Concept", a quarterly journal published by the League of Arab States, New Delhi, during 1980-87.

Jagdish P. Sharma was Head, Department of African Studies, University of Delhi, Delhi. He has extensively written on different aspects of West Asia and North Africa.

John Cherian is Foreign Correspondent and Associate Editor of *Frontline*, Hindu Group of Newspapers. He has extensively written on different aspects of North Africa.

Sebastian N teaches at the Kunjali Marakkar Centre for West Asian and Indian Ocean Studies, University of Calicut, Kerala.

Aftab Kamal Pasha is Professor at the Centre for West Asian and African Studies, School of International Studies, Jawaharlal Nehru University, New Delhi. He has served as Director, Maulana Azad Centre for Indian Culture (MACIC), Cairo, Egypt. He has published over ten books, edited over 12 books and contributed chapters to over 30 books published in India and abroad. His research articles have also been published in numerous national and international journals.

Prakash C. Jain is with the Centre for West Asian Studies, School of International Studies, Jawaharlal Nehru University, New Delhi. His areas of academic interest are: West Asian Studies, Indian Diaspora and the Jain Community. His most recent publication is *Indian Diaspora in West Asia: A Reader* (2007). He has to his credit a number of articles published in Indian and foreign journals.

El Sayed Mekkawi is a Senior Lecturer in the Department of, Faculty of Arts, Minufyia University, Egypt.

P.R. Kumaraswamy is Associate Professor at Centre for West Asian Studies, School of International Studies, Jawaharlal Nehru University, New Delhi.

Bansidhar Pradhan is Associate Professor at the Centre for West Asian and African Studies, School of International Studies, JNU. He is the author of three books, the most recent being Dynamics of Conflict and Peace in West Asia (2003).

Sujata Ashwarya Cheema is a lecturer at the Centre for West Asian Studies, Jamia Millia Islamia, New Delhi. She was awarded the Israeli Government Graduate Fellowship (2002-03) and HERMES Post-Doctoral Fellow (January 07-September 07), France. Her publications include *Structures of Political Violence in Palestinian-Israeli Conflict* (2005) and many research papers and articles.

Part I: Globalisation, India and WANA: Theoretical Dimensions

1

India and West Asia in the Era of Globalisation

Hamid Ansari

The subject is nebulous enough for a speaker to wonder off and allow free play to fancy! The purpose of the organisers, I presume, is to force stray wisdom to return to the fold.

Ours is an age of catchwords and prevailing fashions. The term globalisation falls in that category. Its connotation covers matters economic, technological, cultural and political. The precise content of the package is left to the individual user, and is therefore susceptible to considerable subjectivity. As an umbrella term, it refers to the complex series of economic, social, technological, cultural and political changes seen as increasing interdependence, integration and interaction between people and organisations in disparate locations. In current popular parlance, however, the term is primarily a synonym for global business.

Although an older vintage is claimed for it, the term is of fairly recent origin. A collection of papers entitled *Internationalisation and Domestic Politics*, edited in 1996 by Professors Robert Koehane of Harvard and Helen Milner of Columbia, examined various aspects of internationalisation of the world economy and politics but does not use the term *globalisation*.

For the political and strategic relevance of globalisation, we have to thank Dr. Thomas Barnett. His 2003 book *The Pentagon's New Map* argues for a more effective system of global security as an essential requirements for globalisation; he expressed it in the form of an extended syllogism: stability is essential for markets and growth; growth requires resources, resources need infrastructure, infrastructure depends on money, money on rules, and rules on stability; this stability requires a Leviathan having the will and capability of using force. The United States personifies the Leviathan.

More recently Philip Bobbitt in *The Shield of Achilles* uses the expression 'market state' to describe the new role into which the nation-state has been cast as a result of three factors that operate beyond national frontiers: threats, markets and culture. He visualises a future scenario that would give a menu of three to choose from: a *Meadow* in which the entrepreneurial market-state is predominant, a *Park* in which national governments play a far larger role in defining common interest, and a *Garden* in which the role of governments is supportive rather than regulatory.

These perceptions may be dominant but have not gone unchallenged. Prem Shankar Jha, amongst others, has drawn attention to the negative effects of globalisation. The choice, he says, is between the travails of an empire and the benefits of a cooperative commonwealth.

II

This audience presumably know a good deal about the extent of globalisation in relation to India. For today's discussion, it is equally necessary to be clear about its inroads in West Asian lands. Only then would a discussion about interaction be meaningful.

For the past five years the journal *Foreign Policy* has published in conjunction with *A.T. Kearney Inc.* a Globalisation Index relating to 62 countries that together account for 96 per cent of the world's gross GDP and 85 per cent of the population. It measures 12 variables in four baskets: economic integration, technological connectivity, personal contact, and political engagement.

A study of the Index is relevant to our discussion. The Index is headed by Singapore and only Israel from West Asia is included in the list of the first twenty countries. Beyond it we find Tunisia at serial number 37, Morocco at 40, Saudi Arabia at 45, Egypt at 59 and Iran at the bottom of the list at 62.

Apart from West Asia, Pakistan is at 50, Russia at 52, China 54, Bangladesh at 58, and India at 61, just above Iran. It almost matches our performance in world soccer or Olympics! It is in inverse proportion to our enthusiasm for globalisation, and altogether admirable!!

Another study, by Ali Abdel Gadir Ali of the Kuwait Planning Institute, used the World Bank's trade and FDI measures of globalisation to conclude that barring a few, most of the Arab world was not in the fold.

In a paper published in 2003, the Director General of the Arab Fund for Economic Development Abdlatif Al-Hamad sought to analyse the challenges of globalisation to the Arab world and identified three major deficiencies:

- Failure of liberalisation to go beyond the economic field of free market and private enterprise into political, institutional and cultural liberalisation.
- Failure of modernisation, arising out of the apprehension of diluting Arab and Islamic identity.
- Failure to integrate into the world economy.

Al-Hamad felt globalisation is not a threat but an opportunity to accelerate the slow pace of liberalisation, modernisation and integration. For this to happen, he wrote, Arab countries need to take five initiatives:

- Improve production capacity, information capabilities, and transport systems.
- Create a financial system that is more open and competitive.
- Enhance capacity for technological innovation.
- Reduce levels of unemployment and create more employment opportunities.
- Improve governance both in business circles and at the national levels.

The conclusion that emerges is that in terms of the accepted criteria of globalisation, neither India nor the West Asian countries are considered a success in globalisation. The question of globalisation-induced foreign policy orientations, therefore, has to be approached more in terms of possible future developments rather than for existing ground realities. With this caveat, it would be a useful and interesting exercise in scenario building.

One other conceptual question needs clarification. This relates to the contours of Indian policy towards *West Asia.* It was said in an editorial this week that India does not have a coherent West Asian policy. Is Indian policy region-oriented? Can there be a policy towards East Asia, West Asia, South Asia or any other region of the world having many state entities and considerable diversity? There is also an identifiable subset in the shape of the Arab State system with all its internal contradictions. Beyond it, and on the two extremities, are stand-alone State entities in the shape of Israel and Iran.

The ground reality, therefore, is polycentric. By no stretch of imagination can one visualise a *regional* policy amidst such conflicting diversity. At best, a *regional* policy can address itself to common factors; this necessitates a diligent exercise in discovering such commonality.

A number of other questions come to mind:

- In what manner would the imperatives of globalisation influence policy perceptions at the Indian and the West Asian ends?
- Would globalisation change the core Indian national interest in the region or in relation to individual countries of the region?
- Would the balance of forces, policy perceptions, and the modalities of conducting policy undergo a change?

III

From a general Indian perspective, West Asia has traditionally been considered in two segments: (1) the Persian Gulf littoral and hinterland and (2) other areas of West Asia and North Africa.

The Persian Gulf littoral and hinterland covers the six states of GCC (Bahrain, Kuwait, Oman. Qatar, Saudi Arabia and the United Arab Emirates, Iraq and Iran. Yemen, though not on the Gulf littoral, may be considered a part of it for geo-political reasons on account of its land area, population and location in the Arabian peninsula. Iran occupies the whole of the northern coast of the Gulf and has a coastline of 2440 km; Iraq, by contrast, has 58 km. The narrow entrance to the Gulf in the Straits of Hormuz is controlled on the one side by Iran and on the other by Oman. This entire sub-region is:

- Within the security parameter of India and within the operational radius of the Indian Navy.
- Principal source of imported hydrocarbon energy supplies.
- Principal destination for manpower exports that provides employment to 3.5 million Indian nations whose remittances exceed to US$ 7 billion per annum.
- A major trading partner with overall trade in the vicinity of US$ 18-20 billion.
- An increasingly important destination for Indian projects, and IT services.
- Having an India-friendly and Indian-friendly orientation and desirous of enhancing its political, economic and technological interaction with India.

For each of these reasons, political stability and continued vibrancy of economic activity in all parts of this sub-region is in India's national interest. The globalisation of these economies has to be viewed in this context. The structural changes now underway cover areas of interest to Indian business. These include education, healthcare, construction services, insurance and banking, business and financial services, and tourism. An area of analysis should be the impact on India of possible changes in the skills-mix of manpower requirements of GCC countries.

Political and economic dislocation, induced by domestic or external factors, is not in the interest of India since such dislocation would have an adverse impact on Indian economy. The longer term implications of disruptions, including regime orientation and direction of policies, are difficult to predict.

In West Asia beyond the Gulf, the principal points of interaction are Israel, Egypt, Jordan, Palestine, Syria, Lebanon, Sudan, Libya, Algeria and the other North African States. The principal challenge to Indian policy is of crafting an approach that would maintain equilibrium between the technology-cum-strategic relationship with Israel and the political relations with the larger Arab states some of whom are in the process of becoming partners in the energy calculus.

The Indian position on the Palestinian question is based on well established principles. It is also in consonance with the views of the great majority of the international community. This perception would remain an area of disagreement with Israel and would require careful management. We need to be more articulate on Israeli occupation and its excesses. The latest carnage in Gaza is a case in point.

West Asia has registered the emergence of India as a global power in its vicinity and is anxious to develop new equations. Given the geographical proximity, cultural affinity and the centrality of the region in terms of India's energy and economic security, there would be a continuing need for evolving a distinctly Indian policy approach that would present India as a powerful but benign neighbour to the States of the region. We in turn need to be more responsive in practical terms to their business requirements. Some lessons in this can be taken from Singapore and China. We also need to be less allergic to names and identities.

In West Asian societies, Islamism is an ideology for *change* – for disowning neo-patriarchy and structures of governance associated with it, and for its replacement by a form of governance (democratic, neo-democratic, crypto-democratic) deriving sustenance from Islamic principles, as understood by the group that emerges in control. The democracy-promotion campaign should remain sensitised to this as also to the absence of a linkage between democracy and secularism.

The ideology of globalisation, as articulated by sections of Western opinion, tends to include the Clash of Civilisation as a proven theorem. Neither the Indian experience, nor the Indian national interest, endorses such a thesis.

A combination of domestic compulsions and external

pressures is likely to confront West Asian societies with difficult choices: (a) continuity and no perceptible change; (b) continuity with calibrated change; (c) sudden change with varying degrees of disruption. Policy options with regard to each of these would need to be thought through, in terms of *Indian* interests. Contradictions will emerge as the focus shifts from bilateral linkages to globalisation-induced multilateral impulses. A conceptual framework, and a methodology, would be required for dealing with these.

2

National Interest: A Flawed Notion-Explaining the Shift in Indian Foreign Policy in the Age of Neo-liberal Globalisation and its Implications for WANA Region

Achin Vanaik

Realism and National Interest

The main reason why the notion of national interest is given such enormous, indeed decisive, weight in explaining the foreign policy behaviour of any country, including India, is because of the widespread belief that the Realism paradigm, even in its crudest form, accurately describes and explains the essential character and functioning of the world order[1]. According to this paradigm the world is basically an inter-state system where states are the primary, unitary and rational actors. Moreover, the state is perceived in a cartographic and not sociological sense, i.e. as a 'national-territorial totality' encompassing that whole space marked on any map as the country in question. This, of course, automatically makes the international order an inter-state system where it is the external relations between states that essentially shapes and establishes the character of the world order. And given the uneven distribution of power it is, of course, the strongest states that determine this character which can then either be unipolar, bipolar or multipolar where the latter term only means a very few more than two states. It follows that it is the foreign policies of the most powerful states and of the aspiring major powers that become the key determinant of global politics. And what else determines the foreign policies of states if not the pursuit of their respective national interests?

Such an approach to understanding the world order must *theoretically* exclude from sufficiently serious analytical study the crucial distinctions between government, state and society as well as the multiple and complex permutations and combinations of relationships involving them and other factors, actors and processes, which of course operate within and across the domains of both the domestic and the international. The overall result of such an extraordinarily complex web and intermeshing of multiple relationships and processes is that all too often, in the medium and long term especially, what actually emerges are unintended consequences and unanticipated outcomes rather than the more reassuring assumptions of 'stabilizing' balances of power between states. Indeed, Realism compared to the efforts of other disciplines like Political Science and Historical Sociology, embarrassingly enough, provide much the weaker and more superficial understandings of the very term 'power' that it claims to most highlight and prioritize. Since as a matter of theory and principle the domestic and the international cannot and should not be separated, foreign policy behaviour (and what is supposed to determine it – the national interest) cannot be given the kind of weight that is so casually and routinely given to it for the purposes of explaining the world order.

In fact, national interest does not even determine foreign policy! To understand why this is so we need to investigate its claims more carefully. Three crucial claims are made for this notion. That it is a principle of *legitimation* or *justification* of foreign policy and foreign policy behaviour. That it is a principle of *explanation* for why states behave as they do. That it is a principle of *guidance* for what states should do. The first of these claims is correct. Indeed, that is what it primarily is. The latter two claims are false precisely because, except in the rare cases when there is an obvious national-popular will (fighting for national liberation, against fascist occupation, and so on) there is really no such thing as an objectively grounded *national* interest that can *routinely* serve as the basis for making and following foreign policies. The point is not to doubt or question the sincerity of those who shape and make foreign policy or shape and make opinions about it and therefore constantly make recourse to this benighted term. It is to point out that for the most part there is no such thing as an objective or shared national interest and therefore it is never simply a matter of insisting that there is always a national interest even if subjective perceptions about it invariably differ. States do not try to arrive at, or approximate to, the national interest. They do not search for the 'true' national interest. States pursue state interests. And to dispute that state interests are routinely or regularly or even quite often the interests of the nation or its people as a whole, is to insist that the issue of what and who the state 'represents' must be foregrounded for investigation and questioning. The cartographic understanding of the state that is so basic to Realism, of course, prevents any such consideration, indeed eliminates this issue altogether as a matter of concern.

That is to say, the belief that the state can, does, and should pursue the national interest presupposes that the state in some way or the other represents all sections of the national society. Within the liberal intellectual tradition there have generally been two ways of arguing and justifying this claim even as it recognizes the fallacy of having a map rather than sociological understanding of the state as a 'narrower' set of apparatuses not coterminous with the national society or with the whole territory of the country. The first is to believe that the state stands above society and is therefore socially neutral and impartial in the way that an umpire in a cricket match is. It is this aloofness that then supposedly enables the state to both perceive and follow what is or should be the interest of all – the national interest. The second line of defence is to see the state not as aloof from society but embedded in it in a certain way so that the pulls and pushes of forces in the national society determine the flexibly changing character of the state. Here the state is seen essentially as the *resultant* of an array of interacting forces in society where these separate forces represent different groups and communities. What emerges then is some kind of balance reflecting the intersecting interests of different groupings. To the extent that the state is itself the 'reflector' of this balance of social forces within, it too can be said to more or less fairly represent the overall collective interest.

Dissatisfaction with these two lines of argument even among liberals has led to a third line of argument. Here, it is recognized and conceded that states, even democratic ones, do represent the interests of specific groups and sections (even sub-sections) of society at the expense of others whose interests can never carry similar weight at that point of time. In this case, it becomes much more difficult to claim that there is a routine national interest that explains and guides foreign policy. But insofar as such liberals do not see a highly coherent and solid structure of social relations that itself defines the social character of the state, they are more optimistic than others of more radical and critical persuasion that at least there can be very significant and substantial shifts of power and influence among the various groups of society. So previously subordinate groupings can become the more dominant ones and thus shape state behaviour in ways more consonant with their needs and interests. Thus such liberals are willing to discard the myth of national interest yet hold on to the view that in capitalist democratic societies there is the possibility and eventuality that large subordinate groups reflecting the interests of substantial majorities can for significant lengths of time shape state behaviour internally and externally in ways that suit these wider collective interests.

Marxists and the more radical wing of feminism, however, are more likely to insist on the existence of stable structures of social dominance in society that both shape and are abetted and consolidated by the state itself. That therefore, barring specific contexts of great collective endeavour such as liberation struggles (and even then there will always be small sections of society antithetical and opposed to the interests of the vast majority), such states pursue elite and sectional interests which are always passed off in the name of national interest. Again, the issue is not that of the sincerity or otherwise of senior state personnel who no doubt may be motivated by a belief in the national interest. It is, rather, a matter of objective structures that socialize and shape senior state personnel (and their elite supporters outside the state apparatuses) to think and act in certain ways that help reproduce and extend existing patterns of social power and wealth internally through the pursuit of foreign policies appropriate to such extension and reproduction. The class and social character of the Indian state means that its foreign policy behaviour will be decisively shaped by this fact. It is unfortunate that the Indian left seems all too prone at times to lend credibility to the notion of national interest (or the notion of "enlightened national interest") by subscribing to, and echoing this term, when it above all should be arguing that what we have as a matter of routine is the pursuit of elite sectional interests passed off as national ones – a subterfuge all the more powerful in that so many of its practitioners are unaware that it is a subterfuge, i.e., they are sincere believers in the notion of national interest.

To come back then to the three claims made for the concept of national interest. It is clearly a principle of legitimation or justification. That is where it gets its power and popularity from. It is a new form of legitimization which makes greater internal demands of a state vis-à-vis its own population than was the case in the past. This is because it expresses the fact that modern states are nation-states legitimized in the name of peoples constituted as separate nations. That is why the term used for describing a state's foreign policy in the past was never the 'national interest' but, more accurately, *raison d'etre* or 'reasons of state'. Once the older form of the feudal or royal or patrimonial state transits towards becoming the more modern nation-state then the term of description of its foreign policy behaviour, unsurprisingly, becomes the 'national interest' even though the state continues to represent sectional social interests, albeit different sectional and social interests from those of the past. But it remains the case that any chosen foreign policy or form of behaviour can be justified in its name: hence its repeated and recurrent use by all comers from all avenues and directions.

However, its claim to being an important analytical tool or

concept is greatly weakened once one recognizes how limited is the framework of Realism for grasping the nature of the world order. But even to the extent that the foreign policy of great powers clearly does have some significant impact on the world, national interest is still, analytically speaking, bankrupt. Kenneth Waltz who provides the most elegant, parsimonious and internally coherent theorization of Realism has used a Rational Choice approach derived from the *homo economicus* assumptions of neoclassical economics (widely perceived as the most scientific of the social sciences) to claim that just as one does not require a theory of the firm to provide a theory of the market and how it reaches equilibrium, similarly one can and must abstract away from the internal character of states to have a proper theory of the international system. And just as firms pursue their self-interest so too do states their self-interest or national interest. And in both cases this inter-unit, or more precisely oligopolistic, competition between the most powerful units forced upon them by the anarchy of either the market or the international political system, is regularly stabilized by a market equilibrium (the supply-demand price mechanism) or by a balance of state powers.

This is not merely a Realist analogy. It is a conceptual parallel or equivalent determined by the same structure of rational choice reasoning in both cases. For Morgenthau for whom interest is itself defined as power, the equivalent of interest or power for the firm would be profit, and the pursuit of profit the conceptual equivalent of the pursuit of national interest. For Waltz who insists that power must be seen as means separated from interests but absolutely vital for securing those interests or goals of foreign policy, profit would be the equivalent of power and formally separate from the goals of the firm. But pursuit of profit is so central a goal of firms (given that long term survival is not possible without this) it can be treated as effectively synonymous with a firm's primary self-interests. The pursuit of profit then can be taken as the conceptual equivalent of the state's pursuit of national interest in the Realist framework. But here comes the nub of the problem. Whatever one thinks of the notion of profit, whether one likes it or not, it has an objectively grounded and precise elucidation and is therefore a universally accepted definition. The notion of national interest has no such universally grounded or accepted definition precisely because it is always subjectively defined. Claiming that interest is defined as power *a la* Morgenthau or that the primary national interest for every state is its security *a la* Waltz merely displaces the problem. For both power and security are themselves notoriously vague and open-ended notions not subject to universally accepted definitions or understandings, let alone precise elucidations. Even the claim that survival as a territorial entity is a universally accepted interest of all states, founders on the historical fact that states-governments have on occasions accepted territorial partition or absorption out of choice rather than military compulsion.

It is not the case that there is always an objectively grounded meaning of the national interest though there will always be subjectively different perceptions of it. How often has one heard one or the other Indian strategic thinker or expert parade this superficial claim in order to finesse or avoid recognizing the essentially insubstantial nature of the concept itself and therefore its analytical uselessness. There are *only* subjective perceptions of what the national interest is. States pursue not the national interest, objectively speaking, but sectional interests, passed off as (subjectively perceived) national interests. If the notion is analytically (but certainly not ideologically) useless then it is obvious that it cannot even serve as a compass for guiding foreign policy behaviour. Again, it is not a question of there being some true or objectively grounded national interest whose direction of pursuit must be discerned though many may falsely discern it and thus point in the wrong directions. National interest is not any sort of compass at all because the notion, unlike that of the profit principle, exercises absolutely *no control over the domain of foreign policy choice*. Any course of action *including complete opposites* can be declared as guided or determined by it. You can go to war or push for peace. You can be for or against this or that alliance. You can be for or against such and such country or state.

The profit principle by its very objectivity and its universal acceptability does provide a basis for measuring how well or badly it is being pursued. It also, while allowing some range of options for a firm's behaviour, also rules out a definite array of other choices. This is not the case with the notion of national interest. And the occasions where policy choices are obvious, e.g. having to surrender before a more militarily powerful enemy, these do not require one to be a subscriber to the notion of national interest in order to provide an endorsement for that policy choice.

The Real Explanation

If national interest is not the basis for explaining a country's foreign policy then what is? The real answer is quite simple and obvious. It is the political (and therefore moral) character of the leadership strata that shapes and makes foreign policy decisions. In addition one must also take into consideration that part of what we can call the 'foreign policy establishment', which whether inside or outside the apparatuses of the state, shapes public opinion about foreign policy matters. This political and moral character of these important social layers (usually dominant classes and their middle class support base) changes over time. It is itself shaped by the changes in power relations between classes and social groups nationally and internationally as well as between countries. It is reflective of the changes that take place in the dominant forms of thought and values. It is changed by the complex concatenation of processes and events that have taken place over time domestically and globally.

To understand the shift in Indian foreign policy in the era of neo-liberal globalisation, which is roughly from the end of the Cold War onwards, we cannot separate this story from the much larger and more complex story of why there has been a considerable rightwing shift on all fronts – cultural, political, economic, ideological -- over the last 20 to 25 years in India. This has been caused by a whole complex of factors, domestic and international and by changes objective and subjective, material and cultural. It has involved the substantial Hindutva-ization of the Indian polity and society, the greater economic and social polarization of its people, the insurgency of Indian elites faced with burgeoning pressures from below and angry and uncomfortable about this. Indian official nationalism, i.e., the nationalism of the state, is now more elitist, more insensitive to the poor and indigent, more belligerent and frustrated, more communalized, more arrogant and self-aggrandizing, more desperate to be treated with 'respect' internationally than ever before in its past.

Yes, there were dramatic alterations in the global system that must be factored into any explanation of Indian foreign policy shifts. There was the collapse of the Soviet Union and of its control on Eastern Europe. This collapse of the East bloc clearly rendered non-alignment, at least in the sense of a distancing from alignment with either bloc, a more problematic notion. Insofar as nonalignment meant the pursuit of a more independent (from big powers) foreign policy it could still survive as a meaningful term. But to survive meaningfully and not just ceremonially as a collective, the NAM would have to find a newer unifying rationale. Economic and social changes in the advanced countries in the 1980s greatly strengthened capital at the expense of labour with the dramatic financialization of the world economy being both cause and consequence. Correspondingly, the dominant forms of economic thought shifted from Keynesianism and developmentalism towards the ascendancy ideologically of the mono-economics of neo-liberalism, the most rightwing and conservative form of neoclassical economics. But the view that Indian foreign policy changes after 1991 have been determined essentially by changed external circumstances, thereby altering the national interest, is simply the conceit of a Realist way of thinking. Major changes take place in the world. But their meanings and interpretations are always mediated through the filters of the changing beliefs and values that the senior state personnel of India and their acolytes and supporters hold. There is never any automatic or unavoidable direction in foreign policy that the Indian state must take as a result of such changes, however dramatic.

Consider, however, what is at stake if believers in the notion of national interest are forced to confront the inadequacy of this concept for the purposes of explanation and its indeterminacy for the purposes of guidance; and to acknowledge that it is basically merely a term of justification. Believers have no doubt invested an enormous amount of capital both intellectual and emotional. They would in effect be stripped naked both intellectually and morally. They would be forced to ask themselves the question – if the routines of foreign policy practice are not based on the national interest then whose interests does it represent[2]? Then what is it that those of us who have spent a lifetime talking of the national interest really been doing? Who and what have we been promoting? One of Realism's greatest attractions has always been its complete lack of self-reflexivity inherent, of course, in its crude philosophical positivism as a method of enquiry; its confident belief that what it articulates is the self-evident common sense of international relations thinking. No wonder then that there is so much institutional investment in academia, in government apparatuses, in the corporate media and in the corporate world in sustaining, defending and promoting this myth of an Indian state that genuinely seeks to promote the national interest even if it sometimes makes mistakes and errors in this sincere endeavour.

The Two Key Aims of Indian Foreign Policy since 1991

Since the end of the Cold War the key geo-economic principle guiding Indian foreign policy, regardless of which party or coalition has been in power, has been the extension and consolidation of neo-liberal globalisation. The key geopolitical principle has been the effort to establish, consolidate and deepen the strategic relationship between India and the US, which means acquiescing and participating in the US project of establishing its informal global hegemony. This has, of course, been rationalized and justified in various ways. For example, it has been defended in terms of Indian national interest and the benefits of such a course in helping India to become a major world power which it is presumed should emotionally and psychologically gladden the hearts and minds of the poor and subordinated majority as much as it does the hearts and minds of the Indian elite and middle classes. Neo-liberal economic expansion and strategic partnership with the US will promote the interest of most all Indians at least more than any alternative course of action[3].

What is the reality? Whatever the claimed merits of the neo-liberal form and direction of capitalist development domestically and internationally as a way of bringing prosperity to all or most, the one truly obvious and incontestable characteristic of this form of capitalism is that in the last 25 to 30 years it has led worldwide and within most countries (including India) to the most dramatic accelerations of inequality in the distribution of income, wealth and power between classes and social groups in human history so far. Economic inequality between countries has also grown faster than ever before. It is obvious who has benefited *most and most disproportionately* in India from the 1991 reforms. In this respect whether the majority of others have also benefited (the strongly contested claim that all boats have risen even if some more than others, from the rising tide of production, i.e., from higher average growth rates) is beside the point. The social groups who have indubitably benefited and done so disproportionately are precisely those social constellations at the top and upper-middle of Indian society whose interests the Indian state has most promoted through its neo-liberal policies.

Insofar as various states and the dominant classes and middle classes they most regularly and strongly represent have every interest in sustaining and deepening this neo-liberal global capitalist order, then global politics must to a very large extent be about how to go about providing the necessary longer term stability for the production and reproduction of this form of global capitalism? Here, the question of the US and its global ambitions becomes central. For the principal beneficiaries of such a neo-liberal order it is obvious that such stabilization must be organized through the system of nation states and that this can only be *with* and not against the US state. The issue then is not how best to oppose the US but how best to cooperate with it! And what would be the most desired role for the US to play globally? To be sure there are a whole range of political and other issues that cause dissent and conflict between states. But the processes of neo-liberal economic globalisation while they necessarily contribute to forms of capitalist competition at the level of firms, sectors and even at the level of states, they are nevertheless a crucial factor in containing the scope and depth of such competition in favour of an overall thrust towards promoting the search for a mechanism of global capitalist coordination.

This coordination can only be politically constituted – the establishment of the necessary institutional, infrastructural, legal, punitive, cultural-ideological features that can best assure the expanded reproduction of capital, its uneven distribution, and the ability of states to defuse the pressures created by the sufferings, inequalities and injustices that such a global order will necessarily have. The basic point one is seeking to make here, is that the Indian state representing as it does the interests of dominant groups has a long term and structural basis for pursuing its strategic partnership with the US and therefore to support in howsoever a variable and qualified fashion, its global imperial project. There is then a material foundation as to why after the end of the Cold War the basic shape of the world order, politically speaking, is not the search by other powers to balance against the power of the US but a hub-and-spokes arrangement with the US at the centre and the other powers at the rim of this bicycle wheel, each more concerned to consolidate its bilateral relationship with the US than to join up with others on the rim against the US.

That this outcome should itself be an embarrassment to believers in the Realist paradigm is something that has been registered in parts of American academia where criticism of Realism is fiercer than ever before; but certainly not in Indian academia or in the public strategic discourse here. Furthermore, the US hegemonic enterprise is based not just on its economic, military and political-diplomatic strength but on its cultural capacity to persuade the elites of other countries (including India) of its world view, its values and belief systems and of its stated purposes for conducting the kind of foreign policy it does. One must not underestimate the extent to which the Indian elite and middle classes have come to accept culturally, intellectually, emotionally and morally the particular 'vision' and 'leadership' of the US in its project of global transformation. For the Indian elite and middle classes, what it means for India to become a prosperous, dynamic and powerful country is to be *like* the US. You cannot seriously challenge that which you would most like to emulate!

The implications of all this for the Indian state's foreign policy behaviour towards the WANA region should be obvious. One will make reference here only to the West Asian context which is the area with which the author has more familiarity, though the general argument would apply also to North Africa. This Indian state will not sacrifice its pursuit of consolidating the strategic alliance with the US and as part of this project, its deepening strategic relationship with Israel, for the sake of securing justice for Iraqis, Palestinians or the other peoples and countries of the region be these Syria, Lebanon, and Iran. Ideally, India would have preferred to pursue simultaneously the best of relations with countries like Iran alongside its continuing pursuit of ever deeper relations with the US and Israel. But US and Israeli ambitions make this inconceivable and the Indian state has come out on the expected side in this state of affairs. It might try and cover up this fundamental bias in its foreign policy behaviour by claiming that it is pursuing a 'balanced' relationship with Iran, Israel, Iraq and the US. Or the ideologues for the Indian state might simply acknowledge yet rationalize such biases in the name of national interest. But don't look for an Indian foreign policy that in any serious way represents a genuine commitment to a just resolution of the Palestinian cause and towards creating the necessary pressures that can seriously help in achieving this. A limited degree of economic aid to Palestinians and lip service, is all one should expect. Don't look for a foreign policy that would seriously challenge US and Israel in West Asia, although this alone is the route towards greater dignity and justice for the people of this region.

What is it that can change Indian foreign policy towards West Asia? It can only be the positive and successful outcomes of struggles waged by progressive forces opposed to neo-liberalism and to the US imperial project domestically and internationally. With regard to the first named enemy, this is a struggle being waged by non-state and cross-state actors in India as well as elsewhere. With regard to the second named enemy, this is a struggle being waged by non-state actors and some states in and outside West Asia, the current crucible of world politics. Our responsibility in India is to participate in the struggles to oppose both its neo-liberalism and its strategic partnership with the US and Israel. This is a long-term struggle that is inseparable from the pursuit of radical transformations in Indian society and polity in the direction of greater justice and equalities. The false 'truism' of Realism that morality and the constant and unflinching pursuit of justice has little place in the arena of international politics is another of those myths, like that of the capitalist state as the 'natural' guardian of the 'national interest', that needs to be exposed for the fraud that it is.

Notes

1. In Western academia and to a much more limited extent in Indian academia, there are now various attempts to counter the powerful critiques of Political Realism/Neo-Realism and to 'salvage' it by qualifying it, 'complementing' it, e.g., neo-liberal institutionalism, making it more 'broad church', 'historicizing' it, and so on. But this remains essentially an academic exercise while politicians, the public media and foreign policy bureaucrats for the overwhelming part carry on with their 'common sense' Realist understanding of the world order.

2. As in the case of domestic policy, for foreign policy, public pressure (domestic and external) through political mobilizations and unrest can push particular policy decisions and actions in a progressive direction antithetical to the class and social interests of dominant groups. But as long as the social character of states remains structurally elitist

this capacity to represent the broader and wider interests of subordinate groups is limited and never constitutes the routinized dominant principle guiding foreign policy behaviour.

3. There is an interesting irony at play here. Advocates of economic neo-liberalism, if they possess a measure of theoretical sophistication, would know that the strongest theoretical defence for their position comes from the Chicago School which argucs that 'government failure' is much more dangerous than 'market failure' hence the need to minimize government involvement in the economy unlike welfarists (like Amartya Sen) in the neo-classical tradition who worry overmuch about market failures. The theoretical anchor for this claim is that government personnel (bureaucrats and politicians) pursue like everybody else, their self-interest, which in this case leads to government rent-seeking activity that then militates against economic efficiency. Yet so many of these very same advocates, including professional economists (whom one assumes have sufficient grounding in conventional economics even if their knowledge of radical and Marxist economics can be safely assumed to be quite negligible) like Manmohan Singh, Montek Singh Ahluwalia, P. Chidambaram, et al, have no hesitation in talking of that very same government pursuing the national interest. Self-serving politicians-bureaucrats who are dangerous when it comes to deciding on the best economic policies become through the magic wand of Realist thinking the reliably impartial and genuine pursuers of the collective, public, indeed national interest, when it comes to foreign policies.

3

Neo-liberal Globalist: Transformations in India's Foreign Policy: Implications for West Asia and North Africa

A.K. Ramakrishnan

Introduction

India's policy towards West Asia has been shaped by a number of structural considerations of international politics as well as specific issues and developments in both entities. Contemporary structural constraints for foreign policy making, among other things, include a neo-liberal globalist milieu that define and reorient nation-state behaviour and roles, that reorganize state sovereignty and that unleashes other global phenomena of significant political and economic dimensions. The assertion of American hegemony in military and ideological terms in the international realm is a matter of considerable import and concern.

Specific West Asian issues and areas of significance for India's foreign policy in the present-day context include the continued uncertainties, occupation and violence in Iraq; relations with Iran, Israel and the Palestinians; the petroleum sector; Indian labour force in the Gulf and the prospects for Indian companies in the whole West Asian and North African region.

West Asia and North Africa has much more than bilateral policy significance. The historical, civilizational and regional interactions are of much importance as far as going beyond the bilateral angle of policy making is concerned. The unleashing of forces of globalisation provides new issues of concern and new requirements broader policy orienatations.

This paper tries to capture a few areas of transformations in the thinking and the conduct of foreign policy in the neo-liberal context by analyzing different layers of changes in international politics. It does not address particular issues *per se*, but concentrates on capturing neo-liberal mechanisms of international change. This is looked into as a broad milieu of changing foreign policy orientations of Indian government. It tries to show a few areas of concern and significance in India – WANA interaction in such a context.

Neo-liberal Globalist Transformations and Nation-State

Neo-liberal globalism as an idea and practice envisages global changes through non-state actors like markets, corporations and institutions. State is viewed by conventional neo-liberals as a 'parasite' siphoning out resources from efficient uses. The 'minimum government' notion of the neo-liberals is well-known.

The nation-state has been at the core of contentions between divergent political, economic and cultural entities during the era of neo-liberal globalism. Neo-liberal globalism placed two contradicting claims on the nation-state: that it should be minimal with respect to the market forces and it should be maximum for establishing and maintaining an effective legal regime of 'market-friendly rights', for providing high and comprehensive security for the capital operations, and for reorienting economic and political order within the national milieu for greater market access and smooth business transactions. The implications of this are big for welfare and security of the people. If on the one hand their social security is at risk, they are on the other hand faced with the possibility of increased militarization of their State. As Norberto Bobbio puts it, neo-liberalism "represents an uncompromising commitment to an economic liberty of which political freedom is viewed as no more than a corollary[1]".

This minimum and maximum demands placed on the nation-state not only makes nation-state conduct difficult for policy practitioners but also create numerous legitimacy issues for the state entity. The increasing gap between the haves and have-nots that many observers have pointed out from the very beginning of the current phase of neo-liberal globalisation has come to stay as a major source of social and political concern. The legitimacy crisis that has arisen in many states due to conventional and such new changes has expresses itself in the form of political unrests and state oppression.

Contemporary globalisation in its post-cold war phase was expected to usher in stable and peaceful conduct of international relations where commerce rather than ideologies was supposed to dominate. Commerce did and continues to dominate. But neo-liberal claims of an orderly global transformation not only were not happening along any predictable lines and directions, new crude assertions of power through military might of the dominant nation-state were instead establishing a disorder of war and anarchy in West Asia and elsewhere with implications for the whole world. This dichotomous character of international politics has become a hallmark of neo-liberal globalist reinvention of the world. Another set of claims made on the nation-state have been from extreme nationalism and religious assertion. Both India and the West Asian and North African regions face these phenomena. These movements are supposedly providing a sense of belonging and community feeling in the face of greater alienation of the mass of population in the new global context. They in a way fit well with the neo-liberal environment in as much as providing a non-state realm of politics mostly against the state and most often without much critical positions on the state-market nexus.

One can also see that there is still stress on conventional hard power on the part of the nation-States. The nuclear issue is a significant element of contemporary international discourse. This has become the last bastion of traditional national sovereignty that no state wants to part with and more states want to be in it. The losses in many dimensions of State power under globalisation is sought to be captured back by this dangerous game.

Neo-liberal globalisation entails not merely sovereignty erosion, but also active new roles for nation-states to perform. The global institutional and legal regimes associated with the World Trade Organisation have given new directions to nation-state conduct. Many analysts like Stephen Gill talked about the emergence of "new constitutionalism" at the global level where global legal framework functions as global law in the context of rewriting of national laws in tune with such international changes. Thus the laws in favour of neo-liberal market forces become laws of national conduct. Nation-state is an active entity involved in drafting and implementing such a new institutional order.

Changing Nature of National Sovereignty

State sovereignty that defined 'national interest' and 'national security' throughout the modern era is being affected by innumerable developments associated with contemporary globalisation. They include 1) economic liberalisation, 2) human rights discourses and practices including notions of humanitarian intervention, 3) hegemonic unipolarity and the conceptions and practices of pre-emptive war, 4) international migration and global environmental issues and concerns. If the above phenomena constitute constraints on national sovereignty from outside, there is also an increased propensity for weaker states to implode or fail, thus producing sovereignty challenges internally.

Actually, in our times, many States, especially those which have problems of conformity with the hegemonic global order and those small States with traditionally deep internal challenges and resource depletion live under the ominous threat of state failure. Those with greater inclination to resist the hegemonic order, like the present-day Iraq, are also faced with sovereignty loss. Further, nation-state sovereignty is also affected by political movements of transnational character. Such type of sovereignty-challenging movements has influence in West Asia and North Africa in the form of Islamic movements.

Neo-liberal Globalism and India's Foreign Policy

India's foreign policy making and conduct are influenced by most of the above-mentioned changes in international politics. The changing roles of the State, new sovereignty concerns, the legitimacy questions that arise from a neo-liberal policy orientation, etc. apply in the Indian context as well.

At the institutional level of foreign policy making, one can observe that the centrality of the Foreign Ministry in decision-making is being directly or indirectly undermined due to neo-liberal transformation. In the Indian context, the Ministry of External Affairs has to work within a competing environment that involves other State institutional actors like the Commerce Ministry and also Non-state actors. The chambers of commerce and different state governments in many parts of the country are actors in the scene. Seeking investment, creating the climate for trade within and outside the country, etc. has been placed high on the agenda.

This is not to suggest that such activities were not part of the MEA's functions. The point is that there are more stake-holders in decision-making. The overall implication of neo-liberal non-state influence is the shifting of politics from central locations of decision-making. Neo-liberalism's primary focus on the separation of politics and economy becomes, if not fully, a significant part of our reality.

It has become common currency now to talk about the end of ideology and the ushering in of pragmatism in India's foreign policy in the new global context. I have argued in an earlier paper that the shift in India's public policy, particularly foreign policy, is not from ideology to pragmatism as generally described, but from an earlier developmental statist ideology and practice to a neo-liberal ideology and practice[2]. Foreign policy in India is increasingly becoming an area of intense debates and contestations unlike in the past when everybody was referring to it as a realm of 'consensus'. The new contestations have a lot to do with the neo-liberal transformation.

The increasing tendency to see West Asia through the prism of the American, or supposedly global, "war on terror", is a misplaced approach. K.R. Singh's remarks on the implications of the end of the cold war and the end of the Gulf war of the early nineties are significant to note in the present context:

The earlier East-West divide has now given way to North-South divide and it seems that the framework of the earlier Cold War that the Western Bloc had applied to destabilise the Eastern

Bloc is now being reconditioned for application the North *vis-à-vis* South. While Iraq is the immediate target, the north is interested in fashioning a new international environment that would prevent the countries of the South from confronting, at least militarily, the North as well as pro-North regimes in the South[3].

Girijesh Pant is of the view that: "India-West Asia relations need to be visualized as a strategic option for effective participation in the emerging world order. Though terrorism has clouded the agenda, it cannot be ignored that geo-economics will remain the prime mover of relations among the countries in the twenty-first century. India-West Asia relations are no exception to this"[4].

The linkages between the political and the economic realms need to be stressed in order to avail such a strategic option. An inter-regional mechanism of furthering common interests can be thought about. Regionalism in its present form in our contexts has not taken off as an effective arena of warding off the ill effects of neo-liberal transformations and capturing newer opportunities. India and WANA can utilize resources of inter-linkages of their histories and harness their energies to move beyond the shackles imposed by the 'war on terror' logic of international affairs.

Notes

1. Norberto Bobbio, *Liberalism and Democracy* (London: Verso, 1990).

2. A.K. Ramakrishnan, "Neo-liberal Globalism and India's Foreign Policy: Towards a Critical Rethinking", in Rajen Harshe and K.M. Seethi (eds.), *Engaging with the World: Critical Reflections on India's Foreign Policy* (Hyderabad: Orient Longman, 2005), p.27.

3. K.R. Singh, "Impact of the New World Order", Paper presented at the Seminar on *Post-War Gulf*, Gulf Studies Programme, Centre for West Asian and African Studies, School of International Studies, Jawaharlal Nehru University, New Delhi, March 27, 1992.

4. Girijesh Pant, "India and West Asia Relations: The Changing Economic Matrix", in N.N. Vohra (ed.), *History, Culture and Society in India and West Asia* (New Delhi: India International Centre and Shipra, 2003), p.140.

Part II: Globalisation, India and WANA: Energy Security Dimensions

4

Transnational Gas Pipelines: Global Context, Indian Experience

Gulshan Dietl

The energy pipelines, carrying oil and gas from the production-sites to the consumer centres, often run through two or more States. In the process, they create strategic geography. The route, direction, volume, length, thickness and width of the pipelines are not just the technological and commercial decisions. They are political ones. Their impact, beneficial or otherwise, is determined accordingly.

The location and physical features of States and the distribution of natural resources among them explain the dynamics of interaction among them. The drinkable water, arable land, forests, animal life, and mineral resources are unevenly distributed. Gaining access to or control over them has been the driving force behind much of geopolitics. The rivers, harbours, islands, navigable straits, waterways and channels, coastal zones, roads, railways have been the stakes in the game of geopolitics throughout history. The energy-carrying pipelines can now be added to the list. Through millennia, wars have been fought for God, glory and gold. The contemporary scramble for the oil and gas validates the conventional wisdom.

The oil tankers represent the weakest link in the energy chain, followed by the vulnerable choke points like the narrow straits and waterways close to the coasts that the sea-borne commerce has to traverse. The oil and gas pipelines are the next points of vulnerability in the energy trade. There are more gas and oil pipelines crossing the international border than ever before. Many of them are mega projects envisioning lines that run across several countries – at times, connecting an entire continent, at others, going beyond across water bodies. Very often, they are submerged below water; and not always hugging the coastline. The Baku-Tblisi-Ceyhan (BTC) pipeline, the Trans-Afghan Gas Pipeline (TAGP) and the Asia Energy Grid are the most ambitious of the global pipeline projects at present.

In the circumstances, they have assumed a critical role in international security affairs. American soldiers are now helping to defend such conduits against attacks in Iraq, Colombia, and Georgia. President George W Bush has authorised the deployment of US military personnel in Georgia to help train the Georgian troops that will be responsible for protecting the BTC line. Pipeline protection has become a major concern for Saudi Arabia, Sudan, Algeria, Nigeria, Burma and other strife-torn producers.

There are several reasons to take a closer look at the gas pipelines in particular. One, the gas pipelines are much more prone to political influences than the oil pipelines. The price and production of crude oil are largely set by the agreements of the Organisation of Petroleum Exporting Countries (OPEC). The oil trade is centralised to that extent. The gas deals, on the other hand, are bilateral or multilateral between/among the concerned parties. Two, they are long-term agreements and conditional upon infrastructures involving large-scale investments. Once entered into, they are there to stay for decades. The calculations that go into their building are that much more rigorous than the oil trade. Three, the share of gas will incrementally go up in the global energy basket in future. According to the US Government's Energy Information Administration forecasts, global natural gas consumption in 2025 will amount to 152 trillion cubic feet (tcf) – a seventy per cent increase on the 2001 total of 90 tcf. Four, while oil production is expected to peak as early as 2010, gas is likely to reach there several decades from now. And five, there is a shift in production sites to less accessible and land-locked areas contributing to an increasing importance of the pipelines.

The paper proposes to examine three gas pipelines in this context. The pipelines chosen are the Turkmenistan-Russia-Ukraine pipeline, El Gran Gasoducto del Sur and the Iran-

Pakistan-India pipeline. No three gas pipelines could be more unlike one another as the above ones. They are located in diverse regions geographically and are in different stages of development. The first is an old functioning grid that was a domestic line within a single sovereign space. Now, it runs through three States. The second is an ambitious project that proposes to run across most of South America. It is still in the planning stage. The third is intended to run through three States. After years of deliberations, however, it is still not finalised.

Turkmenistan-Russia-Ukraine Gasgrid

The Ukraine-Russia-Turkmen gas pipeline, till the break-up of the Soviet Union was a domestic grid. Today, the gas trade between Turkmenistan, Russia and Ukraine is not just a commercial proposition, but an illustration of triangular dependencies of the three countries. The key issues in terms of transit are that all Turkmenistan's gas exports outside Central Asia pass through Russia, which puts the latter in complete control of around three-quarters of Turkmenistan's exports. Russia's position vis-à-vis Ukraine is extremely vulnerable in that more than ninety per cent of its gas exports to Europe pass through that country.

Thus, Ukraine is the transit point as well as the choke point of the Turkmen and Russian exports. It has also been a leaking point of the deliveries. In early 1990s, there were serious disruptions as Ukraine pilfered the gas for its own domestic use. Since then the gas deliveries have become an important issue in the political and security relationship between Russia and Ukraine, having featured in the package of agreements which have included issues such as the future of the Black Sea Fleet and Ukrainian nuclear weapons. There was a serious stand-off between the two last winter, when the Russians cut off natural gas supplies to Ukraine over price dispute. A compromise was reached only after Ukraine agreed to pay more for the gas that was, till then, subsidised.

The Russian diplomacy to retain control over its former space and the US diplomacy to extend its control over the same have repeatedly to come to a collision. Till recently, Ukraine was pointedly excluded from both the EU and the NATO expansions; as also from the list of possible invitees. Since the "Orange Revolution", the situation has radically changed. How the energy pipeline politics plays out in the changed circumstances remains to be seen.

El Gran Gasoducto del Sur

Venezuela is the only OPEC member-State from the Western Hemisphere. Its proven oil reserves of 77 bb would go up to 300 bb, if its extra-heavy oil is also accounted for. That would put the country at the top of the oil-rich states. Besides, it has substantial gas reserves of 150 tcf.

El Gran Gasoducto del Sur, or the Great Gas Pipeline of the South, is an ambitious 6,600 kilometre, US$ 23 billion project that would link Venezuela's natural gas supplies to Brazil and Argentina. Apart from physical and economic magnitude, the project is expected to provide one million jobs during the construction period in Venezuela, Brazil, Uruguay, Paraguay and Argentina. It would be the most ambitious gas-distribution project in the history of the world. What makes it unique, however, is its political significance. The Venezuelan President Hugo Chavez's bid for regional leadership, his quest for regional economic integration and his objective of limiting US presence in the region are the oft-repeated goals of the entire endeavour. The pipeline is slated for completion in 2017. Bolivia, a country with nearly 50 tcf of gas, has formally joined the project in the meanwhile.

The member-states have set up Petrosur, a ministerial body responsible for co-ordinating the planning and execution of energy policies and the activities of the state-owned enterprises. And they have approved US$ 9.2 m in funding for engineering design and environmental studies.

There are many question marks over its completion and operation. One, it makes very little economic sense; it would be much cheaper to build liquefaction terminals and ship the gas by tankers. Two, there is a poor record in pipeline maintenance in the region and a lack of expertise in constructing one. Three, the proposed capital outlay envisages huge investment that may not be forthcoming. Four, in view of Brazil's quest for energy self-sufficiency, the pipeline could be redundant in long term.

Iran-Pakistan-India Gas Pipeline

The Iran-Pakistan-India gas pipeline project has been under consideration for nearly two decades. There are three possible routes for the proposed project: one, overland, from Iranian gasfields terminal at Assaluyeh to the Pakistani border on to India; two, offshore, hugging the Pakistani coast along Baluchistan; and three, deep sea, under the Pakistani Exclusive Economic Zone (EEZ). The overland option would involve 56 inch-diameter pipeline stretching 2,000 km; 850km in Iran, 700km in Pakistan and 1120km in India with initial estimate of US$ 700million.

The Indian defence experts reject the option of an overland route through Pakistan, as it empowers Pakistan to cut off supplies to India whenever it wants. International guarantees can reduce, but not eliminate the chances of such a cut off. Additionally, it could also be disrupted and/or damaged by Pakistani opposition in a purely internal circumstance in the country. Pakistan favours an overland route as this will assure its own gas supplies while giving it a stranglehold over supplies to India. India favours the laying of the pipeline through the Pakistani Exclusive Economic Zone. Such a pipeline will need to be sunk 3,000 metres, and would be the first experiment in pipeline construction at such depth. Till recently, Pakistan declined to permit it citing various techno-economic, defence and strategic reasons. It maintained that the project would cost one and a half time more if laid under water, with an estimated cost touching US$ 10 to 12 billion. There were talks of involving stakeholders like the World Bank, the Asian Development Bank, international financial institutions and the private sector in both India and Pakistan.

In early 1997, India, Iran and Pakistan agreed in principle to officially pursue the matter with urgency. During the Indian Foreign Minister Jaswant Singh's visit to Iran in July 2000, a

Joint Working Committee was set up to examine the security, political, technical and economic issues related to the transportation of the Iranian gas. In November, the Iranian Deputy Foreign Minister S.M.H. Adeli visited India with a fresh proposal in this regard. According to it, India and Iran would consider the project "bilateral", none of them would need to enter into any contractual obligation with Pakistan or rely on its security assurances. That responsibility would lie with the international consortium that would run the project and manage the risks of disruption involved.

After the change of government in India in mid-2004, the then Foreign Minister K Natwar Singh expressed India's willingness to consider the overland route, if Pakistan was willing to give required guarantees. Interestingly, his statement did not reiterate the Indian condition that Pakistan should confer the status of the Most Favoured Nation on India. The Pakistani response, predictably, was prompt and positive.

Early next year, there were positive developments as the Indian government agreed to give it a fresh look. Speaking in Islamabad on 16 February, the Indian Foreign Secretary Shyam Saran said at a press conference that India had agreed to go ahead with the project and that three countries were moving forward in a pragmatic fashion to make it a reality. He also spoke of an overarching trilateral agreement on the issue. The statement was significant in view of the fact that India, till then, was in favour of separate agreements with Iran and Pakistan.

In the meanwhile, there were major deals on oil and gas between India and Iran. The two countries signed a preliminary agreement estimated at US$ 40 billion that committed India to import LNG and develop Iranian oilfields and a gasfield. The ONGC Videsh Limited (OVL) would help in developing the oilfields in exchange for 90,000 bd of crude. India would also import 7.5million tonnes of LNG starting 2009 for a period of twenty-five years. India would pay US$ 1.2 plus 0.065 of Brent crude average, with an upper ceiling of US$ 31 per barrel of LNG. Iran would ship 5 million tonnes of LNG annually with a provision to increase the quantity to 7.5 million. OVL gets twenty per cent share in the development of onshore oilfield Yadavaran, which translates into 60,000 bd. China would retain its fifty per cent share in Yadavaran, Iran's share would go down to twenty per cent and India would acquire the rest of the thirty per cent. India also acquired a hundred per cent right in the Juffair oilfield that is estimated to yield 3,00,000 bd.

It is necessary, at this stage, to put the trilateral project into a broader context. The US considers Iran as a hostile State and enforces unilateral economic sanctions against it. The US companies cannot enter Iranian gas market under the Executive Order 12959, which was signed by President Bill Clinton in 1995 and renewed by President Bush in March 2004. Notwithstanding comprehensive unilateral sanctions against Iran [and Libya since1986], the Iran and Libya Sanctions Act (ILSA) was enacted by Congress in August 1996. ILSA has many of the same objectives as the unilateral sanctions, but is different in jurisdictional scope. Unlike the embargoes against Iran and Libya, which are primary sanctions, ILSA imposes a secondary boycott. The legislation was designed essentially to force foreign companies into choosing to do business with Iran and Libya or the United States.

ILSA mandates the U.S. President to impose sanctions on any US or foreign person, company or country who, after August 5, 1997, invests US$ 20 million or more in an Iranian project [US$ 40 million for Libya; this was lowered to US$ 20 million in August 2001 and has now been lifted], if the investment directly and significantly contributes to the enhancement of Iran's [or Libya's] ability to explore for, extract, refine, or transport by pipeline its oil and natural gas reserves. ILSA requires that sanctions be imposed for a minimum of two years.

It is also necessary to put the trilateral project into the Indo-US context. From the time India and the US entered into an agreement on civil nuclear co-operation in July 2005, there has been an increasing strategic relationship between the two States. The Indo-Iran relations, and especially the Iran-Pakistan-India pipeline, have been affected by this development. There have been several instances of US seeking to prise India away from the project.

In March 2005, the US Secretary of State, Condoleezza Rice visited India and Pakistan. Speaking in New Delhi, she said that the US had conveyed its "concerns" to India on the gas pipeline. "Our ambassador [to India] has made statements in that regard. So, those concerns are well known to India." As an incentive to wean India away from the project, she said, "...we believe that a broad energy dialogue should be launched with India."

On the same day, either as a consequence thereof or in an unfortunate coincidence, the Indian Petroleum Minister Mani Shankar Aiyar called on Iran to set a reasonable price for its gas sale to India and Pakistan in view of the fact that the consumer countries constituted an attractive market of about 200mcm a day. "Otherwise we would be forced to look at other options", he said. In an unseemly taunt, obliquely referring to the US sanctions, he added that if Iran had alternative markets in the United States, China and Japan, then these could be tapped by it.

The US made several diplomatic moves on the issue in quick succession thereafter. The US Under-Secretary of State Nicholas Burns wrote an article in **Washington Post** encouraging New Delhi to establish energy ties with Central Asian States and to reduce "the lure of long-term contracts with Iran". The US Energy Secretary Samuel Bodman queried his Indian counter-part Murli Deora regarding the pipeline during his visit to India; declaring that Washington needed to "stop" it. The Chairman of the Foreign Affairs Committee of the US House of Representatives, Sam Lantos, led a group of US Congressmen in writing a letter to the Indian Prime Minister suggesting that India pull back not just from the pipeline but also from the LNG deal with Iran. He has, since then, introduced a bill in the US Congress entitled "Iran Counter-Proliferation Act". If and when passed, it could adversely impact the already poor prospects of the pipeline. And to cap it all, the then Assistant Secretary of State for Non-proliferation and International Security, Stephen G Rademaker, stated in New

Delhi that India's votes in the International Atomic Energy Agency against Iranian nuclear programme were "coerced."

The US concerns on the Iran-Pakistan-India gas pipelines are, in the circumstances, well known. They have been expressed repeatedly, publicly, and at various levels and through many influential voices in the US administration.

Geopolitics of Transnational Gas Pipelines

The location and physical features of States and the distribution of natural resources among them explain the dynamics of interaction among them. The drinkable water, arable land, forests, animal life, and mineral resources are unevenly distributed. Gaining access to or control over them has been the driving force behind much of geopolitics. The rivers, harbours, islands, navigable straits, waterways and channels, coastal zones, roads, railways have been the stakes in the game of geopolitics throughout history. The energy-carrying pipelines can now be added to the list.

The oil tankers represent the weakest link in the energy chain, followed by the vulnerable choke points like the narrow straits and waterways close to the coasts that the sea-borne commerce has to traverse. The oil and gas pipelines are the next points of vulnerability in the energy trade. In the circumstances, they have assumed a critical role in international security affairs.

A gas pipeline is the result of a specific agreement between the concerned parties. The agreement could be conditional, time-bound and mutually beneficial. It could also reflect the relative power balance between the parties; have asymmetrical impact on each of them; and be prone to adjustments/disruptions with changing times.

The pipeline politics could be excruciatingly long-drawn and often kill the most sensible and mutually beneficial constructions. At times, it could lead to fruitful compromises and eventual positive consequences. And those consequences may also have a spill-over effect in other areas of co-operation between/among the parties.

The three cases scrutinised in the paper amply bring out extraneous considerations that go into formulating and executing mega gas-projects. The Indian policies through the long time-span of deliberations over the Iran-Pakistan-India gas pipeline are particularly illustrative in this regard.

5

Can West Asia Retain its Position in the Oil Market? Implications for India

Shebonti Ray Dadwal

Since oil was first discovered in the region, the oil-rich West Asian countries have been the mainstay of the industrialised world's energy supplies, and particularly the Western world, led by the US. Yet it took one incident of terrorism targeting the US mainland for the US President to exhort his fellow Americans and US allies to reduce their dependence on Gulf oil by 75 per cent by 2025 on the basis that the region was no longer a "reliable" source of energy supplies. Yet US energy consumption patterns do not indicate that the country is seriously attempting to reduce its consumption. Neither do any of its policies vis-à-vis that region indicate that the region's importance in terms of its status as an important supplier of energy, particularly oil, has, or will diminish in the future.

According to the Energy Information Administration's, International Energy Outlook 2006, (EIA IEO 2006) total petroleum supply in 2030 will need to increase by 38 million barrels per day (mbd) to 118 mbd, from the 2003 level of 80 mbd. OPEC producers are expected to provide 14.6 mbd of the increase[1].

As of January 1, 2006, proved world oil reserves, as reported by *Oil & Gas Journal*, were estimated at 1,293 billion barrels (bb), that is, 15 bb (about 1 per cent) higher than the estimate for 2005. The largest increase in proved oil reserve estimates was made in Iran, whose oil reserves increased by 5 per cent, from 125.8 bb in 2005 to 132.5 bb in 2006. Higher reserve estimates were also reported by Saudi Arabia, where reserves increased by 4.9 bb (2 per cent) in 2006, and Kuwait, where reserves increased by 2.5 bb (3 per cent). Other increases were reported from Venezuela (by 3 per cent) and Chad, (with 1.5 bb proven oil reserves in 2006). Declining oil reserves were reported in Mexico (down by 1.7 bb), with smaller losses in Norway (0.8 bb), the US (0.5 bb), and the UK (0.5 bb), among others.

However, there is no doubt that of the world's total proved oil reserves of easily accessible and cheap resources are located in West Asia, although the amounts projected range from 71 per cent as quoted by the EIA to *Oil and Gas Journal's* estimate of 57.1 per cent. Although Canada too has huge reserves, these include 174.1 bb of oil sands which are much more expensive to produce). Among the top 10 oil reserve holders, six are from the Gulf region, with Russia holding the eighth position with 60 bb, Nigeria 10th with 36 bb, Algeria 15th with 11.4 bb, Kazakhstan 17th with less than 10 bb and Azerbaijan at 19th position with 7 bb[2]. Moreover, although there is a growing tendency to believe that African oil will occupy a position of even greater strategic importance to the US, Europe and Asia (particularly China) over the next decade to diversify their oil import sources away from West Asia, there is sufficient evidence to show that the 50-year turmoil over oil extraction in Africa continues unabated with reports of hostage-taking and takeovers of oil platforms in the Niger Delta by marginalised communities demanding justice and compensation from foreign oil companies and the government. The conflict in Sudan too shows little signs of ending; and rampant corruption continues in most of the African countries[3].

Under these circumstances, the importance of the Gulf's strategic position in the oil market cannot be over-emphasised. Therefore, despite technological advances delaying depletion from fields in other regions, there is no doubt that in the ultimate analysis, no other region can come close to the Gulf region in terms of oil reserves. The same is true for natural gas reserves. Although Russia and Central Asia also have large gas reserves, the whole of Eurasia, including the FSU states have around 1,953 trillion cubic feet (tcf) of gas while the West Asian region's reserves are around 2565 tcf[4].

Recently, doubts have been raised about West Asia's reserves position due to lack of updated and accurate information and even basic statistics on the same. Before the second oil shock in the late 1970, early 1980s, the major oil companies had excellent information regarding supplies and reserves. But soon after, fundamental changes occurred in the market related to market information. First, the number of suppliers increased; also there was a move away from long-term contract deals to spot markets and short-term deals. Also, take-overs of marketing from the international oil companies to governments made access to information difficult. Almost all the Gulf countries claim that their reserves have increased. In 1985, Kuwait revised its official reserve figure upwards by 50 per cent and other countries followed. Yet there are indications suggesting that many of the Gulf countries' oil reserves are far below the amount being claimed by the government. According to some geologists, even after a decade of production from a particular field, reserve estimates remain unchanged with no explanation if and to what extent new field discoveries may be compensating for depletion of reserves in existing fields. Neither is there much information on whether the huge revenues earned during the 1970s and 80s by these countries were used for reinvestments into their energy sectors or more specifically into exploration and production (E&P)[5]. Hence there are concerns that, despite predictions, that OPEC member states will increase capacity by an additional 20-25 mbd over the next two decades may not bear out. In fact, OPEC's capacity has come down over the past 25 years from 38.76 mbd in 1979 to 31 mbd currently[6].

However, others say that the earlier data provided by the oil majors – the Seven Sisters who controlled Gulf production till the 1970s – were manipulated. Their policy was to cap oil output to avoid over-production to prevent flooding of the market, along with the proclivity to underestimate official reserves in order to resist the host countries' pressures to increase output so they could pocket more revenues. But once the host countries had nationalised their concessions, the artificial measuring system collapsed and a more consistent and realistic assessment of reserves became possible. Also, many of these countries undertook exploration campaigns which yielded new discoveries at the end of the 1970s or '80s. Coupled with higher prices that allowed them to convert what were possible reserves to proven reserves explains the upward revision of reserves estimates[7].

Nevertheless, barring Saudi Aramco, the majority of the national oil companies do not have access to the latest technology or human resource capabilities crucial for increasing production from ageing oilfields. And with many of the oil sectors off limits to foreign oil companies, there is a concern that this may affect production. Moreover, the fact that the region is increasingly being perceived as "unstable" gives room for thought as to its status as a reliable supplier. More than any other region, events arising from political, economic or military issues that take place in the West Asian region have an immediate and direct impact on global oil prices. Several reasons have contributed to this.

First, the upsurge in anti-American sentiments in the Gulf, following the 1990-91 Iraq war and the 2003 Iraq invasion and the concurrent rise of Islamic extremism, with Islamist groups calling for an end to US hegemony in the region and regaining control of the region's energy resources. Stating that "the biggest reason for our enemies' control over our lands is to steal our oil," Osama bin Laden exhorted his followers in December 2004 to "give everything you can to stop the greatest theft of oil in history." Subsequently there have been a spare of attacks – albeit unsuccessful – on oil facilities in Saudi Arabia, with the intention of increasing the price of oil to over US$ 100 a barrel, and affecting Western economies. The frequency of insurgent attacks in Iraq has also increased against the Iraqi oil industry, ensuring that Iraqi oil production remains well below its pre-war level. Moreover, there is growing concern that the escalating sectarian violence in Iraq could spread across the entire region[8].

Neither is the demand for higher oil prices restricted to the extremists. Economic hardship, anti-Americanism and rising nationalistic sentiments have led to similar demands from the

Arab streets, leading the governments to try and extract higher rents for their natural resources from the international community. Hence the temptation for producers' to cut back production to ensure higher oil prices may grow.

Currently, world attention is focused on the looming confrontation between the West and Iran over the latter's suspected nuclear weapons programme, and fears that this could lead to a regional military conflict with subsequent repercussions on global supplies. Oil being a fungible commodity, the impact of supply disruptions from any one region or country would reverberate throughout the entire oil market in terms of price. Concerns are raised that the West Asian region displays an abundance of all the characteristics of the worst conflict zones of the 20th Century while economic volatility has remained pronounced in the region. Iraq has experienced severe economic volatility due to UN sanctions and the US invasion and subsequent sectarian violence, while the threat of conflict involving Iran continues. As a result, the GDP growth rate in the country has decreased drastically while inflation and unemployment remains high.

Neither is the situation in the rest of the region much better. All six countries bordering Iraq have also experienced ups and downs. Iran's per capita GDP ranged between 0.3 per cent to 7.3 per cent over the last 5 years; Jordan between 0.3 per cent to 5.1 per cent; Kuwait -5.5 per cent to 6.9 per cent; Saudi Arabia -6 per cent and 3.3 per cent, Syria between -0.4 per cent and 3.3 per cent; Turkey -9 per cent to 7.4 per cent[9].

Secondly, given the fact that most of the Gulf economies are dependent on oil revenues, they support high oil prices, and many see OPEC manipulating prices to increase prices. Recently, President Bush asked OPEC members not to raise prices by cutting output, warning them that it could "wreck economies" and reduce demand for their products if it follows through with the cuts to shore up prices[10]. Although it is generally accepted that OPEC has lost its ability to influence prices, many of the cartel's members have advocated setting higher price benchmarks for their basket of crude. Recently, when there was a large reduction in oil prices, OPEC announced that it would cut production by 1.2 mbd, which succeeded in arresting the fall, although prices have subsequently gone up marginally. However, given its status as the largest holders of oil reserve, the time may come when OPEC will regain its lost market share as well as control over prices. Given most of the member's preference for higher prices, concerns have been raised that once OPEC regains control over market share and hence price, they will ensure that prices remain on the higher side. OPEC's reputation as a leader in the oil market came from the fact that the members had excess production capacity. However, while its spare capacity was around 11 mbd till the early 1990s, today, this has shrunk to around 1.3-1.8 mbd. Of more concern is that Saudi Arabia alone holds the ability to increase production at short notice. All the other members are producing to capacity[11].

Another issue of concern is the growth in domestic demand for energy resource in the region. Most of the oil exporting countries experienced high economic growth in 2005 and the first half of 2006, leading to high domestic consumption of oil due to increasing populations, higher sales of automobiles and higher production of petrochemicals, particularly in the West Asian countries[12]. As a result, demand for oil is projected to grow at an average annual rate of 2.1 per cent, from 5.4 mbd in 2001 to 8.9 mbd in 2025. Oil's share in the energy mix was about 53 per cent in 2001 and is projected to remain near that level through 2025 given the availability of oil and gas. Iran and Saudi Arabia, the two largest oil consumers in the region, each surpassed the one mbd consumption mark in the 1990s. Iran's domestic consumption of oil totaled at 1.5 mbd in 2002, representing more than one-third of its oil production capacity due to a large working-age population and heavily subsidised prices for transportation fuels. In Saudi Arabia, the transportation sector and the massive petrochemical sector have been driving rapid growth in oil demand since the mid-1990s, although much of the oil will be replaced by natural gas. It is expected that around 2.6 bcf per day of additional natural gas will be used by 2015[13].

Although currently, the industrialised countries continue to the major consumers, with the US, EU and Japan consuming up to half of total annual output, their share has steadily been overtaken by growing consumption in the Asian industrialising countries with China and India contributing 35 per cent to incremental oil consumption between 1990 and 2003. As oil intensity and hence consumption in the industrialized countries decrease, Asia will become the major oil customer of the Gulf oil producers. In fact, China, Japan, South Korea and India now takes around 60 per cent of Saudi Arabia's crude oil exports, as well as the majority of its refined petroleum product exports, while Kuwait exports over 60 per cent of its oil to Japan, India, Singapore, South Korea, Taiwan, and Thailand. The same is the case for Oman and Bahrain[14].

With the demand for oil in India projected to double over the next two decades, it is in New Delhi's interest to ensure augmentation of international production, for reasons pertaining to supply security as well prices. However, as far as conventional oil is concerned, the supply pool will become smaller, with growth coming mainly in the Persian Gulf region. Projections by the EIA and IEA indicate that the world's oil supplies from the Persian Gulf region will rise from less than one-third in 2003 to nearly half by 2030. Saudi Arabia alone has stated that by 2009, it would increase its capacity to over 12 mbd, while Iran and Iraq are both known to be sitting on several billion barrels of unexploited reserves.

Therefore, to ensure energy security, a new order needs to be introduced in the oil market. First of all, it has to be understood that there is only one oil market, whose security is contingent upon its stability[15]. This, in turn, is dependent on adequate spare production and storage capacity as well as access to timely and accurate information. Often, price volatility in the markets is a result of rumours, conspiracy theories and lack of information, leading to panic buying and speculation.

Since the health of the world oil market and sustenance of economic growth has strong linkages with energy security, both in terms of demand as well as supply, energy interdependence, not only between producers and consumers, but also international and national oil companies and governments, is crucial. An important factor in this respect is the need for cross investments in producers' and consumers' energy sectors. Today, the tightness in the oil market, both for crude as well as refined products, is largely due to lack of adequate and timely investments, both in the upstream as well as downstream sectors of producing and consuming countries. The IEA estimates that around US$ 17 trillion will be required over the next 25 years to ensure a well supplied market.

However, this would require some changes in the energy sectors of many of the Gulf producing countries. There are indications that many of these countries, which had nationalised their oil sectors, are thinking afresh on this. For instance, although the Kuwaiti Constitution forbids foreign ownership of the country's mineral resources, the government is exploring allowing foreign investment in upstream oil development under new terms that would allow foreign firms to earn per-barrel fees instead of the traditional production sharing agreements[16]. Saudi Arabia has opened it upstream gas sector to foreign participation, although its oil sector remains closed. UAE has allowed US and Japanese companies to take stakes in their oil fields, both to enhance production from older fields as well as new E&P projects[17], and Iran, despite being under sanctions, is planning to reformulate the unpopular buyback contracts to allow foreign firms more time to recoup their investments. There is a growing realisation that without access to new technology and funds, they will lose market share to other producers as well as to other fuels.

Today, the oil market is facing several threats – from regional conflicts, terrorist threats and domestic political problems in producing states as well as growing concerns over environmental pollution. It is only through cooperation – bilateral as well as multilateral – that individual countries can ensure their energy security.

Notes

1. World Oil Markets 2006, EIA, DoE, June 2006, www.eia.doe.gov/oiaf/ieo/oil.html.

2. Ibid., Oil & Gas Journal, Vol. 103, No. 47, December 19, 2005 from: US Energy Information Administration, http://www.eia.doe.gov/emeu/international/petroleu.html.

3. Salih Booker & Ann-Louise Colgan, Africa Policy Outlook, 2006, Foreign Policy in Focus, March 16, 2006, http://www.fpif.org/fpiftxt/3157.

4. Energy Information Administration, October 5, 2006, http://www.eia.doe.gov/emeu/international/reserves.html.

5. Paul Stevens, "The Role of the Gulf in World Energy: Lessons from the Past", *Gulf Energy and the World: Challenges and Threats,* ECSSR, 1997.

6. Joe Barnes & Amy Myers Jaffe, "The Persian Gulf and the Geopolitics of Oil, *Survival*, Vol.48, No. 1, Spring 2006.

7. Leonardo Maugeri, The Age of Oil: The Mythology, History and Future of the World's most Controversial Resource, Praeger, 2006.

8. The Threat of Oil Jihad, Rand Corporation, March 3, 2006, http://www.rand.org/commentary/030306UPI.html.

9. Niall Ferguson, The Next War of the Worlds, Foreign Affairs, Sept-Oct 2006.

10. Reuters, October 24, 2006

11. Energy Information Administration, Short-Term Energy Outlook, October 2006, http://www.eia.doe.gov/emeu/steo/pub/3atab.html.

12. Randy Kirk, Explosive Oil Consumption Growth in the Top Oil Exporting States, Energy Bulletin, July 25, 2006, http://www.energybulletin.net/18475.html.

13. World Oil Markets, IEO 2003, EIA, www.stat-usa.gov/.../e5b3666e3baaf1c385256ecf004f8afb/$FILE/IEO2003_ch004.pdf.

14. Middle East oil market witnesses significant changes, Alexander's Oil and Gas Connections, Vol 10, No.18, September 28, 2005, http://www.gasandoil.com/GOC/news/ntm53967.htm.

15. Daniel Yergin, Ensuring Energy Security, Foreign Affairs, Vol. 85, No. 2, March/April 2006.

16. www.eia.doe.gov/emeu/international/kuwait.html.

17. http://www.eia.doe.gov/emeu/cabs/UAE/Full.html.

Part III: Globalisation, India and Gulf: Economic Dimensions

6

India and Arab Gulf's Look East Policy: Strengthening Economic Relations since 1995

Javed Ahmad Khan

Introduction

There can be hardly any doubting that during the last one and half decades of economic liberalization and privatization in the Arab world has enhanced the economic growth in the region. In fact, this new development has also given various dimensions to the policy makers and even individual enterprises to expand their economic and trade relations not only with their traditional business partners; US and Western Europe but with the rest of the world especially in Asian and East Asian countries which was not possible at such a big scale in the decades of 1970s and 1980s because of the cold war rivalry and the mobility of capital and goods as it is possible in today's globalised environment. According to a survey released in January 2006, of 140 senior executives interviewed in 14 countries by Price Waterhouse Coopers and the Dubai-based Moutamarat group, 83 per cent saw Arab companies were willing to open up their markets, at a time when global corporations are looking for new opportunities[1].

There are, however, some other factors that facilitated the Arab Gulf's 'Look East' policy in recent years. At a recent workshop on GCC-Asia relations in Dubai on January 2006, the analysts pointed that since the two regions are heavily exchanging energy, trade and expatriates, it is logical that they must grow beyond the cooperation. For India too, the Arab Gulf's massive oil revenues are creating attractive markets for business communities here[2].

Arab Economies towards Transition

In this regard, the WTO accession of these Gulf States have provided new opportunities to look new partners in the Asian region on purely economic and rational basis, which is different from 'alliance in the cold war period. The rising oil revenues stimulated stock and real estate market in the Gulf and made investors aware of opportunities nearer to home. For example, the accession of Saudi Arabia to the World Trade Organization in 2005 has also given an added impetus to exploit Saudi Arabia's comparative advantage in certain sectors of energy, especially petrochemicals and large scale Saudi private sector investments are under way in this investment climate. Similar boom in Dubai, Qatar and Bahrain has provided regional investors with a wider variety of investment potential and have opened up the trading and investment links with China, India, Malaysia and other developing economies, here, the 'Free Trade' concept must be given the prime importance. Another phenomenon that can be noticed is the new approach to 'regional integration' and here an urgency to get freedom from the 'clutches of Western power' can be seen, especially in deliberations of Organization of Islamic Conference (OIC) camp. Now, the local institutions in the region such as OIC, Islamic Development Bank (IBD), International Islamic Finance Corporation (IIFC) and Islamic Chambers of Commerce and Industry are making new economic strategies, where a shift from the West is emerging, though at a very small level, with the anti-West feelings especially with regard to the economic and trade issues. For example, the blasphemous cartoon of Prophet Mohammad created much hue and cry not among individuals in the Gulf region but also regional governments took strong note of it and threatened to see its impact on economic relations with the concerned countries.

In fact, since the 9/11 incident, there is a rise in anxiety among Arab investors over the best and safest havens for foreign direct investment, and the US does not look a safe and best bet to many, especially in the region. This has also forced some of the larger Gulf economies to try and diversify their economic and investment relationships with a wider number of Asian developing countries that might be prone to recessions following 9/11. Since the US is not an attractive market for investment mainly because of its sluggish economy and mounting deficits, the Arab economists have begun to suspect that the long delayed 9/11 American recession is coming[3].

Gulf Look towards Asia and India for Investment

Why the GCC countries are taking interest in Asia for integration? Two major factors point toward this shift. First, the resurgent Gulf economies are flush with money from oil sales and need fresh pastures to invest and diversify. Secondly, the increase in Asia's oil consumption with both energy-starved China and India needing the fuel to boost their growth engine.

But the main question is why under such a situation Asia will be their priority of investment and trade? Here, we can argue purely on economic term that this region is comparatively more profitable than their conventional Western trading partners. Because, the sluggish US economy is no more attractive for investment purpose as it was in early 70s and 80s, when money got its ultimate destination in Western non-communist block. Similarly, and most importantly, these Asian countries were then also not such growth oriented much profitable as are in today's liberalized environment.

In Table 6.1, look at the Asian GDP growth of the emerging Asian countries and also of India, which reflect the growing economic and investment activities in these countries. Naturally, the foreign investors will opt an 'economies of scale' and will look where the rate of return is higher. In fact, the King Abdullah of Saudi Arabia's tour to these Asian countries in January 2006, is purely on this economic rationality, to diversify their investments in the region where the prospects of returns are higher than those highly deficit economies of the US and Western Europe.

As the table shows, the Asian developing economies as a whole are growing by 5.5 per cent in 2005 compared to developed countries of US, Western Europe witnessing the growth of merely

2.3 per cent throughout the decades reflecting a depressed domestic demand. It is now global observation that the US economy is 'running out of steam' Even the OECD forecast growth is indicating the further declining trend for the year 2007. However, on the contrary to the US and European economies, the economic growth in Asian developing economies was mainly driven by a combination of strong foreign demand and robust domestic demand and where the rising, exports have been a major driving force. Like the China's share of exports in 2004 (34 per cent), India became second with (18 per cent), during the same year. In fact, India has undergone significant growth in manufacturing and exports of its related services and business process outsourcing[4].

Table 6.1: World Output Growth, 1990-2005
(Percentage change over previous year)

Region/ Country	1990-2000	1999	2000	2001	2002	2003	2004	2005
	Average							
Developed Countries	2.4	2.7	3.5	1.8	1.3	1.7	3	2.3
Japan	1.4	0.1	2.8	0.4	0.3	1.4	2.6	1.8
United States	3.4	4.1	3.8	0.3	2.4	3	4.4	3.5
European Union	2.1	2.9	3.6	1.7	1.1	0.9	2.1	1.5
South-East Europe, CIS	4.3	3.4	8.1	5.6	4.9	6.9	7.5	6
Developing Countries	4.8	3.5	5.4	2.4	3.5	4.7	6.4	5.4
India	6	7.1	4	5.5	4.3	7.8	6.7	6.5

Source: UNCTAD Trade and Development Report, 2005.

Since one of the main reason for the Arab investor's inclination towards the developing economies is because of the profitable avenues here. For example, China and India are among the countries that AGCC is working on signing free trade agreements (FTAs), based on the volume of reciprocal trade. According to Dubai Chamber of Commerce and Industry (DCCI), Dubai's exports to China stood at a total value of Dh 210, 889,563 in 2003. The major export products to China accounted for a combined share of 94.5 per cent of Dubai's total exports to China in 2003. Similarly, in 2003, exports to India accounted for a total volume of Dh 415,744,825. The top exports to India constituted a share of 80 per cent of Dubai's total exports to the country[5].

The basic argument in this context is that Arab Gulf's preference of India for enhancing their economic cooperation is not because both have a thousand years of civilizational links, but it is mainly because, in a competitive economic environment, India is more attractive in recent years than some two or three decades back. In other words, the liberalized economy of India is now more transparent and its investment policies have given more confidence to these countries. Moreover, because of the political stability and democracies, India is becoming safer place to the business. Thus, the center of gravity of the global economy is shifting toward China and India as both are poised to become the new economic powerhouses of the 21st century.

India: An Attractive Market for GCC

Arab companies have not looked towards India till very recently as we have discussed up till now. The Arab countries concentrated their investment in the economies of US and Western Europe, but the economic reform of 1990s, provided a new impetus of oil rich Gulf States to see the economically more viable and alternative investments where future is sound.

The Arab Gulf's economic inclination towards India can be seen among the individual countries of the region. Even at the World Economic Forum – 'Asia and the Middle East', discussion drew attention as the strengthening of trade relations between the Asia-Middle East economic relations has the potential to develop into a strategic block[6].

Now the GCC has emerged as India's fasted growing trading

partner with two-way trade moving above US$ 16 billion, surpassing the China and only left behind the US. India is negotiating a free trade agreement (FTA) with GCC although there is still a roadblock with Indian petrochemical industry, which rather fears that Gulf countries have comparative advantage since they get fuel cheap. India's petroleum sector wants its petroleum products to be put on the sensitive or negative list so that it is not subject to tariff reduction under the FTA. In fact, the production capacities in the GCC countries are projected to expand and this would be an added threat to Indian companies[7].

The following Table 8.2 shows India's direction of trade in various regions during the last one decade – (1996-2006). Although there is a general trend of rising trade relations with these regions, but in WANA region, India's export and import needs special attention. We can see that from 1996 to the year 2000, India's import from the WANA is almost doubled but from the 2001 onward, only the export column is shown to be rising because government of India has stopped mixing the oil import volume with the general import items. We should not be in delusion that our import with WANA is lessening. This however also reflects the sensitive aspect of India's energy import from that particular region as our dependency on this particular commodity is steadily rising. In case of India, however, there is a strategic shift in the foreign policy of the country. It is energy that has become the driving force, and the WANA region is becoming the largest supplier of oil to India where both the private and public sector oil companies are heavily engaged.

Table 6.2 shows India's trade pattern during the last one decade, 1996-2006 with the various region. The most phenomenal growth in the non-oil trade can be seen especially with the West Asian and North African Region, (WANA) from the year 2000 onwards, as the data in this table and figure bellow also include the value of oil imports during the years 1996-2000.

There is more clear picture of India and WANA regions trade relations during the 1996-2006 in the figure 1 given below, where from 2000-01 onwards figure is showing the non-oil trade (and

Table 6.2: India's Direction of Trade - Region Wise, 1996-2006 (US Million)

	EU Countries		ASEAN Region		WANA Region		South Asian Region	
Years	Export	Imports	Export	Imports	Export	Imports	Export	Imports
1996-97	8844.45	10522.67	2934	2934	3344.96	6219.08	1724.39	242
1997-98	9311.41	10806.74	3396.44	3396.44	2464.79	6529.61	1632.2	245
1998-99	9177.47	10840.21	4317.38	4317.38	4214.79	5864.18	1692.02	493.7
1999-2000	9645.95	11076.37	2237.5	4629.16	4545.71	9671.93	1427.83	418.7
2000-01	10670.44	10640.31	2913.78	4147.48	5613.58	3618.39	1954.41	492.49
2001-02	10136.31	10584.24	3457.02	4387.22	5777.83	3170.19	2050.78	589.04
2002-03	11847.87	12780.42	4618.54	5150.17	7863.64	3587.09	2784.9	530
2003-04	14443.58	14991.8	5821.74	7433.16	10185.03	4926.23	4293.55	709
2004-05	18118.3	19115.68	8425.89	9114.66	13232.44	9526.51	4606.14	997.19
2005-06	23120.38	25704.03	10411.3	10883.68	16226.1	10853.89	5547.65	1413.31

Source: Ministry of Commerce, Government of India.

before 2000, the data includes the oil import also). But this should not be seen only in the context of who is gaining more and who is in the deficit position. In fact, this figure would be more revealing if we visualize the future scenario, especially the emerging opportunities in a liberalized market. For, India's huge oil import from the Gulf and other part of the globe also means that the developmental activities in the country is picking up and the ultimate GDP growth would be the net result of what India is striving for. This would also mean that India's export capacity of finished goods would accelerate, as the buoyancy of Indian economy is already indicating. In a globalised market situation, this development ultimately invite the foreign investment because, unlike the US and Europe's sluggish economies, with no much attraction for foreign investors, the dynamics and the investment potentials in India is bound to gain in full, in the years to come as the China is experiencing till now. We can support this argument in the context of Arab Gulf's new trend of investing in India which is accelerating as more and more private investors from the Gulf are turning towards India. The Foreign Direct Investment is clearly proving that once you create an atmosphere of investment and trust, the finance will automatically pour in. Moreover, the same logic applies with the Gulf region also. For example, till hardly one decade back, India could not penetrate in the region despite claiming the thousand years of civilizational links. But once the economic reforms took place, the same Arab world began more economically rational. They found new destination and alternative market in the East and also a space to distance from the traditional Western partners.

Thus, in an economic and business environment under the WTO regulations, a growing tide of confidence is contributing to a more stable future across Asia and the Gulf. India's largest construction and engineering firm, Larsen & Toubro Limited (L&T) has joint ventures in Saudi Arabia and Oman, and operates projects in the United Arab Emirates and Qatar. The company, the largest manufacturer of low-voltage electrical switchgear in India, expects revenues from the Gulf to be doubled to more than US$ 1 billion by 2009. The company is building on the growing Indo-Saudi relations, especially in the economic sector, the local YBA Kanoo Group formed a joint venture at a cost of US$ 15 million in the Second Industrial Area of Dammam to produce electrical switchgears with India's leading engineering company[8].

Huge opportunities for setting up educational institutions and collaborations also exist, particularly because of the big expat Indian population. Now India is also penetrating in the Gulf market through its educational and training institutes. Indian educational institutions like IITs and IIMs have a bright future in the Gulf. The prestigious Indian Institute of Management-Ahmedabad (IIM-A) has entered into a tie-up with Oman's competence HR to offer its short-term 'executive educational programme' in Muscat, Qatar and Abu Dhabi. Recently, the region has been an area of major growth for Satyam, where its revenues grew by almost 60 per cent. Al-Rajhi Bank, Oman Polypropylene, Dubai Holding, Wataniya Telecom and M. H. Al-Shaya are some of Satyam's GCC reference customers.

Another major factor towards Arab Gulf's inclination towards India is the image of 5 million Indian workers in the GCC which is praiseworthy among the business class, as compared to other Asian workers in the region. Consequently, we see that since the year 2000, there has started an increasing flow of Indian expatriates in the region.

The increasing trends of India's FDI from the Gulf countries during 1990-2005 can be seen in Table 6.3. This shows that confidence in the Indian economy is building up among the Arab investors and it is expected to go up in the years to come.

Since India has embarked upon its developmental projects, it needs nearly US$ 320 billion for this over one decade. In the recent bilateral trade discussions, India has invited the Gulf investors to make use of the favorable climate in the country.

Arab investors are tying up with major Indian real estate firms to grab a share of the billion-dollar industry. Some of the large real estate developers in the Arab world — Emaar Properties, Al Ghurair Group's ETA Star, Al Rostamani Enterprises' KM

Properties, Nakheel LLC, Dubai Properties and Kingdom Hotel-investments are betting big on India. ETA Star has commenced work on new projects in Bangalore, Chennai, Kolkata and Hyderabad. Emaar-MGF Land Private Limited, a joint venture company formed by Emaar Properties PJSC - the world's largest listed real estate company, and MGF Developments Limited of India are investing in real estate amounting to over half a billion dollars for projects with a capital outlay of US$ 4 billion (Rs. 18,000 crore). The projects are planned for Delhi, Andhra Pradesh, Karnataka, Tamil Nadu and Maharashtra[9]. Oman's Commerce and Industry Minister Maqbool Ali Sultan has recently indicated that Omani companies too are studying investment openings in India. Citing the US$ 1 billion Oman-India Fertiliser Company (Omifco) as a cornerstone of joint venture between the two countries that has helped Oman to raise its exports from US$ 64 million in 2000 to US$ 366 million in 2005 under the Indian commitment to buy the total production from the plant in fact opened up the possibilities of other similar ventures. On investment plans in India, Oman Oil Company is in talks with Bharat Petroleum Company for possible increase in stake in the long delayed 6 million tonnes Bharat Oman refinery project at Bina in Madhya Pradesh. State-owned Oman Oil Company currently holds three per cent stake in Bharat Oman Refineries Ltd. The refinery is slated for completion in 2009.

Table 6.3: India: Share of Top West Asian Countries FDI Inflows, 1991-2006 (Amount in Millions)

Country	US Dollars	Rupees
UAE	156.27	6,991.16
Israel	43.75	1,623.11
Oman	24.03	1,075.93
Saudi Arabia	19.14	795.38
Kuwait	6.09	263.16
Qatar	0.09	4.01

Source: Ministry of Commerce, Government of India.

With the changing geo-strategic situations in the Gulf, mainly after the September 11, 2001, a sense has developed among the policy makers in India that the time has come to lure the Gulf investors. Turning away from the their traditional favorites like US and Europe, oil rich Gulf countries began to saw partnership especially in energy and oil sector, telecommunication, hotels and real estate[10]. Moreover, the Arab tourist traffic to India, which grew 10.2 per cent to 1,26,873 in 2005, was set for a 20 per cent surge in 2006. There has been an increase of 26.8 per cent during 2004 and 13.2 per cent during 2005 in foreign tourist arrival to the country. With its increased interaction with the trade fraternity from the WANA region, Kerala is now seeing continuous rise of Arab visitors for health tourism raising the revenues by 20 per cent to Rs. 15.2 billion. Kerala is confident that the Smart City project to be developed by Dubai Technology and Media Free Zone (Tecom) and its subsidiary Dubai Internet City (DIC) at the port city of Kochi will go ahead and benefit the state[11].

Moreover, Gulf States are also wooing Asian investments into their ongoing developmental projects after the massive oil revenues increased since 2000 onwards. For example, Saudi Arabia, which is mostly oriented to America and Europe for its strategic relations, is also searching new opportunities of investments in the Asia. The Kingdom has also softened regulations to woo foreign investors[12]. Similarly, Dubai's government has started a push to attract direct investment from Asia's manufacturers, as it tries to broaden its economic base. According to industry leaders speaking at a *MEED* forum on project finance in the Arab World, new projects in the GCC – already at a record high –are expected to grow by up to 50 per cent in 2006. Here, it can be seen that plenty of new investment opportunities exist in India for Gulf corporate majors and vice versa. Moreover, following the decisions of several Emirate states to permit foreign ownership of real estate, there has been substantial interest on the part of Indian investors in purchase of houses and apartments in the UAE. In the last few years, about a third of all investment in real estate in the UAE has originated from the Indian subcontinent[13]. The Dubai Chamber of Commerce and Industry hosted in June 15, 2006, the Indo-Gulf Partnership Summit where the Federation of Indian Chambers of Commerce and Industry (FICCI) and Indian International Film Academy (IIIFA) in association with Dubai Chamber of Commerce and Industry took active part[14].

In this context, the Indo-Arab economic relations have also got much focused and at the governmental level there are increasing efforts to strengthen this as it is the first time that both have come to benefit from each other in the real sense of economic freedom and enterprises.

Although the Arab States are eager to see India a trustable partner much more than an economic partner, however, from time to time, we can notice some acrimonious feelings among the Arabs towards India. For example, in August 2006, the Indian government's ban on Arab television stations was seen in complete contrast to the friendship that Arab countries imagine exists with their neighbors and a work of 'pro-Israeli lobby' in India who wish to drive a wedge between India and its Arab allies. According to Nabila Al-Bassam, a Saudi businesswomen who was on a trip to Mumbai, 'it is a game of double standard that India is playing. One the one hand India establishes friendship with the Arab world while simultaneously it joins with Israel and the US in defaming Arabs[15].

Oil and Gas Market

With the rising demand for hydrocarbon energy for Asian economies to boost their growth engine, the economic integration between Asia and the GCC is increasing and the Asian market is becoming a major target for GCC oil exports, as its exports to Asia are two-thirds of its output. More than half of total GCC exports go to Asian countries while a third of GCC imports are from Asia.

The prospects of energy relations between the Gulf and India are expected to have significant consequences for the geopolitics of the region. GCC countries now realize that their future economic security depend only on their ability to manage oil resources effectively and to engage in successful regional integration. Asia imports more than two-thirds of its daily oil needs with about 80 per cent coming from the Gulf region. In the globalize world energy market, Indo-Gulf relations has taken a significant turn in the sense that conventional view of intra-regional trade, loaded with the heavy energy dependence and its impact on geo-politics and economy come now under no fear of energy supply disruption, all seems to be diminishing under new liberal business environment. This can be seen especially in the context of Asian Oil Market conference at New Delhi in June 2005, were the oil minister's of Asian and Gulf countries examined the market situation from the consumers and producer's perspectives. This also marks a significant development in the area of Indo-Gulf energy relations.

The impact of this new development can now be seen in the countries of Gulf oil producers. Saudi Arabia pumps 60 per cent of its overseas sales to Asia and is looking for new opportunities across the region to secure an outlet for its supplies. Speaking at Asian Oil Market Conference Saudi Oil minister, Naimi rightly pointed out that 'Asia has become our number one customer.

The Gulf region provided about 65 per cent of India's oil imports. In the fiscal year 2004-05, India imported 105 million tons of crude oil and petroleum products at a cost of US$ 29.8 billion the 45 per cent increase over the bill for the previous year. According to one recent estimate, including crude oil and petroleum products, India's imports from the Middle East increased from US$ 5.4 billion in fiscal year 1996-97 to approximately US$ 27.5 billion in fiscal year 2004-05.

As a matter of fact, despite the increasing volume of oil from the Gulf countries, India dependence on the Arab world is not of threatening nature for its exports to the region is also proportionally moving up in the liberalized regime.

But, in the era of globalisation, Indo-Gulf trade relations are now heading towards interdependency. This mean 'the fear of oil dependency on this volatile region would not be same as it was in

1970s or 1980s and the oil and gas, the so-called 'sensitive items' would not pose much threat to India. In fact, the concept of oil supply disruption is not any issue as for India's future economic relations with this region is concerned[16].

Another important development in Gulf hydrocarbon sector can be seen in the re-opening of oil and gas fields to the international oil companies (IOC), previously too, IOCs were in the Gulf countries, but the main dominance was of US and Western oil companies. With the new economic climate and also being conscious of the Western biased attitudes, the Arabs Gulf is trying not to be wholly dependent on Western oil companies. This became possible also because now the de-regulated global oil market has provided them the economically competitive companies from Asian countries.

A new element in the energy relation is the Arab Gulf's readiness to supply natural gas to India. Since the beginning of 1990s India has been eyeing for the liquefied natural gas (LNG) from the Gulf region. Early in 2005, India agreed to import 7.5 million tons of liquefied natural gas annually from Qatar over a 25-year period. The Indian government is also close to realising the long-standing project to build a pipeline from Iran, which if materialized, could start supplying India with natural gas by 2010[17].

After the development of oil production in the Gulf region from 1960's onwards, India's economic relationship with the region became broader and more complex. India became an important customer for crude oil and petroleum products from the Gulf although its dependency of energy outside the Gulf is projected to be safer[18]. Today, India's economic relationship with the Arab Gulf countries is undergoing new and potentially profound changes. The economic and political liberalization in these oil rich Arab Gulf states are opening up investment opportunities to foreign investments for which India is an important partner.

Among downstream players, India's state-owned refiners Indian Oil Corporation Ltd. and Bharat Petroleum Corporation

Ltd., besides private sector entities like Reliance Industries Ltd. and Essar Oil Ltd. are operating in the Gulf's oil fields.

Conclusion

India's new image of a growing economic power in Asia is almost well established, and its major economic partner emerging in recent years are the oil-rich Gulf States. But this has not happened in a sudden, as various global geo-strategic factors have come into it. Foremost among these is the wave of economic liberalization that has taken place in both the regions, paving the way for a potential business and investment climate, which were almost unthinkable till the late 1980s – the period of cold war era. Today, the Arab Gulf's oil wealth inflated by high oil prices, is increasingly finding its way into Asian assets ranging from property and infrastructure to stocks. Asia is now seen as strategically and economically better and a lot of the Gulf investment both public and private funds are being very aggressive in Asia, particularly China and India. Even the Arab Gulf governments are looking in the developing Asian economics as a numbers of the Heads of the States have already toured the countries like China, India, and Malaysia. Historically, Gulf oil money has been invested in Western assets such as US Treasuries and European properties. There is also prevailing an atmosphere of distrust because of the hostile US and Western attitudes towards the Islamic world since the September 11, 2001. But how far this may affect the Arab world's mindset is quite unclear. For India however, its fastest growing economy is a center of attraction for the international investors. Indian manufacturers and traders are moving in the Gulf region with increasing confidence, and are the main competitors to Western names. But in this new competitive environment India's rival from Asian and East Asian regions like China, Malaysia and Pakistan are also in the race to penetrate in the Gulf market. In this challenging scenario, India should must be more transparent while enhancing friendship with Arabs and remove unnecessary barriers in order to attract the Gulf markets.

Notes

1. *Gulf Daily News*, January 28, 2006

2. Mark Thirwell & Anthony Bublo, 'India Looks West', the GCC Looks East', *GCC-India Research Bulletin* (Dubai), Vol.2, June 2006, pp.5-6.

3. Mohamed A. Ramady, '9/11 Changes the Face of Gulf Economies', Arab News, September 25, 2006.

4. *UNCTD Trade and Development Report 2005*, p.9

5. *Khaleej Tiimes* February 22, 2005

6. www.weforum.org/site/homepublic.nsf/Content/Asia+and+the+Middle+East+draw+closer - 36k -

7. *The Economic Times*, September 15, 2006.

8. *Arab News*, March 28, 2006

9. www.menareport.com. 21-12-05

10. *The Economic Times* October 17, 2006.

11. *Khaleej Times*, May 5, 2006

12. Tariq Alhomayed, 'Why do Saudis travel to India and China? *Al-Sharqul Awsat*, January 23, 2006.

13. *Gulf Daily News,* January 28, 2006.

14. Details available at; http://www.dcci.ae/contents.asp?Page=news 1282&cookie per cent5Ftest=1

15. *Arab News* August 6, 2006

16. Javed Ahmad Khan, *India's Energy Security and the Arabian Gulf – Oil and Gas Market in the Decontrolled Regime*, New Delhi: Arise Publishers & Distributors, 2005, ch.4.

17. Javed Ahmad Khan, *India's Search for Natural Gas in the Persian Gulf*, New Delhi: Academy of Third World Studies, JMI, 2004. (Monograph)

18. See for details on India's energy search in various regions, SD Muni and Girjesh Pant, *India's Energy Security – Prospects for Cooperation With Extended Neighborhood,* New Delhi: Rupa Publications, 2005.

7

GCC-India Relations: What Next?

N. Janardhan

Introduction

While being rooted in the prevalent economic dynamics, the aim of this paper is to raise ideas and elicit responses on what the future course of the relationship between the Gulf Cooperation Council (GCC) and India could be beyond the economic realm. While the GCC countries are looking East and India economically still looks West, the premise is that the GCC's new 'Look East' policy has to go beyond preferential trading arrangements and newfound political warmth, and address security strategies as well. The focus is not to lay out a formula, but to try and build an argument that looks beyond the US-centric security paradigm that prevails in the Gulf. The premise again is that the GCC countries would take India seriously only if it is willing to be involved beyond trade.

GCC-Asia Ties

There is little doubt that GCC-India ties are its best and hold even more promise for the future. To understand the changing relations, one needs to see it through the prism of GCC's new approach toward Asia. There is a growing recognition of the increasing significance of Asia as an economic ally at a time when, first, the GCC economies are robust following high oil prices and need new avenues to invest and diversify; and, second, when Asia's oil consumption is soaring amid an economic boom.

The fact that the Saudi king and crown prince chose Asian countries – China, India, Malaysia, Pakistan, Japan and Singapore – on their first tours in 2006 after taking up new offices, and that the Kuwaiti emir's toured Asia in May point to the recognition of

Asia's roles in international stability and security based on their political positions and membership in international organizations, as well as their economic achievements and nuclear power status[1].

The GCC countries are at a stage where they do not want to put all eggs in one basket anymore. They perhaps realize that if the 19th century belonged to the British and the 20th to America, then 21st century could well belong to Asia. Its friendship is widening with a spectrum of nations, which marks its new strategy for separate alliances in the security and economic spheres. In this context, the 'look East' policy is not a replacement for its traditional ally – the United States – but could, however, be an effort to restrict Washington's influence.

Economically, it is a win-win situation based purely on complementarity of interests. They are attempting to make sure that the future Asian economic growth has a GCC contribution through uninterrupted energy supply. Saudi Aramco, for example, now does almost half its business in Asia and has more offices here than anywhere else in the world.

The GCC countries also realize that solutions to many of its problems – including unemployment, need for better education, economic diversification, advancement in the field of science and technology, etc. – lie in linking up with Asia. Helping in the process is the fact that their relations they carry no excess political baggage. Asian countries are not interested in linking political reforms in the Gulf region to economic ties. Both have come to terms with the need for greater liberalization and are positioning themselves to take advantage of a globalised business environment.

At a broader level, the GCC's evolving shift toward Asia is logical. It consumes over 23 million barrels per day, which is 30 per cent of the world's demand. The GCC exports two-third of its oil output to Asia, which could more than double by 2020. Further, more than half of the GCC exports go to Asian countries, while a third of the GCC imports are from Asia. Together, the GCC-Asia oil and non-oil trade figure is over US$ 200 billion. This figure will certainly grow as free trade agreements are being considered with China, India, Japan and Pakistan, and perhaps Singapore and South Korea as well[2].

Beyond the oil and trade dynamic is the human element. Approximately 70 per cent of the GCC's labor force is made up of expatriates, who send home nearly US$ 30 billion as remittances annually. Again, of the 12.5 million expatriates in the region, about 70 per cent of them are Asians.

Recognizing these factors, the GCC Chambers of Commerce and Industry has called for giving priority to activating economic cooperation with Asian countries. This 'Look East' policy in the economic realm comes at a time of regional introspection in the political arena too.

Cooperation and greater linkages between the two regional blocs in the oil sector is thus a key element to ensuring both security of supply for Asian consumers and of demand for GCC oil producers. The rise in energy demand by Asian countries is likely to influence the long-term political economy of the GCC countries and shape international relations in the coming decades[3].

GCC-India Relations

With bilateral non-oil trade almost touching the US$ 20 billion mark in 2005-06 (the oil bill from the Gulf amounted to about US$ 26 billion), relations between the GCC countries and India have evolved greatly since Bombay's days as a premier marketing centre for pearls and dates from the region, and Indian currency and postage stamps were in circulation in the Gulf[4].

The GCC countries account for more than 12 per cent of India's total global exports, supply nearly two-thirds of India's energy needs and host over four million Indians who contribute to the region's economic development. There is also little dispute about the importance to the Indian economy of remittances sent by Indian expatriates and of the increasing Indian dependence on Gulf crude oil, which may grow to 91.6 per cent by 2020.

There is the profitability of business ventures too. India is selling its ideas with the slogan of 'more value for your money'. Indian officials are suggesting that what costs the GCC countries

US$ 100 in the West, only costs US$ 15 in the East. This sets the stage for GCC investment in India's infrastructure projects, while also opening the GCC economies for Indian investment. For example, the Saudi Arabian Investment Authority is putting about US$ 5 billion investment abroad annually, and India plans to build about 28 new airports. Similarly, the Kingdom has chalked US$ 624 billion investments in various sectors over the next five to 10 years and two Indian oil companies are in discussions with Saudi Aramco for possible Saudi investment, which is, in turn, associated with possible investment by Indian companies in the Yanbu refinery[5].

Table 7.1: Select World Oil Consumption Pattern (Thousand Barrels a Day)

Country	1995	2000	2004	2005	Change 2005 over 2004 (%)	2005 share of total (%)
USA	17725	19701	20732	20655	−0.2	24.6
China	3395	4772	6772	6988	2.9	8.5
India	1580	2254	2573	2485	−3.5	3.0
Brazil	1498	1855	1776	1819	2.4	2.2
World	69506	75779	81444	82459	1.3	100.0

Source: Adapted from the BP Statistical Review of World Energy 2006.

Energy Diplomacy

The GCC countries need to watch India's energy diplomacy closely. India's willingness to invest up to US$ 25 billion for acquiring oil and gas fields overseas means its state-owned oil firms have stakes in a dozen countries – Russia, Sudan, Iran, Iraq, Libya, Egypt, Qatar, Ivory Coast, Australia, Vietnam, Bangladesh and Myanmar. It is also exploring possibilities in Kazakhstan,

Turkmenistan, Kuwait, Oman, Yemen, Ecuador and Venezuela.

To meet its forecasted growth rates, though India has also revealed plans to buy up to one million tons of crude annually from Qatar and encourage higher imports of liquefied natural gas (LNG), it is important for the GCC countries to safeguard their business interests with India with regard to the 'fuel of the future'. A US$ 22 billion deal to buy five million tons of LNG annually from Iran over 25 years, starting 2009, will also contribute toward developing clean fuel. The quantity of imports could go up to 7.5 million tons in 2011.

The gas is required to meet industrial and vehicular demand, and for domestic cooking, estimated at 170 million cubic meters per day (mcmpd) and projected to increase to 400 mcmpd over the next 20 years. Domestic gas supply is about 85 mcmpd, with imports expected to cover bulk of the future demand. The number of vehicles sold in India in the year ending March 2005 rose 16 per cent to 7.9 million, in addition to the 50 million already plying on the roads. The thirst for fuel is bound to grow with the increase in internal business and leisure travel, which has triggered a budget airline race and the likelihood of India's aviation market growing by 20 per cent annually.

Aiding in meeting that requirement are talks between India and Pakistan over building a US$ 4-billion, 2,775-kilometer pipeline to bring Iranian natural gas to India through Pakistan – a plan proposed in 1996, but repeatedly hit by roadblocks. Yet, optimistic quarters suggest that pumping gas could be possible by 2012. India's expansion of its energy supply basket has even touched nuclear frontiers. As part of the US-India Energy Dialogue, Washington has agreed to share civilian nuclear technology with India, reversing decades of US policies aimed at discouraging countries from developing nuclear technology. Once approved by the Congress, India could buy nuclear fuel and shop for at least six nuclear power reactors[6].

Common Interests

Politically, GCC-India ties are hampered by one major strain–

the sensitive Indo-Pak border conflict over nuclear flashpoint Kashmir. The hesitation of the GCC countries to fully support India has stymied their cooperation with it. But with the GCC now stressing a bilateral peace process – based on the existing Shimla and Lahore agreements – there is acceptance that a solution, as sought by Pakistan, cannot be decoupled from India's concerns relating to cross-border infiltration.

In a similar vein, in dealing with India without linking it to Pakistan, the GCC countries have put economic pragmatism ahead of religious ideology. India has also joined the GCC's exclusive club as a "dialogue partner" – Japan, the US and Pakistan are the only other countries to have that privilege.

Strategically, by guaranteeing oil supplies, it could be a calculated political move to prompt a decisive tilt by New Delhi away from Iran, which is a big competitor in the energy market. The economic dynamics could have a political angle as well. While it could also serve as a tool to erode Iran's ties with India, the GCC countries may be using India's influence to contribute in any way toward diffusing the current nuclear stand-off.

In the social realm, the time when expatriates remitted all their earnings to their home countries has passed. This can be illustrated by recent decisions in Bahrain – where expatriates with more than 15 years of work experience and a healthy bank balance can now reside in the country even without work permits– and Dubai, which now allows foreigners to own real estate and even trade on the stock exchanges, meaning that money that was hitherto channeled out of the country as savings will soon be reinvested in the economies of Gulf countries. The fruits of engagement in GCC-India ties can therefore be seen to be mutually beneficial.

Beyond the economy and politics, given that the GCC countries and India have several mutual concerns – terrorism being notable among them – maintaining closer ties becomes inevitable and, given the subcontinent's volatile security milieu and the critical developments in the Gulf, even acquires a sense of urgency.

Tracking India's Resurgence

It is important to mention here the changing perception of India and Indians in the Gulf. After being the major source of unskilled and semi-skilled workforce to the Gulf for decades, India is now ready to increase its share of skilled and professional workforce in the region, which is bound to alter the composition of the Indian workforce in the region to some degree[7]. The wealth of resources India has on offer in the realm of the knowledge economy is an encouraging prospect for the GCC countries – more than 380 universities, 11,200 colleges and 1,500 research institutions; as well as the increase in the IT workforce – from 6,800 in 1986 to 650,000 in 2003 to over two million by 2010.

While characteristics such as India being the world's largest democracy, home to 150 million Muslims, fourth largest economy in the world in terms of purchasing power parity and world's largest provider of peacekeepers are well documented, India's strategic importance is being viewed in what the country is shaping to be – the fourth largest consumer of energy by 2010, which is indicative of the economy's momentum; hi-tech plans to develop super-computers, complete nuclear fuel cycle facilities and placement of own satellites in orbit; replicating IT success in biotechnology, biogenetics and pharmaceuticals; and more importantly, a strategic partner of the United States, which is willing to share nuclear technology for civilian use and even share roles in joint space missions.

It is now evident to the GCC countries that the beneficiaries of India's knowledge economy include the United States and Europe, which will help India play a bigger role in the region's service industry. Further, the expanding private sector in the region has given Indians a level playing field over Western expatriates, and an opportunity to showcase their professional skills.

Prominent Gulf Arabs are taking note of changes in India and voicing their opinion. Comparing Indian youth who were finding easy employment in the services sector as part of the outsourcing drive in the last few years, Khaled Al-Maeena, Editor-in-Chief of

Jeddah-based *Arab News*, wrote: "In the same period, I wonder how many of our young people found jobs. I also wonder how many of our young people have a good command of English and the necessary IT skills. I am afraid of the answer, and I am really afraid of finding out how many of our young people have good work ethics"[8].

Similarly, Bahrain-based intellectual Abdullah Madani said: "(The Gulf's) recognition of India's advancement in numerous vital areas and its political willingness to learn and benefit from India…is a new Gulf rhetoric, given the prevailing preconceived idea in the region that India is no more than a backward nation that is only capable of supplying poor quality goods and unskilled labour. In fact, there is now a sound base for the two sides to establish a long-term strategic partnership"[9].

Of course, there is a pervasive feeling all around that economic sense is common sense. The GCC has finally realized the significance of reinforcing and expanding cooperation with India, while maintaining its strong ties with Pakistan, a key element that was missing in its diplomacy armour in the past. As a result, after years of hesitation, ideology – in the form of Islamic solidarity – took a backseat and the GCC dealt with India and Pakistan on a level playing ground by signing the framework agreement on economic co-operation.

While having a non-Hindu president, prime minister and leader of the largest party in the parliament, as well as King Abdullah bin Abdulaziz's visit – the first by a Saudi head of state in 60 years – contributed positively to India's image, more importantly, the Gulf is also taking note of India's renewed interest in the region.

Security Dynamics: GCC Perspective

Moving on to the not-so-explored territory of security dynamics, the need for alternate strategies in the Gulf and the possibility of India playing a role in it arises as a result of changing developments on both sides.

In the Gulf, the United States has been inept in dealing with the Iraqi and Iranian security dilemmas. Given the added pressure of the region's leadership being unable to provide the necessary vision, two schools of thought prevail in the region: one urging less international involvement in the region's affairs and the other, more.

Those arguing that the way out of the dilemma is through the withdrawal of external powers from the Gulf feel that external powers have precipitated the crises rather than contribute positively. They feel the region may be better off dealing with the crises itself; and that the Gulf has become so complacent that it is unwilling to evolve indigenous mechanisms for conflict prevention and resolution, as well as shying away from confidence-building measures with potential rivals. Therefore, the new mantra, even elucidated by the GCC countries, is that "a lasting Gulf security system can only function if it is based on a regional initiative".

But the situation on the ground is really not conducive to the complete removal of external forces. The GCC countries "neither practice nor engage in any sort of cooperative security exchange," and there is a sense of distrust even among the members of this homogenous bloc[10]. As a result, an indigenous alternative and viable security architecture is highly unlikely.

In such a situation, the alternative is further internationalization of the region. The dominant view is that the United States is a spent force – not militarily or economically, but politically. "What remains is a facade of a relationship." The GCC countries realize that they require American military power for protection in a volatile region. "For the moment, they rather have the US in their back pocket despite all its problematic policies than have Iran breathe down their neck."

This school argues that all the US approaches in the region – relying on Iran and Saudi Arabia as part of the twin-pillar policy in the 1970s; propping up Iraq to counter Iran as part of the balance of power in the 1980s; and invasion of Iraq in 2003 – have failed to guarantee the desired level of security. Yet, the US pursues a "balance-of-power approach" by playing one country against another in the bloc. As a result, the GCC countries are willing to consider intense political, economic and social ties with other countries to counter the prevailing notion that only (US) military power counts.

Two examples from the Saudi experience illustrate these changes. Frustrated by the impasse in the Arab-Israeli conflict even before September 11, 2001, then Crown Prince Abdullah instructed the Saudi ambassador to the US to deliver the following message: "Starting from today, you're from Uruguay, as they say. You (Americans) go your way, I (Saudi Arabia) go my way. From now on, we will protect our national interests, regardless of where America's interests lie in the region." In a more diplomatic suggestion, Saudi Foreign Minister Saud Al-Faisal told the Gulf Dialogue meeting in Bahrain in December 2004 that guarantees for Gulf security cannot be provided unilaterally "even by the only superpower in the world". The region requires guarantees "provided by the collective will of the international community."

The events leading to these and similar reactions in the region have forced the GCC countries to build ties with a host of alternatives, particularly in Europe and Asia. Some of the countries here have one factor in common: they are "regional plus" powers; their political weight goes well beyond their geographical borders, though not as far as to give them a global reach or global ambitions. This gives them a perfect stake in developing a multi-polar world that can resist any single nation's efforts to achieve dominance[11]. While cultivating the new relationship, the region is linking its economic interests and security needs. And, apart from the importance of energy, Europe and Asia are showing signs of relating to the relevance of the Gulf region to transnational security issues such as proliferation of weapons, crime, drugs and terrorism, and their impact on their domestic scenarios. Further, to many, the fact that the Arab Gulf countries are even willing to consider alternatives despite US objections is the "real strategic shift occurring in the region"[12].

Indian Perspective

While energy security is certainly a factor, India is now

willing to showcase its power and influence in the region. This expanded security perspective is driven by necessity, ambition and opportunity. The desire to lead coincides with its rise as a major power with continental aspirations. Former premier Atal Behari Vajpayee and current Prime Minister Dr. Manmohan Singh urged looking beyond the immediate neighbourhood. Singh said "the Gulf region is a part of our natural economic hinterland. We must pursue closer economic relations with all neighbors in our wider Asian neighborhood"[13].

After Pakistan, China, Russia and the US, the Gulf is the focus to ensure against any maritime or landward threat to it from the region, serve as a base to pursue India's interests, confront terrorism and extremism, as well as tap the investment potential. By focusing on the Gulf and restoring traditional linkages with the immediate and extended neighbourhood, India is seeking to address its "four deficits" in the historical, security, economic and global decision-making realms[14].

India is now talking about "soft power" and diplomacy – the security of the Gulf countries, as well as the wider Middle East, is of "paramount concern" and New Delhi is ready to contribute to the stability of the region by sharing its experience in combating terrorism, maritime security and military training. India stresses that events in Iraq have brought home the fact that a politically unstable area can become the spawning ground of terrorists.

"Linkages with illicit trafficking in narcotics, as well as in small arms have enhanced the destructive potential and lethal reach of the terrorists. The fight against terrorism has to be long-term, sustained and comprehensive. It cannot be ad hoc, selective or compartmentalized in terms of region or religion"[15].

According to India's National Security Adviser M.K. Narayanan: "The key focus in our external relations today is ensuring the stability and security of the region, comprising the arc of nations from the Gulf to East Asia...India's decision to enter into cooperative strategic relationship with China fully mirrors this approach[16]."

India is keen on cooperation with the GCC countries to ensure safety and security of sea-lanes and of communications; safety and freedom of navigation in the shipping lanes and trade routes; positively influence religious extremism and/or transnational terrorism, narcotics trafficking and proliferation of weapons in the region; and achieve peace in the subcontinent, given Pakistan's bond with the region.

Further, portraying India as "a core state" in the emerging global order and offering to help secure the busy Malacca Straits against high-seas pirates at the Asia Security Summit in Singapore in June 2006, Mukherjee said: "(New Delhi's) role is crucial for ensuring and maintaining long-term peace, stable balance of power, economic growth, and security in Asia...India is one of the important legs of the Asian juggernaut along with China, Japan, and Indonesia[17]."

The latest military build-up plan dates back to 2001. On a visit to Washington, then external affairs minister Jaswant Singh said: "For a long time, India has not been seen in its true dimensions. How many people know that Indonesia is only 65 miles from the southernmost Indian island? Or that but for Pakistan-occupied (*sic*) Kashmir, Tajikistan is just 27 miles from India. That we had a border with Iran in 1947? Or that the legal tender of Kuwait till 1938 was the rupee? So when we talk about Indonesia or central Asia or the Gulf, it is because of our interest and our sphere of influence."

With this in mind, the government launched "a 20-year program to become a world power whose influence is felt across the Indian Ocean, the Arabian Gulf, and all of Asia"[18] in November 2003.

In order to highlight its potential and achieve its objectives, the Indian military services are undertaking a major build-up of conventional arms, creating ways of delivering nuclear weapons and defending against them, planning construction of warships, enhancing military logistics in Central Asia and negotiating with the US for an Asian version of NATO. All these come in the wake of India's existing maritime security involvement involving Asian, African, European and Gulf countries (Oman), as well as

Russia and the US. Further, the Indian Coast Guard and Navy have been active in anti-piracy, disaster relief, and environmental management and response operations, which was evident after the 2004 tsunami.

A key role in this program is that of the Indian Navy. In October 2003, then navy chief Admiral Madhvendra Singh said: "Fulfilling India's dream to have a full-fledged blue-water navy would need at least three aircraft carriers, 20 more frigates, 20 more destroyers with helicopters, and large numbers of missile corvettes and anti-submarine warfare corvettes." The Navy's acquisitions program was then worth US$ 20 billion. The plan includes acquiring or constructing a submarine that could launch nuclear missiles, aircraft carriers, and long-range missiles with a reach of over 2,500 kilometers.

The Navy's aim is not just to patrol the seas, but have the capacity to create and "deploy battalion-sized forces at various strategic points... [on] short notice, and disperse them quickly from the landing or dropping zone before any adequate enemy response". The inference is that the expansion program envisions possible intervention in countries in India's "sphere of influence".

These plans were reflected in the government's Maritime Doctrine in 2004. According to a US War College study:

"Whereas (India's) earlier doctrine focused on inward-looking strategies, the new doctrine attempts to deal with conflict with (an) extra-regional power and protecting persons of Indian origin and interest abroad," (which perhaps brings the Gulf on the radar screens)[19].

Maintaining that the 'challenge' lies in India becoming a maritime power, former Indian Navy chief Admiral Arun Prakash promised in August 2006 a fully balanced, technologically fighting fit force in the next decade.

"We are back on track on the submarine front (and) in a few years time would be back to the desired levels on the naval air operations front as well....With fantastic support by the indigenous shipbuilding infrastructure and other acquisitions, within the next 10 years, the Indian Navy would be a fully-balanced, technologically fighting fit, all-purpose maritime force to be reckoned with...The challenge, therefore, lies in India becoming a maritime power. No one can stop India from becoming a maritime power...Though our maritime interests are now all over, anything that happens between the east coast of Africa and the Malacca Straits is of immediate concern to India. We have the business to know what is happening in this part of the Indian Ocean. So, this is the immediate footprint of the Indian Navy...All our maritime strategies, plans and growth takes into account the matrix of economic interests and military threats. All that the force is planning is done keeping in view of the bigger role of the country in world affairs in the 21st century and safeguarding all the vital interests of India....There's total consensus on this issue and we are not going back from this approach to Indian maritime strategies or planning. China and Pakistan are only a small part of it, nothing more"[20].

The naval build-up can be gauged from the 8,000-acre Seabird naval base near Goa, which would bring together warships, aircraft carriers and long-range aircraft, among others, capable of impacting waters that stretch from Aden to the Malacca Strait. Further, Israeli-built Heron UAVs in Kochi would give India a surveillance capability that is unrivalled in the region.

Conclusion

Notwithstanding the historic ties between the GCC and India, which have been sustained by the current oil, trade and expatriate dynamics, the way forward for a robust bilateral relationship rests on developing a paradigm that hinges on strategic political, economic and security dimensions.

The common political and security concerns translate into efforts for peace and stability in the Gulf region and South Asia. The emerging perceptions create further opportunities for GCC-India cooperation in the future. While the GCC countries are going through important changes and transformations, the process of understanding and integration needs to intensify beyond the traditional issues. This involves joint efforts to meet domestic and regional challenges.

In acknowledging that the existing cooperation was not proportional to their historical ties, geographical proximity, and deep-rooted interactions between their people since ancient times, and signing the ground-breaking framework agreement, the two sides indicated that they were ready to move away from oil and rhetoric and not allow political and ideological differences to puncture economic ties.

Aiding the process is the change of political guard in India. As part of the Congress Party-led coalition government's stated policy of reverting to more traditional ties with the Arab world, as opposed to the former government's perceived close relations with Israel, the ideological barrier has and should incrementally make way for constructive dialogue and mutually-trustworthy relationship between the two sides.

But while many dub King Abdullah's visit to India in early 2006 as "a strategic shift" in Saudi foreign policy, others believe that the visit and its implications are highly exaggerated. The pessimistic view could be a result of the lack of any follow-up action on India's part. For example, the Chinese President Hu Jintao reciprocated Saudi diplomacy in April, three months after King Abdullah's visit. But there is nothing yet to suggest that a visit by the Indian prime minister is on the anvil.

With India viewing the Gulf, South Asia and Central Asia as "strategically interactive and interrelated regions", it is time for the GCC to reciprocate in a commensurate way. Given the prevailing anti-West sentiment among Arabs, it is the appropriate time for upgrading GCC-India ties.

A GCC-India relationship based purely on selling and buying of oil is untenable in the long run. The GCC countries need to take note of the fact that India's basket of energy suppliers are widening. It is not impossible that India may follow the United Sates, which gets more oil from Africa than the Middle East, or China which gets more crude supplies from Angola than Saudi Arabia. With a view to strengthening and diversifying relations, it is imperative for both to acquire fresh dimensions to consolidate their positions in a fast-changing world.

Further, while the GCC countries may be uncomfortable with India's ties with Israel and Iran, there is no doubt that New Delhi will not compromise on its own strategic interests and downgrade its relationship with Tel Aviv and Tehran to accommodate the GCC countries reservations. Instead, the GCC countries could use the India-Iran bonhomie to its advantage. Since India has maintained good relations with Iran, including a military cooperation agreement in 2003, improved GCC-India ties could be used as a tool to engage New Delhi in the role of an honest broker in the GCC-Iran relations.

The GCC countries and India share a common desire for peace, stability and security in the region and value the independence, sovereignty and territorial integrity of the countries concerned. However, in the process of moving forward, the real challenge is how to turn the Indian military strength into a factor of regional security. The dilemmas in the Gulf region could ease if the GCC countries and India evolve new ideas of collective security that go beyond the restrictive paradigms of the past. But by suggesting that it is willing to play a proactive role by sharing its experience in combating terrorism, maritime security and military training, New Delhi may also be indicating just how far it is willing to go, which, in fact, is not far enough for the long-term security concerns of the Gulf countries.

This raises many questions.

- Will India stick to involvement only in soft security issues?
- If it goes beyond, will it mirror the US approach or will it be distinct and non-controversial?
- Even if it is interested in a wider role, what will public opinion be and how effective will India's role be?
- How will India's increasing military cooperation with the United States pan out in the GCC countries?
- More crucially, are the GCC countries looking 'out of the box' for their security or is the US making a mountain out of a molehill while expressing long-term fears about China's intentions in the regional security architecture, and possibly

India's in the future?

Notes

1. Three of these countries are nuclear powers.

2. Negotiations for the GCC-India free trade agreement began in 2004 after the idea was mooted at the inaugural GCC-India Business Conference in Mumbai in February 2004, which served as a springboard to transform a traditional relationship into a robust one. The GCC-India Framework Agreement, which was signed in August that year, was aimed at enabling exploration of possibilities of mutually beneficial economic and industrial cooperation, with particular emphasis on supply of energy, oil and natural gas to India, development of small- and medium-scale enterprise sectors, meaningful privatization programs, Indian participation in the petrochemical and energy-intensive industries in the GCC and tie-ups with Indian information technology companies. A clause that would prevent another fiasco like the Saudi displeasure with the Bahrain-US FTA was also inserted – "individual member states are free to undertake bilateral activities with India in various fields". After the last round of talkṣ at the second GCC-India Business Conference in Muscat in March 2006, the two parties are hopeful of an agreement in 2007; more details on the race for FTAs on both sides are available in N. Janardhan, "For the GCC and India, escalating opportunities," *The Daily Star* (Lebanon), January 10, 2006.

3. For more details, read N. Janardhan, "GCC-Asia ties: economy first; what next?" *Khaleej Times* (UAE), January 31, 2006.

4. India's oil import .bill in 2005-06 was US$ 43.8 billion as opposed to US$ 29.8 billion the previous year, increase of 46.8 per cent.

5. For suggestions on how to intensify GCC-India economic cooperation, see A.C. Patankar, "Economic and Industrial Cooperation – Future Challenges," *GCC-India Research Bulletin*, (Gulf Research Center, Dubai, June 2006).

6. N. Janardhan, "What oils the wheels of GCC-Indian cooperation?" *The Daily Star*, August 12, 2006.

7. India now annually produces more engineers than the European Union. The Indian embassy in Abu Dhabi estimates that currently 25 per cent of the Indian working population can be categorized as unskilled, 50 per cent as semi-skilled/skilled, and the remaining as professionals and businessmen.

8. "14,000 jobs and a bitter lesson in skills," *Gulf News* (UAE), February 23, 2004.

9. "The GCC finally takes a note of the Indian giant," *Gulf News*, September 5, 2004.

10. Recent examples include serious differences between Saudi Arabia and Bahrain over the latter signing the free trade agreement with the United States, which resulted in the Saudi crown prince boycotting the December 2004 GCC Summit in Manama; and the widening rift between Saudi Arabia and Qatar over Al-Jazeera's coverage of political events in the Gulf, which has manifested in several forms, including the US shifting from the Prince Sultan Air Base in Saudi Arabia to Al-Udaid in Qatar starting 2002, and unconfirmed Saudi objection to a Qatar-UAE (Dolphin) gas project in 2006.

11. Read Jonathan Steele, "India's revival means it can pick and choose its friends," *Guardian* (UK), February 24, 2006.

12. For more on these issues, read Christian Koch, "Gulf region makes strategic shift in new global system," *Arab News* (Saudi Arabia), 22 October 2006; Christian Koch, "Gulf needs more, not less, external involvement," *Gulf in the Media (UAE),* January 27, 2006; and Tanvir Ahmad Khan, "Taking a broader view of security in the Gulf," *Gulf News*, 13 July 2006.)

13. "PM keen on building strong ties with Gulf states", Sify.com (India), August 7, 2005.

14. Part of a statement by former Indian defense minister Pranab Mukherjee at the Carnegie Endowment for International Peace, Washington, DC, June 27, 2005.

15. Statement by India's Special Envoy to the Middle East Chinmaya Gharekhan at the second Gulf Security Conference in Bahrain, 2-3 December 2005.

16. These views were part of his presentation titled "China and India: The Asian rising powers debate – An Indian perspective," at the third Global Strategic Review Conference of the International Institute for Strategic Studies in Geneva on September 18, 2005.

17. "India is a core state for Asian security: Pranab Mukherjee," *The Hindu* (India), June 4, 2006.

18. India's defense expenditure doubled from US$ 11.6 billion in 1998-99 to US$ 21.5 billion in 2005-06. More details available in "India's place in the US strategic order," Research Unit for Political Economy (Mumbai), December 2005.

19. For more on GCC-India tactical dimensions, see Khadija Arafah Muhammad Amin, "Need for strategic cooperation," *GCC-India Research Bulletin* (Gulf Research Center, Dubai, January 2006).

20. "Navy chief promises technologically fighting fit force," *Indo Asian News Service,* August 8, 2006; such assertions have led to question if India's naval modernization effort is aimed at turning the Indian Ocean into India's ocean. For more, see "US, China, India flex muscle over energy-critical sea lanes," *Freerepublic.com*, June 10, 2006.

Part IV: Globalisation, India and WANA: Political Dimensions

8

American Hegemony in WANA Region: Challenges for India

Chintamani Mahapatra

American hegemony is not a new phenomenon in world history. But the slow emergence of the US as a powerful hegemonic power is rooted in birth and evolution of the United States. The birth of this country itself is the outcome of European expansionism. The establishment of settlements by European colonists along a narrow strip of land along the Atlantic coast soon gave birth to a policy of expansion, which is an important aspect of colonial history of the US. This territorial expansion by the European, largely British settlers, was at the cost of Indian tribes. The post-independent history of the US was primarily a story of westward expansion of the US. Even before the continental expansion was complete, the US Administrations began to focus on expanding political influence and economic presence, if not territorial, over the rest of the countries of the Western Hemisphere on the basis of the Monroe Doctrine[1]. The US industrial expansion was still limited with little need for overseas market when the ideologues in that country advocated foreign adventures, naval expansion, overseas naval bases and a colonial possession in the Pacific[2].

Soon after the quick victory in a war with Spain in 1989 and eventual colonization of the Philippines, the US propounded an "Open Door" policy for facilitating penetration of American capital and goods into the Chinese market. By the beginning of the 20th century, the US was one among many major powers and certainly not the strongest one. But its hegemony over the Western Hemisphere was unrivalled, which continues until today. As far as Asia was concerned, US motivation to establish a hegemonic presence was clear, but European colonial powers and Japan were not prepared to let that happen.

Not until after the Second World War could the US establish a hegemonic presence in other parts of the world. This war ended the European empires and led to the establishment of an American empire albeit with a difference. The decolonization process gave birth to a number of independent nation-states and contributed to an altered political geography of the globe. Armed with the deadly nuclear weapons and possessing unparalleled economic and technological resources, the US co-opted almost all major powers, both the victors and the vanquished of the Second World War, and sought to build a global order in its own image.

The challenge to US hegemony came from an erstwhile ally during World War II and that was the former Soviet Union. There was not a single other major power that supported the Soviet Union in the latter's struggle against American hegemony in different parts of the world. Nonetheless, Moscow benefited from the unwillingness of a vast number of newly independent countries to join the US-led bloc that executed a Cold War against the Soviet Union and a political war against the ideology of "Communism." The so-called "non-aligned" group of countries did not join the Soviet bloc either, but most of them had long colonial experiences and detested anything that had the potential of turning them into neo-colonial powers. The US did not rule most of these countries as a colonial power and had only a few colonial possessions compared to Europeans, but it considered it essential to seek the support of the former colonial powers in the Cold War against the Soviet Communists and thus antagonized the nationalists in the developing world by doing so. The end result of all this was political isolation of the US in the vast majority of non-aligned countries.

The Soviet opposition and the non-aligned movement made it difficult for the US to establish and run a global empire, which was part of the American dream, as has been specified in the doctrine of "Manifest Destiny." As the two superpowers remained engaged in the Cold War, West Europe and Japan recovered their war-torn economies and a few regional powers equipped with sophisticated weapons, including nuclear weapons and deadly delivery systems, surfaced on the world stage. By the 1970s, the US was a declining power and Manifest Destiny was far from being realized.

When the Cold War ended with the collapse of the Soviet Union, the bipolar power structure of the international system was dismantled. By this time, the European Union, Japan, ASEAN, China, and India had already emerged as important actors in the world stage. The severe psychological blow of the Soviet disintegration created political hallucinations, strategic dreams and utter disappointments in various parts of the world, including in the US. Some in America and many elsewhere concluded that the world had turned unipolar, the US had become a hyper-power and the American empire had spread around the globe. Those who had theorized the existence of a multipolar international system during the Cold War also came to be persuaded that there was only one remaining superpower in the world and thus there was no discernible second pole of power anywhere.

As events unfolded and analysts woke up to emerging realities, the world slowly and slowly came to look different. The prevailing discourse of American unilateralism is actually a myth. First of all, the US was more powerful in the immediate aftermath of the Second World War than it is today. It was much richer and prosperous in terms of wealth generation then and it is now. Secondly, there was less number of political or military heavy weights at that time than is the case now. Thirdly, Russia with ten time zones and tens of thousands of nuclear weapons and missiles still possess the overkill capacity and can threaten the physical existence of the US and the globe. Fourthly, a smaller strategic ally like Pakistan could send its foreign secretary to Washington to declare the country's achievement of a nuclear capability within a couple of years after Washington imposed the Pressler Amendment against the nuclear programme. Fifthly, India could defy the West and refuse to sign the CTBT and eventually conduct a series of nuclear weapon tests and announce itself as a nuclear weapon power. Sixthly, two members of the so-called axis-of-evil continue to defy the hyper power, one by conducting a nuclear test and the other refusing to stop uranium enrichment. Seventhly, one may ponder over the following questions to examine the nature and extent of American unilateralism: could the US have gone into Kuwait to liberate it from Iraqi occupation all by itself? Could the US have gone alone to fix Bosnia or even Kosovo? Could the US resort to retribution against the Al Qaeda by bombing Afghanistan all by itself? Could the US have gone into Iraq in 2003 all by itself? Was the US alone in opposing the Kyoto Protocol, refusing to adopt the landmine ban or hesitating from joining the International Criminal Court? Or, there are some developing or newly industrialized countries, which have also been able to be defiant? Was the US alone in being able to bypass the UN when it suited its purpose? Or, there are also other instances where lesser powers also did so?

Seen from a different angle, the US certainly is the richest country in the world. But it is also the largest debtor nation. After World War II the US represented half of the global out put, but by the closing years of the 20th Century it accounted for about a fifth of the world GDP. Does the richest country, the USA, represent an equitable society, if not an equal society? As a matter of fact, the US, despite its high democratic credentials, is not an equal or equitable society. Racism still persists in the American society and the income inequality is one of the worst. Is it a completely healthy society? No, deaths from diabetes, TB, flu, cancer are a regular feature and 39 states in the US have detected AIDS. More than 40 per cent of American people do not have health insurance in the US. According to analysts, the US is the only industrialized country where health care is regarded as a privilege and not a basic necessity. Has there been perfect law and order in the US? No, some commentators have point out that the US cannot maintain order in its own capital and speaks loudly about its responsibility to maintain global order. According to an Amnesty International Report of June 2001, about half a million murders took place in America since 1977. The US accounts for the globe's largest prison population, which comes to about a quarter of the world total or 2 million.

All these facts indicate that there is no global hegemony and there exists no unipolar world contrary to several theoretical constructs by international relations scholars. The realist and neo-realist school of scholars do not deny the existence of a unipolar power structure and only argue that it is a temporary phenomenon sooner than later to be replaced by a new balance of power. Some of them wonder as to why no real balancing is taking place yet and others try to explain in terms of realist structures. The neo-liberal scholars interestingly believe in the durability of the present hegemonic power structure and provide explanations by referring to less threatening posture of the US to other major powers and existence of myriad inter-locking international institutions where the US plays a role along with other powerful nations. There are some scholars who argue that the existence of nuclear weapons in Russia and China are enough to deter the US and thus there is no unipolarity. Critics point out that such an argument is based on an analysis that counts only the military power as the important variable and thus lacks conviction.

However, even if some other criteria are included in the analyses, it would be difficult to establish that there is anything called American global empire, a globocop, American century or American hegemony around the globe. There is no doubt that:

- The US has the most potent and sophisticated military machine in the world.
- The US spends more on military than other members of the G8 combined.
- The US spends almost as much money on defense as the rest of the world put together[3].
- But it is the spread of small arms that poses the real danger to human life. Half billion small arms spread around the globe take about 300, 000 lives every year in armed conflict, although another 200, 000 are killed due to suicide or homicide. About 80 per cent of all these casualties are civilian and about 90 per cent of those killed are by small arms.

Almost every minute one person falls dead by the use of a gun. More than a 1000 companies in above 90 countries are responsible for production and sale of small arms. About 90 countries have the capacity to produce small arms and half of them belong to developing countries. Can the US be a globocop in such circumstances?

- It is true that the US is the biggest arms seller in the world. It accounts for about 40 per cent of the global market and about 50 per cent of the developing world's market. But then there are several others who compete with the US and share the rest 60 per cent and 50 per cent of the arms bazaar[4].
- The US is the wealthiest country[5], but its economy is not completely self-dependent. While the US provides a huge market to very many countries in the world, including Russia, China and India, it depends on the world market for its survival and prosperity. More than 20,000 US companies are spread out in the nook and corner of the world and producing goods in other countries and buying those back. While less than 2 per cent of American people produce more than enough agricultural products for domestic consumption and exports, they still depend on huge subsidies[6]. It is ironic that US farm lobby was instrumental in getting a portion of US sanctions against Pakistan lifted after Chagai nuclear explosions[7]. The US economy and the US military R & D depend on conflicts in the Third World and arms race abroad.

US Hegemony in WANA Region

If hegemony or unipolar system would mean absolute dominance, it has never been there in world history. If it would mean less than that in terms of degree of dominance or relative predominance, the currently perceived "unipolarity" is anything but inimitable. As William R. Thompson writes, "...unipolarity in global politics—a high concentration of power favoring one state is a recurring, if nonpermanent, phenomenon[8]."

Having said that, there is little doubt that the US is relatively the most dominant actor in the politics and security of the WANA region. It is probably the biggest investor in the region, but its foreign direct investment, mostly in the oil industry, is only 5 per cent of its global total. It is probably the largest trading partner of most of the countries in the region, but its trade in non-oil sector is abysmally low. The US with five per cent of world's people consume huge amount of world energy. The Americans consume more oil per day than combined consumption in China, Japan, Russia, Germany and India—the next five largest oil consumers[9]. It is also the largest importer of oil, but except Saudi Arabia no other country in this region figures in the list of top ten oil exporter to the US.

However, the WANA region has 8 out of top 15 major oil exporters in the world and they include Saudi Arabia, Iran, UAE, Kuwait, Algeria, Libya, Iraq and Qatar. It is Saudi Arabia alone that sells most quantity of oil to the US, but America's allies and potential adversaries buy oil from these countries. Moreover, these oil producers are crucial to maintaining the oil price stability in the international market. Secondly, 5 out of top 14 oil producers in the world are part of WANA and they are Saudi Arabia, Iran, UAE, Kuwait and Algeria. Hence the US continues to play a substantial role in the region by establishing cordial ties with the regimes, maintaining military bases and a modest troop presence.

It is a myth that the US is dependent on Middle Eastern oil. First of all, the US is the third largest producer of oil. Secondly, the US import of oil originates from very many countries, including the OPEC and a large number of non-OPEC members. In August 2006, for instance, the US imported oil from many countries at the rate of 13, 334 barrels per day. Out of this, the Persian Gulf accounted for only 2,310 barrels per day. Out of this, Saudi Arabia alone accounted for 1, 513 barrels per day[10]. And thus when the US officials make declarations about the need for assured supply of oil, its nuances have to be examined properly.

Having taken serious measures to prevent the volatile WANA region from directly disrupting life and security of the American people, the US has devised a policy that makes it the dominant player in this region. First, it has established very close relationship with the undemocratic regimes of the region by promising to guarantee their security and durability. Secondly, it has maintained a robust military presence in the region to guard against the entry of any other major power into the region, to prevent the emergence of any regional heavy-weight in WANA region that could pose a challenge to US interests, to ensure the energy security of allies and to be able to disrupt energy supply to any future adversary.

Such American strategy appears to be frightening. It is partly because other major international actors today are not prepared to take risk. Russia is energy resource rich and is a net exporter of oil and gas. China has become a net oil importer and its dependence on imported oil is rising day by day, but it does not have the wherewithal to play a dominant role in WANA region. The EU and Japan are economic power houses and logically should be interested in maintaining a strong military and political presence in WANA region. But both Brussels and Tokyo have been outsourcing their security to the US for long and have been largely followers of the US lead.

Even then, the US policy in this region has not always been successful, because there is no absolute dominance or hegemony of the US. First of all, Israel, the closest strategic ally of the US has never been able to live at peace. The military might of Israel, its successive victory in wars against Arab countries in 1950s, 1960s and 1970s, its occupation of Arab land, its refusal to concede a sovereign Palestinian State look very impressive from one angle. But seen from another perspective, Israel has been living under constant threat to peace and stability within its borders. It has been the largest recipient of American foreign assistance and the US has also certain amount of leverage in the Arab world, but the regional peace has been eluding for decades. The US and Israel have failed to dictate peace, despite massive military, including nuclear capability. A hegemon in true sense of the term would have been expected to do so.

Secondly, the US has miserably failed in its Iran policy for now more than quarter of a century. The successful Iranian Islamic revolution, ejection of US military presence from that country, the hostage crisis, failure of the containment strategy, long spell of sanctions against Iran as well as on foreign entities seeking big business opportunity in Iran indicate the degree to which one should look at the US as a hegemon in this region. Without any open support from the international community, Iran recently has been able to defy the wishes of the US, the EU-3 and the UN Security Council to desist from enriching uranium as part of its efforts to establish a full cycle civilian nuclear programme.

Thirdly, nothing illustrates better the plight of the so-called hegemon than the insurgency against the US and other coalition troops raging in Iraq since 2003. Although the neo-conservative foreign policy team in the Bush Administration, which perceives the US as a sole superpower running a unipolar world, wished to remove the Saddam regime in Baghdad, majority of the major powers and a vast majority of the international community could not be convinced of the US rationale and thus backed away from supporting the US military intervention. Washington certainly succeeded in breaking up the European Union and the NATO alliance on Iraq issue, but failed to constructively engage them in its Iraq strategy. The Arab neighbours, who did not hesitate to back US military action against the Taliban, also kept distance from US military misadventure into Iraq. The Bush Administration could neither cajole nor pressurize the Arab countries to join forces in removing the Saddam regime. Now it is increasingly becoming evident that Iraq intervention was a great strategic blunder. The Vietnam Syndrome is often being revisited by American people, pundits and political leaders alike.

Fourthly, no major power has been as badly challenged by non-state entities as has been the United States—the sole superpower! The term "clash of civilization" was first used in September 1990 by Bernard Lewis in an article in the *Atlantic Monthly*, entitled "The Roots of Muslim Rage". This was a time when the Cold War and the Soviet Union were on their last legs. It appears as if some American scholars were already looking for a new enemy. A little more than a year after this article was published, the USSR disintegrated. Samuel Huntington then popularized this concept in an article published in *Foreign Affairs* in 1993. He then wrote a book entitled—*The Clash of Civilizations: Remaking of World Order*—published in 1996. Five years later, the clash of civilization seemed to have started when a handful of terrorists attacked the symbols of US prosperity, the World Trade Centre in New York and the symbol of US military power, the Pentagon building in Washington, D.C. Huntington's ideas, which were criticized and condemned around the world, came to be revisited after September 11 incidents. Irrespective of scholarly views in favour of or against the concept of "clash of civilizations", Osama bin Laden and members of his organization, Al Qaeda, believed in this theory. Perceiving that Islam was under threat, Osama bin Laden took on the US by engineering the September attacks.

There are so many inter-state wars and a few world wars recorded in history, but for the first time, the only remaining superpower of the post-Cold War era declared a global war against terrorists—the non-state actors. The war is still on and Osama is still at large. The two countries that came under heavy US military fire power—Afghanistan and Iraq—are yet to concede defeat. Taliban appears to be re-emerging as a force. Iraqi insurgency just does not show any sign of ending. The Second World War continued for about six years. The US war against terror has entered the sixth year! The recent inability of Israel to handle the challenge posed by Hezbollah forces in Lebanon and to replicate its earlier spectacular military successes is also seen as an American defeat.

Last but not the least, the US has been facing a rampant and violent anti-Americanism in the WANA region in recent years without any such precedence in its entire history. It has been widely recognized as a dangerous development across the entire political spectrum in the US. The Bush Administration has been trying to come to terms with this phenomenon without much success. The Middle East Partnership Initiative, the free trade area proposals, intense public diplomacy to reach out to the common men and experiments with promotion of democracy in the region have not shown tangible and satisfactory results. In fact, democracy promotion initiative has given rude shock to the Bush Administration after the HAMAS victory in the elections held in the Palestinian Area. Going against the grain of the democratic peace theory, the Bush Administration is strategizing hard to corner and isolate the HAMAS government.

Challenges for India

The US is not a hegemon in absolute sense of the term. But it happens to be the only country with global reach. It cannot force its will on other countries all the time, but its cooperation is necessary for conflict resolution, regional developments and global peace. It is no wonder that majority of the countries in the WANA region seek friendship and cooperation with the US. Except Iran, no other country in this region has raised a banner of protest or has adopted a confrontational approach. Iraq once did, but it is now in shambles. Libya once did, but it has now adopted a cooperative strategy even to the extent of abandoning its nuclear ambition. Egypt, the most populous country in WANA region, is the largest recipient of American assistance among the Arab countries and the second largest in the world. Saudi Arabia is probably the richest country, but has enormous economic ties and strategic understanding with Washington.

The WANA region has so much of contradictions, ethnic, tribal and other societal divisions that no country feels comfortable with the idea of a regional dominant power and would ever be ready to cooperate with an external power to prevent the rise of a regional power. External powers, other than the US, are not prepared to replace the US as the major actor in the questions of peace and stability in this region. The European countries and China are big stake holders, but look to Washington to take the lead. The EU has of late shown interest in distancing itself from the US policies and charting an independent course, but still looks at the US as the ultimate guardian of peace deals.

China and Russia adopt policies that aim more at restraining the US than in supporting the regional challengers.

India has to factor all these into its calculations in approaching this region to ensure its energy security. India is fast becoming a big stake holder in the peace and stability of WANA region. India's high-speed economic growth requires more and more energy and thus India's dependence on West Asia and North Africa is likely to increase in years to come.

History, culture, economy and security bind India with this region. As India aspires to play a major role in international affairs, it has to take hard decisions on issues and developments in WANA region in years to come. India's efforts to forge a "strategic partnership" with the US have coincided with rising anti-Americanism in WANA region. India faces an enormous task of public diplomacy to prevent any impression among the people in this region that it is teaming up with the US against them.

In its swift drive towards ensuring energy security, India has signed a nuclear deal with the United States. But its requirements of oil and gas will continue deep into the 21st century, unless a miracle happens and commercial alternative to oil is available. The challenge and dilemma in this area was clearly visible in India's efforts to give shape to its "strategic partnership" with Iran and simultaneously enhance its "strategic partnership" with the United States. This dilemma is still hunting the mandarins of the South Bloc.

The bigger challenge of the future will come from our policy towards Israel. There is a strong constituency in India against developing closer ties with Israel. But a section of the Indian foreign policy community sees enormous benefits in developing a cooperative relationship with Israel. Given the sentimental opposition to Israel in WANA region, India has to trade very carefully to enhance its ties with Israel. The US has been able to forge closer ties with Arab governments as well as Israel. But Washington's unquestioned support to Israel is the main cause of anti-Americanism in the Arab World/Muslim World. India is not the US. And it may not be able to befriend both the Arabs and the

Israelis. Traditionally, India followed a pro-Palestinian policy. It was also apparently anti-Israeli in content. But the evolving ties with Israel indicate that such a policy could be counterproductive.

Can India support the principle of a Palestinian State and still forge cooperative ties with Israel? Will it be credible in the eyes of the Arabs? Can India maintain a neutral policy in the Arab-Israeli dispute? The power of the Jews lobby in the US and the rising cooperation with Israel in matters of defense purchases on the one hand and India's energy needs and other economic relations with the regional countries would continue to pose dilemmas and difficulties for India.

In the ultimate analysis, India is not a major player in this region. What India says or does would have little impact on the ground in the conflict situations in WANA region. But India is increasingly becoming a stake holder. Stakes without adequate clout or power pose the central challenge for India. India cannot fully support the US policy in this region. India cannot robustly oppose the US policy. And India may not be able to stay neutral either. Developing a viable and long term strategy is the need of the time.

Notes

1. Mark S. Joy, American Expansionism, 1783-1860 (London, New York, Pearson, Longman, 2003). American history is a history of expansion. American people believed in the concept of "Manifest Destiny". This term was actually first used by John O'Sullivan who wrote that it was "...the right of our manifest destiny to overspread and to possess the whole of the continent which Providence has given us for the development of Liberty and federated self-government entrusted to us...." Ever since the birth of the nation Americans sought to spread American ideals and culture; actually American interests, by a combination of war and diplomacy. This book also discusses the historiography of this subject. Another recent book that throws adequate light on this theme is Anders Stephanson, Manifest Destiny: American expansion and the empire of Right (New York, Hill and Wang, 1995). A review of this book in Foreign Affairs in March/April 1995 said: "This provocative volume, by a Columbia University historian, examines the idea of manifest destiny from 1600 to 1990. The dominant impression

conveyed is of an infatuated people driven to expansion and genocide by the delusional belief that they were God's chosen."

2. Alfred T Mahan, Theodore Roosevelt, Henry Cabot Lodge and many other American idelogues ardently supported the idea of overseas possessions even before US industries were in need of foreign markets.

3. See www.globalissues.org

4. Ibid.

5. The US replaced Britain as the richest country in the world in 1903 and has since remained in that position.

6. Less than two per cent of people in US depend on agriculture for their sustenance Almost one-third of their produce is meant for the export markets.

http://www.globalissues.org/Geopolitics/ArmsTrade/BigBusiness.asp

7. Chintamani Mahapatra, *Indo-US Relations into the 21st Century* (New Delhi, Knowledge World, 1998)

8. There were times in world history when Portugal, Netherlands and Britain enjoyed this status. William R. Thompsn, "Systemic Leadership, Evolutionary Processes, and International Relations Theory: The Unipolarity Question," *International Studies Review*, vol.8, issue 1, March 2006, p.5.

9. The figures are for 2005 and prepared by the US Department of Energy. See, www. eia.doe.gov

10. Ibid.

9

Indo-Arab Relations: The Pakistan Factor

Qamar Agha

India and the Arab nations are maintaining friendly ties since ancient times. The people belonging to two different civilizations are interacting with each other and have contributed in different fields of science, art and culture, much before the advent of Islam. Relations continued to develop throughout the Islamic era. During this period, Arab rulers were mostly looking towards North Africa and Europe for expansion of their empires whereas trade and commercial ties with India continued to expand. Later, both the people came under the colonial rule and suffered more or less similar experience. This has helped the national leaders in both the regions to forge closer ties with each other while they were still colonized.

The powerful nationalist movement in India had greatly influenced Arab political leaders. The national movements in India as well as the Arab World remained secular, anti-colonial and anti-imperialist in nature. This was the major source of worry for the then European colonial powers. British colonial rulers introduced policy of divide and rule in both the regions to contain India and the Arab world. As a result, the Arabs, who overwhelmingly follow one religion, one culture and one language, found themselves divided between religious and secular camps. Similarly, the British colonial rulers in India encouraged the Hindu-Muslim divide. Before leaving India and the Arab world, Great Britain partitioned both the nations. Pakistan and Israel were created to serve the Westerns Nations interests in the respective region.

During the freedom struggle, Mahatma Gandhi, Jawaharlal Nehru and other leaders of the Indian National Congress had acquainted themselves with the various issues and committed to pursue a foreign policy compatible with the aspirations of the people. Their experience of leading the freedom struggle had helped evolve certain principles, which later became the cornerstone of the India's foreign policy. Self-determination for all the colonial people was one such principle. Another important aspect of the Indian foreign policy was its opposition to military blocs and refusal to be dragged into Cold War. India believed that by joining a power bloc it might dilute its hard won independence and make India dependent- militarily, politically and economically- on one or the other big power. To counter the pressure of the rival blocs, India put forward the concept of non-alignment, which in effect meant pursuit of an independent foreign policy. National leaders were opposed to foreign interference in its domestic as well as foreign policy and wanted to achieve self-reliance in economic development.

The conduct of India's foreign policy towards West Asia was guided by these principles as well as its perceived national interest. India's national interest demanded that the Arab countries remained free and friendly so that no threat to its territorial security could be possible from that quarter. Besides, India was keen both to promote its trade with the countries of the West Asia and to have access to the trade routes lying across the region. The policy has worked for most of the period and the ties between the two people continued to develop in the postcolonial period.

Indian national leaders fully understood the game plan of the big powers for South and West Asian regions and extended full support to the Arab people in their fight against colonial and imperialist domination. Nehru also recognized the vital geopolitical importance of the West Asian region to India that is often termed as Middle East because it is on the way to British possessions in India and Far East. Geopolitical experts have described the region as the "gateway of Asia and Africa." Middle East is comprised of "those regions of Asia which extended up to the borders of India." Therefore, India's security has been historically linked with the development in West Asia. Nehru acknowledged this fact in a speech before the Constituent Assembly in 1949: "If you have to consider any question effecting the Middle East, India inevitably comes into picture. If you have to consider any question concerning South-East Asia, you cannot do so without India. While Middle East may not be directly connected with South- East Asia, both are connected with India".

Besides security interests, Nehru had felt that the struggle against colonialism and imperialism were interdependent therefore the need was to coordinate the freedom struggles in these countries. Congress Party under his leadership developed ties with several Pan-Arab Nationalist leaders and extended India's support to their independence. Mahatma Gandhi and Jawaharlal Nehru backed the struggle of the Palestinian Arab people since the British announcement of Balfour Declaration, which accepted the Zionist demand for Jewish National Home in Palestine. The response of leaders of India's national movement towards the Palestinian cause before independence of India has formed the backdrop of India's Palestine policy ever since. The Mandate system was also condemned by the Congress Party as "plot to cover imperialist greed" and later expressed itself against the partition of Palestine. This is because "the Arab countries have looked upon Israel as an outpost from which their freedom might at any time be threatened", Nehru observed.

The problem that has directly affected India was the Baghdad Pact, comprising Britain, Iraq, Iran, Turkey and Pakistan. Basically, the Baghdad Pact was intended to form the "northern Tier" of the Western defense system against the Soviet Union. Yet Pakistan, which had little to fear from the Soviet Union, had joined the Pact mainly in its bid to create military bloc of Islamic nations against India. Such attempts in the past to create a pan-Islamic bloc were shrugged off by the Arabs. As Nehru put it in the Lok Sabha on March 29, 1956: "But surely, nobody here imagines that Pakistan government entered into this pact because it expected some imminent or distant invasion or aggression from the Soviet Union".

The government and the press in Pakistan made it perfectly

clear that they had joined the Baghdad Pact because of India so that they can speak from strength. Nehru elaborated the point in another speech in the Lok Sabha on August 26, 1958, spelling out the reasons for India's concerns:" Pakistan, our neighbor country with whom we want to be friendly is a part of the Baghdad pact and thereby gets the help and assurances and backing of some of the most powerful nations in the World. As a result, Pakistan itself is prevented from adopting such friendly attitude to us, which it otherwise might have adopted. Moreover there is a question of the supply of large quantities of military equipment". In the same speech, he also wanted to know that "whether, there were any foreign bases in Pakistan, and the Pakistan government denied it. And even if we accept the Pakistan's denial, the fact is that the military equipment of Pakistan has grown and vast airfields have been built all over. Whether one calls them foreign or domestic bases, they are there. All this arming of Pakistan is a matter of some concern."

The Baghdad Pact did not find much favor in the Arab World either. Even some conservative Arab regimes, which had been traditionally pro-Western, could not afford to ignore the popular sentiment against a security system imposed from outside. The Saudi rulers denounced Pakistan's membership of the western sponsored military pact. They were surprised to find an "Islamic state of Pakistan should accede to those who have joined hands with the Zionist Jews" and urged it "to return to right path" by withdrawing from unpopular Baghdad Pact which they described as a "stab in the heart of the Arab and Muslim states". This was the period when the Arab world unitedly supportive of the Indian policies and particularly its ties with the Saudi Arabia was growing. Indo-Saudi ties were further consolidated in 1955 when King Saud visited India and appreciated India's support to the cause. The joint statement issued at the end of the visit reflected a certain "harmony" in the political outlook of King Saud and Prime Minister Nehru. Both the leaders emphasize, "A peaceful and non militant approach to the issues which divide the world is an urgent necessity." During the stay in Delhi, King Saud also said: "I desire to say to my Muslim brethrens all over the world with satisfaction that the fate of the Indian Muslims is in safe hands" and thanked Nehru and his government for their policy towards the Muslims. Later when Nehru visited Saudi Arabia in 1956, he was accorded with the title "Rasool as salaam" or "messenger of peace". Pakistan immediately objected the title conferred on Nehru and enter into a bitter controversy with the Saudi Kingdom.

The forming of Baghdad Pact was soon followed by Egypt's arms deal with Czechoslovakia. The move has brought sharp division in the Arab ranks. Thus, instead of lending stability to West Asia, Baghdad Pact engulfed it into the Cold War. Egypt under Nasser and other nationalist regimes sought support from the Soviet Union to deal with Israel. They believed that the Zionist regime in Israel backed by the Western nations was a major threat to peace and stability to the Arab nations. This provided Soviet Union an opportunity to gain its entry in Middle East extended its support to the nationalist regimes to undermine the Baghdad Pact and to weaken western influence in the region. The whole region plunged into an acrimonious controversy. To counter the Egyptian moves in the region, the conservative Arab regimes, which were earlier opposing the Pact, sought support from the western nations. Saudi Arabia and other conservative regimes articulated that the immediate threat to their rule comes from Soviet backed Pan-Arab nationalist movement. The powerful Wahabite Islamic movement also declared that the anti-religious international communist movement poses threat to Islam.

Baghdad Pact has in fact created greater tension and conflict in West Asia and it has created wedge between India and the pro-west conservative Arab regimes in the Arab World. In Nehru's words: "it has certainly put one country against another among countries that were friendly to one another. I do not know how any one can say that this has brought security and stability to western Asia". Nehru consistently maintained that military alliances have no meaning in the nuclear age. To small countries, these "do not add to their defensive power for they have little or no military value." They only increase the country's dependence on its partner, which in turn scuttle the country's freedom. Besides, the military alliances sometime defeat the very purpose they were meant to serve. This is what exactly happened in the case of Pakistan when it tried to get help from its western allies in its 1965 and 1971 war with India but without success. Similarly Arabs also failed to get sufficient support form western nations to help solve the Palestinian problem.

In the re-alignment of forces, India developed much closer ties with the pro-Soviet anti-imperialist; nationalist-secular regimes while continuing to maintain economic relations with the pro-West conservatives Arab Islamic regimes. Therefore, India never had a problem in dealing with both the Arab camps mainly because of its unwavering support to the just Arab cause whether it was the Palestinian problem, Suez crisis, Eisenhower Doctrine, Arab-Israeli conflict or any other issue concerning the Arab people. Through out the period, Indian policy was not to meddle in their intra-Arab dispute or their internal matters. Besides this, India continues to play an active role in the economic development of the Pro-West Arab States of the Persian Gulf region where more than 3.5 million Indians are working. Most of the Indian public as well as private sector companies are operating in the region. This has helped India to earn a good reputation in West Asia. India's political relations with the conservative Arab states might have suffered a set back but economic ties continue to grow throughout the cold war era.

However, Egypt, India's most trusted ally in the Arab world, was defeated in 1967 Arab-Israeli war and after the death of Egyptian Gamaal Abdul Nasser, Anwer Sadaat became the President. He made a peace deal with Israel and joined the Western Camp. This was the major setback to the nationalist movement in the Arab world and India lost a major ally in West Asia. Then, civil war erupted in Lebanon in 1976 and the subsequent Israeli attack in 1982 to degrade Palestine Liberation Organization's (PLO) military capability weakened both the

Lebanon as well as PLO- the two major power centers of the nationalist movement in the Arab World. The Ba'ath nationalist movement in Iraq suffered a major set back due to its eight years long Iran-Iraq war which resulted in mutual destruction in 1980's. Later, Iraq's occupation of Kuwait further complicated the situation in the region because of the arrival of the US troops in Saudi Arabia and other Gulf States to liberate Kuwait. The Iran-Iraq war also brought financial difficulties in Saudi Arabia, Kuwait and other oil producing oil countries of the region that were providing financial assistance to Iraq in War against Iran. Later, Saudi Arabia, Kuwait and other Arab countries had to pay their bid to cover the cost of the coalition forces came in to liberate Kuwait. These developments in West Asia had direct bearings on India, mainly because; these countries were major trading partner and a source of oil supply to India. Besides other factors, all these developments gave rise to the militant Islamic movement in the West Asian region that was a major source of worry for India. Pak-Saudi support to Islamic resistance to the Soviet occupation of Afghanistan further complicated the matters for India.

Throughout the Cold War era, conservative regimes in West Asia remained united in their opposition to the nationalist movement. Supper Power rivalry and the division in the Arab ranks has provided Pakistan an opportunity to align itself with Saudi Arabia and other pro-West conservative Arab States. The division in the Arab ranks helped conservatives to form OIC to counter the Arab League dominated by the nationalists. Soon, it has developed Pak-Saudi-US axis to counter the nationalist regimes in the West Asian region. In order to consolidate its ties with the oil rich Saudi Kingdom, Pakistani government as well as its politico-religious organizations like Jamaat-e-Islami and Jamiat Ulema-e Islam projected Saudi rulers as the leader of the Islamic nations at a time when the powerful liberal Islamic movement in the entire Indian sub-continent was refusing to accept Wahabite Islamic rule in Arabia where the Islam's two most holy shrines are located. In return Pakistan's government and religious organizations received massive economic assistance from the oil rich Arab States of the Persian Gulf region. Islamabad policy was to exploit religion to further its political, economic and diplomatic gains in Islamic Arab nations. Since then it is using religion to counter India's policy in the region waging propaganda war to damage India's image as a secular State. Its closer ties with the conservative Arab States helped in blocking India's entry in the OIC and have succeeded in getting their support for its two major wars with India. Pakistan has also managed to get backing of some of the Arab States in OIC for its anti Indian stance on Kashmir. Islamabad is projecting Kashmir as an "Indian occupied territory" and equating it with Palestine while continue to indulge in cross-border terrorism in India.

Over the years, Pakistan with the help of its Islamic organizations has been consistently working towards taking Islamic society globally from conservatism to militancy and finally to terrorism that has done great damage to the Arab cause. Many countries, including India, Russia, China and the newly independent Central Asian Republics that were earlier refusing to develop ties with Israel are now seeking support from the Jewish States to counter Pakistan backed Islamic insurgency in their respective countries. As a result, traditional support from the international community to Arab Palestinian cause weekend. Besides, Indian policy planners have to spend lot of time in countering Pakistan's propaganda in the Arab-Islamic countries. Pakistan might have succeeded in getting the support of some of the oil-rich Arab rulers but failed to get sympathy among the masses who looked towards the Islamabad with suspicion. Islamabad's policies have not helped the Arabs at all, rather contributed in further division of the Arab nations and helped the Western Nations to consolidate their hold over the region.

However, situation is fast changing in these countries as well. Arab nations are now realizing that policies adopted during the Cold War era are no longer valid. On the contrary, many of them have now become counter productive. Islamic militancy that they were earlier backing, has now become a major source of problem for them. Now the Arabs are facing the threat from the forces that they have encouraged to counter nationalism and communism. With the arrival of the US troops in Saudi Arabia, it has brought division within the Saudi backed Wahabite Islamic movement; many of them have now joined the ranks of al-Qaida and waging Jihad against the pro-West Arab governments. Islamic movement is weakening these regimes, forcing them to rely on US for security and have joined the US backed "war on terror" to deal with the growing Islamic militancy in the region. In the fast changing regional and international situation, Pakistan is no longer fits in their scheme of things. Rather, it has become part of their problem. Now, their policy is to contain militancy, role back Jihad and promote their economic and commercial interests. Hence to achieve their objectives and for mutually beneficial relations, Arabs States are willing to further enlarge their dealing with India. In the new economic set up Pakistan has very little to offer its allies in the Arab World.

Now, the globalization has set a new agenda where economic rather than the ideological issues in foreign policy of the countries. The forces of globalization also influenced Indian foreign policy where economic interests have become prime factor in foreign relations and ideological issues have taken a back seat. In the new global setup, Indian policy is also directed to protect and promote its economic and commercial interests and to exploit the opportunity thrown up by the forces of globalization. The government believes that the fundamentals of Indian economy have now become much stronger due to steady growth; therefore, it is also working hard to project India as an "emerging Economic Power" in international scene to attract foreign investments to bridge the gap in our resources to have access to technologies and markets

The other factors forcing India to come closer to the West Asian States are the geographical proximity and strategic relevance of the Persian Gulf region. By focusing on Gulf and restoring traditional linkages with the immediate and extended neighbor, India is suggesting that the security of the Gulf States as well as the wider West Asia is of "paramount concern" and "New Delhi is willing to contribute to the stability of the region by sharing its experience in combating terrorism, maritime security and military training." India believes that the region now goes beyond historical, cultural, and economic realms. India is keen on their cooperation in ensuring "safety and security of the sea-lanes of communications, safety and freedom of navigation in shipping lanes and trade routes. India's policy in the region finds echo in the world of Prime Minister Manmohan Singh who said that: "the Gulf region is a part of our natural economic hinterland. We must pursue closer economic relations with all neighbors in our wider hinterland." The new "look-west initiative towards the oil rich Arab States will bring the economies of the Persian Gulf closer to India". Since independence, the successive governments in India have been taking special interest in boosting economic ties with countries of the Gulf region, which have been showing a remarkable surge over the past years, with the GCC countries accounting for 11 per cent of India's exports. India has already entered into a framework agreement on economic cooperation with the GCC countries. The new economic order demands India's closer ties with the Arab nations.

Besides, The Persian Gulf region remains a major source of oil supply for the growing energy demands in India; more than 60 per cent oil comes from this region. The Arab States account for 45 per cent of the oil reserves and 20 per cent of the natural gas resources of the World. India ranks sixth in global petroleum demand and by 2020, it is projected to emerge as a fourth-largest consumer of the hydrocarbon energy resources, after the United States, China and Japan. India wants to ensure stable price and uninterrupted oil and gas supplies from the Persian Gulf region since that is necessary for its economic growth. The sudden hike in global oil prices fuelled inflation remains a constant source of worry for the Indian policy makers who have now decided to go beyond imports and "seek equity access to foreign oil and gas resources and achieve strategic energy security." The opening of the oil and gas sector in the Arab World is welcomed in India and its oil companies are exploring the possibilities for investment in oil sector.

In a situation like this, India will have to adopt ways and means to deal with high oil prices, which is having direct impact on our economy. The rise in oil and gas consumption and increase in its prices is further contributing to loss of revenue. Besides, these products are highly subsidized in India. However, the government is taking measures to avoid further losses by deciding to go beyond imports and "seek equity access to foreign oil and gas resources" and achieve strategic energy security. The opening of the oil and gas sector in the Arab nations is welcomed in India and the government is exploring opportunities in the Arab world. India has already acquired stakes in oil and gas fields in more than a dozen countries of the world including in Sudan and considering investing another US$ 25 billion in this sector. This is additional attraction for the oil producing countries of the Persian Gulf region. In order to achieve oil security, India is searching new reserves of oil and gas in India and augmenting supplies from its traditional suppliers by striking new deals abroad. The government has also planned to build strategic oil reserves of 5mn tons by 2008 to cover 15 days of domestic demand for oil products.

Besides oil supplies to India, there are more than 3.5 million Indians work in the oil producing countries of the Persian Gulf region that sends more than 10 billion dollars back home annually. India is the second largest trading partner of the Gulf Co-operation Council (GCC). It is also the largest single origin of imports into India and the second largest destination for exports from India. Bilateral trade rose to US$ 18 billion, excluding oil and gas imports by India that are worth about US$ 20 billion.

Ever since India has introduced economic liberalization policy, new dimensions were added to Indo-Arab economic cooperation. Now, there are more avenues for foreign investors and the countries of the GCC and they have responded positively to the liberalization policy. It has also borne fruits in the form of joint ventures between the two countries. But, still there is immense potential for economic cooperation between India and the Arab States with stability in the region being a key factor where India can help support the goals of spreading democracy and fighting extremism. The Arab States of the Gulf region face the "challenge of human resource development and the diversification of their economy, while India, on the other hand, face the challenge of securing its oil resources to sustain its economy." These challenges offer tremendous opportunities for cooperation between India and the Arab world. Besides the oil sector, India and the Arab nations could cooperate in knowledge-based industries. India, being the hub of the knowledge-based products, offers good potential for the Arab nations to tap. An Indo-Gulf joint commerce and trade committee has defined the contours of a preferential free trade agreement (FTA) with the GCC. The framework agreement will provide better banking arrangements is aimed at exploring opportunities in the areas of oil and gas, knowledge-based industries, education, health and other areas for investments. This move would further strengthen the economic and commercial ties between the two people.

India continues to be a factor in their trade and development. Growing energy demand in India provides them stable market. Therefore, they are promising "uninterrupted oil supplies to India" and wants to benefit from the growing Indian economy through trade and investments. Besides the oil-rich Arab countries are also embark on massive economic development that led to demand for skilled manpower and labor supplies from India which has surplus manpower resources. Besides, the oil rich Arab States are trying hard to shed their dependence on oil revenues and focus on encouraging more trade, commerce and industrialization. It's a mutually beneficial policy for India as well as the Arab nations where both can help in each other's development. In fact, in the present global environment there is a convergence of economic interests between India and the Arab States. The liberalization of Indian economy has also been beneficial for them; both can invest in each other's economy and can make enormous profit through the development of both the regions. The policy is to promote

India as a source of cheap technology and a safe destination for investment

Now there is a noticeable change in attitude of the Arab States towards India. They recognize India's unique position in international community where it enjoys considerable support in developing as well as developed nations. Arabs also see, India not only a major market for their hydrocarbon products like oil and natural gas but providing an opportunity to invest in its growing market. The importance of India was reflected in the two high profile visits paid by the Saudi King after fifty years and the Emir of Kuwait after thirty years. During his stay in India, King Abdullah of Saudi Arabia promised Indian leaders not only uninterrupted oil supplies but also government as well as private investments in different sectors of Indian economy. In fact, the Arab leaders are anxious with the growing Indo-Iran relations, including a military cooperation agreement and the proposed Indo-Iran and Indo-Turkmenistan gas pipelines projects that would lead to a major loss to their oil markets. They don't want to loose their share in Indian market to the rivals in Iran or the emerging markets in Caspian Sea basin. Arab leaders see pipelines projects would ultimately connect the South Asian region with the emerging Central Asian oil *bazaar*. In this scenario, the Arab States would be relegated to a marginal supplier of oil in India and other South Asian countries. They believe that the pipelines would also bring Iranian influence in Pakistan and Afghanistan-the two pro-Saudi Islamic states of the South Asian region. The recent visits of King Abdullah of Saudi Arabia followed by the Emir of Kuwait to India were basically to impress Indian leadership that dealing with the Arabs more profitable than to make huge investments in Indo-Iran gas pipeline project. What ever be the reasons for their visit to India, it was certainly a major setback to Pakistan's diplomatic efforts in the Arab World also. Islamabad was consistent in its approach to prevent these countries coming closer to India. It shows that the pro-west Arab States do not have much in common with the Pakistan. Their vested interest is forcing them to develop mutually beneficial ties with the emerging nations like India. They want to gain from the relationship.

Earlier, the policy was to invest mainly in Western Nations. But, now, in the fast moving situation, the Arabs are looking for other avenues also to invest their surplus money. In the last four years, the oil producing countries of the Persian Gulf region have accumulated more than US$ 500 billion as surplus revenue and it continues to increase at much faster rate. At present, their surplus money is parked in Western banks. Some of this money, the Arabs want to invest in India and China as part of their "look East Policy." These two countries are also emerging major oil consumers in Asia and providing the Arab States an opportunity to invest in their fast growing economies. The surplus money they have acquired mainly because of sudden rise in oil prices and it is possible that oil prices may not come down to a level, which existed just before the regime change in Iraq. The upward trend in oil prices is due to instable situation in West Asian region mainly because of the US occupation of Iraq, the spread of Islamic militancy and the growing confrontation between Iran and the Western Nations over Iranian nuclear programme. The sudden increase in consumption of oil and gas in India and other Southeast Asian nations has also attributed to rise in oil prices. These factors are not going to be eliminated in the near future. Though the oil producing Arab States are stable but the sectarian violence in neighboring Iraq and the presence of large number of American troops in the region and the continuing Arab-Israeli conflict is posing threat to their peace and stability. However, the plan to contain Islamic militancy is there but they have no control over the external factors that are encouraging extremism among the Arab masses. There is no charismatic political or spiritual leader in the Arab world who could bring unity among the people of the region.

As far as the economic ties are concerned there is no problem in India but political issues remain to be solved. The policies persuaded by some of the countries towards Pakistan were a constant source of worry for India. The problem came in early

1970's when Saudi Arabia and other conservative Islamic States in the region extended moral and material support to the Mujahideens who were waging Jihad against the Soviet troops in Afghanistan and later helped install Pakistan backed government by replacing pro-Indian government in Kabul. Saudi Arabia and the United Arab Emirates were the two countries in the world that even recognized the then Pakistan backed extremist Islamic Taliban regime in Afghanistan. They also continue to back Islamabad sponsored resolutions on Kashmir in OIC and other international forums. India was also disturbed with the Saudi support to Pakistan based Islamic organizations whose militant wing is involved in terrorist activities in Kashmir and other parts of the country. In addition, some of these governments are not governed by the secular modern laws and have tendency to mix their version of religion with politics. They have legal system that even allows those people to move freely in their respective countries who committed crimes in other countries. Some of these criminals wanted in India are staying in the region. These are sensitive issues and will have to be addressed before embarking on any major trade or commerce dealings. These issues are raised not with the intention to discourage ties with the West Asian nations but to sort out the differences in advance so that no problem emerged in future. The need is to take up the confidence building measures to solve the long-standing concerns of both the regions. Besides, the pro-West Arab regimes are major source of financial support to Pakistan and maintain strategic ties with Islamabad. Therefore, they should play a constructive role by putting pressure on Pakistan to contain Islamic militancy and not to allow its soil for cross boarder terrorism as Islamabad has promised to Indian leaders in 2005, instead of asking India to sort out its differences with Pakistan.

It is important to know that India's strategic ties with Israel and the Western Nations have not affected our relations with the Arab nations. Arabs don't care much about the growing Indo-Israeli relations. As a matter of fact, trade with the Arab nations has gone up many folds since India established diplomatic ties with Israel. Now, several Arab countries are also maintaining relations with the Jewish State, therefore, it is no more an issue with them. Now, the realization has set in that their total opposition to Israel or undeserving support to Pakistan would ultimately isolate them in international community. The Islamic Arabs States are trying to adjust their policies towards India who maintains closer ties with Israel or having dispute with Pakistan.

Geographic and historical cultural affinity is additional factor that prompts both sides to join hands for a partnership of progress and development for their people. Pakistan or any other country cannot hold ancient ties between the two people hostage indefinitely. Traditional trade and investment partners like the Arab States will always occupy an important place in India's foreign policy.

References

Government of India, Ministry of External Affairs, Annual Reports, New Delhi, 2000-2005.

Hamid Ansari, The OIC and India: Signal of a Rethink

http:// www.observerindia.com/analysis/A566.htm

Vimla Vasan, CII agenda to boost trade with GCC

http://wwwthehindubusinessline.com/2004/04/21/stories/200404210179 0400.htm

India, Gulf nations to expand trade ties

http://www.the hindubusinessline.com/2004/01/10/stories/2004011002190400.htm

India and GCC relations, Embassy of India, Riyadh

http://www.indianembassy.org.sa/Pages/ComWing/India-GCC (EC)/India...

Dr N. Janardhan, GCC-India FTA Talks Give Fillip to 'Asian Community'

Dr N. Janardhan, Saudi Arabia Scripts New Chapter in GCC-Asia Ties Pakistan Observer

http://www.pakobserver.net/200605/03/news/world02.asp

Dr N. Janardhan, GCC-Asia Ties First; What Next?

http://www.sagia.gov.sa/InvestInSaudi/Newsroom_7566.htm

Dr N. Janardhan, What Oils the Wheels of GCC-India Cooperation?

http://www.gasandoil.com/goc/news/ntm53511.htm

Stephen Blank, India and the Gulf after Saddam

Stretegic Insights, Volume 111, Issue 4 (April 2004)
http://www.ccc.nps.navy.mil/si/2004/apr/blankApr04.asp
Kuwat Chamber sees Huge Scope for Enlarging Ties with India
http://72.14.221.104/search?q=cache:39_xGUX8tCkJ:
Www.ficci.com? Press/90/KUWAIT.doc+...
http://www.arabnews.com /services/print/print.asp?artid=75773&d...
Atul Aneja, India and the Gulf-cementing ties
http://www.thehindu.com/2006/03/31/stories/2006033108561100.htm
Atul Anaja, India, GCC to sign comprehensive economic pact next year
http://www.thehindu.com/2006/03/26/stories/2006032602541100.htm
"Strengthening Ties between Asia and GCC", Address by Ong Keng Yong, Secretary General of ASEAN, at GRC Annual Conference, Dubai, UAE, 4 January 2006
http://www,aseansec.org/18164.htm
Joint Press Communique- Visit of GCC Secretary General to India
http://mea.gov.in/declarestatement/2004/02/16js01.htm
Consulate General of India, Jeddah, India-GCC Trade
http://www.egijeddah.com
GRC Workshop Urges Asian Role In Gulf Security
http://www.tmcnet.com
India Working on Economic Cooperation Pact With India
People's Daily Online—http://www.English.people.com.cn/
Regional Economic Outlook-Middle East and Central Asia, 2005-2006, International Monetary Fund, Washington.
International Energy Agency, World Energy outlook 2005-2006
http://www.unctad.org/en/doc
http://www.menareport.com
http://www.gulfinvestmentcorp.com
http://www.assocham.org
http://www.energytribune.com
Girijesh Pant, India Energy Security: The Gulf Factor, GSP Occasional Paper Series, 2002/2 (New Delhi: Gulf Study Programme, 2002)
Rakesh Mani, Rational Exuberance: Invest Big in the Gulf
http://www.chowk.com

Part V: Globalisation, India and WANA: Cultural and Diasporic Dimensions

10

India's Cultural Diplomacy in West Asia and North Africa

Aftab Kamal Pasha

Trade between India and the Arab world not only opened new avenues of approach to each other but greatly influenced both the societies, because trade granted an opportunity for cultural exchange between the two societies. When people move from one place to another along the trade routes, they carry ideas, religions, philosophy, customs, traditions, rituals, as also books, handicrafts and artistic items with which people of different societies get familiarized. Markets opened up and aided this process. Due to the long sea coast both India and the Arab world had, both derived considerable revenues from trade in ancient period. As during the modern period, in ancient times also culture and civilizational aspects followed trade and commerce between India and the Arabs. Along with the vibrant maritime contacts, there existed considerable trade through the land route via Iran, Babylonia, Oman, Aden and Palestine. The economic interactions closed distances and brought societies and communities together. These cemented relations which had huge implications for future. Experts agree that commercial ties gradually paved the way for cultural relations. The long association in the field of trade and commerce, religion and philosophy, medicine and mathematics, music, arts and many other cultural activities has left a strong impression on both the people[1].

The island of Hormouz and the Gulf region since times immemorial have been meeting place for Indians and Arabs but also for people as far away as China and others. Due to its strategic location at the cross roads of very ancient trade routes as also near the several great river based civilizations, Arab people of the Gulf region have been interacting with traders, seafarers and others. Hormouz welcomed merchants of different religions and from all regions of the world and the city was called the "citadel of security". Even though the Arabs were fascinated by China and things made of China and for the Arabs, the Red Sea was 'Sea of China' and the lure of China was "irresistible," but by far the most robust or vigorous interaction was between the Gulf Arabs and Indians from all along the West Coast. Not only basic goods went from but Indian teak wood and iron swords were especially in great demand. Indian traders settled all along the coasts from Basra to Muscat, Aden and up to Suez[2].

The spread of Islam under Amr-ibn-al-As in major parts of Egypt brought Arabs from the heart of Arabian Peninsula to a country where idolatry, and temples existed. Pharonic culture was widespread despite the growth of Christianity, but modest trade especially Egyptian imports of Indian textiles continued. Fragments of Indian fabric were found at Al Fustat near Cairo which functioned as a major trading centre in Egypt. Initially the direct maritime trade contacts appear to have declined since the rise of Islam between India and Egypt as the Arabs from Oman, Yemen and others like Persians began to interact with Indians on a bigger scale converting the Indian Ocean as a Muslim lake. Muslim merchants especially Arabs were now firmly established from Malacca, Malabar to Maghreb to China. The Arab traders and mariners [Muslims] now virtually controlled land and sea routes and used camels and ships to transport mainly Indian goods. The Jews were also active with the Muslims. Indian goods especially spices continued to reach Cairo in modest quantities for onward transmission to Europe in return for furs and amber from the Baltic's; slaves, timber and metals from the Alps and the Balkans. To one writer "pepper has perhaps been the oldest continuous link between India and Egypt and also between Asia and Europe and one that has survived, battered but intact, ever since"[3].

With the rise of Islam in 7th century AD Arab traders spread Islam to Indian coastal towns especially in Kerala and married local women and their children are known as Mappillas. Large member of Indian scholars went to Baghdad during 7-12th centuries at the invitation of the Abbasid Caliphs. The Indians took with them books in Sanskrit in numerous fields and helped in translation to Arabic. This is known as the golden period in Indo-Arab cultural ties. India not only shared its culture but has also received from others. Unfortunately this mutually beneficial interaction came to an abrupt end due to the savage Mongol invasion and destruction of Baghdad in 1258 AD. According to an Indian scholar the following Arab scholars helped the cause of transmitting Indian culture and knowledge to the Arab world. They are Abu Zayd al Sirafi, Suleiman al-Tajir, Al Masudi, Ibn Hauqal, al-Jahiz, al-Istakhri, al Maqidsi, Ibn Hazm, Ibn al Nadim, Ibn Abi Usaybia, Ibn al Ibari, Ibn Battuta and a host of other translators, scientists and philosophers like al Kindi, al Sarakhsi, Qustab, Luqa, al Fazari, al Khuwarizmi, Thabit b. Qurra, Thinan b. Thabit and the Caliphs and the Vazirs like al Mammon, Yahya b. Khalid and the Barmakids. In particular Yahya bin Khalid al Barmaki (805 AD) minister under the famous Abbasid Caliph Haroon al Rashid took keen interest in Indian science, technology, philosophy and literature. He invited Indian physicians, scientists, astronomers and other scientists to Baghdad and got Indian texts in Sanskrit translated into Arabic[4].

Al-Beruini's book Kitab-al-Hind highlights Indian achievements in science and other fields as also its religious tolerance. An Egyptian scholar of 15th century Al Qalqashandi says the Indian people are bestowed with wisdom, peace and justice to be seen in the entire country. Another Egyptian scholar Abu Zohra said Indians have a glorious history and civilization. Despite the Mongol destruction of the Abbasid Caliphate and the subsequent domination of the Arabs by the Ottomans; it did not substantially disrupt the links between India and the Arabs[5].

Under these circumstances Alexandria became once again the terminus of transcontinental trade as it had become famous earlier during the Romans. Trade ties between India and Egypt were revived through the Red Sea and there was brisk trade. During this period the "Syrian" i.e. Byzantine merchants [Constantinople still remained the capital of the Eastern Roman empire until 1453 when the Turks took over] and the Jewish traders also began to play an important role in the trade between India and Egypt. The Jews were uniquely placed as a link between the Christians and Muslims. Many writers refer to a loose alliance of Jewish merchants known as the Rhadanites whose name appears in the **Book of Routes** composed around 850 by Ibn Khordabeh, Director of Posts to the Caliphs at Baghdad. The Jews were present all along the old silk route from Gaul to China. Interestingly the arrival of Muslims [Islam] at the gates of Arles and Marseilles [France] and at Saint Peter's Basilica in 846 propelled the Jews to prominence as even Charlemagne and his Frankish nobles were forced to rely on Jewish merchants for their luxuries.

Due to their new role, Christian persecution of Jews virtually stopped as also forced conversions common during the Frankish Dynasty Merovingians dynasty [476-750] in Europe. It must be noted that one of the oldest surviving decrees of the Venetian Senate forbade Jews from traveling in Venetian ships[6]. The Jewish presence was noticeable due to the Fatimid Dynasty's [969-1171] connections with Maghreb areas. Like the Romans, the Fatimids also encouraged trade through the Red Sea by maintaining a strong navy and providing security to merchants from all over the world. According to one writer: "Cairo was then embarking on the period of its greatest commercial splendor, drawing commerce, merchants, and travelers like filings to a magnet. Alexandria regained the position it had occupied in classical antiquity as Europe's chief point of access to the exotic goods of the East"[7]. In 996, a traveler to Cairo counted 160 merchants from Amalfi alone. Nahray ibn Nissim, a Tunisian Jew settled in Egypt, was dealing in products as diverse as Spanish tin and coral, Moroccan antimony, Indian spices, Armenian clothes, rhubarb from Tibet and spikenard from Nepal. The Jewish trade connections came to light from the remarkable collection of business papers, belonging to Jewish merchants, discovered in a

Synagogue of Old Cairo. The documents, letters, etc. cover the period 1000 to 1250. The commercial contacts of the Genizah (Cairo) Jewish merchants under the trading guild known as the Karimis existed through their agents from China through India to Morocco and were an important link between India and Egypt. The intermediaries in most cases were Jews themselves[8].

According to K.N. Chaudhri, "Business was done by consigning goods to friends and relatives in Fustat or Aden, which the principal remained in India. It is significant from the point of view of commercial organization that the leading Jewish merchants of the period with business connections in distant countries did not find it necessary to travel with their own goods"[9]. The major items imported from India were spices but also included sandalwood, camphor, cloves, nutmegs, cubebs, coconuts, flaxen and cotton fabrics and ivory, pepper, lead, Kutla drug, bamboo, cane precious stones, cardamom, cinnamon, aloes, marjoram, myrrh, galangal, mastic, vermilion, parrots, saffron, mustard, cassia, garlic, musk, ginger, pearls, crystals and Sanbazaj (used for polishing stones). Wine and scents were imported from Egypt. Many Arab Egyptian merchants settled on India's western coast like Gujarat, Konkan and on the Coromandel Coast. Jeddah now became an important link for trade between India and Egypt due to the trade being in Arab hands and also due to its proximity to Mecca – the pilgrimage centre for Muslims from all over the world. As seen earlier large number of Indian scholars visited several parts of the Arab world especially to Baghdad the capital of the Abbasid Empire taking with them their works in Sanskrit on astronomy, mathematics and medicine which were translated into Arabic and Greek. Gradually Islam began to influence India first through Arab traders in the coastal areas and later from Sind, Persia and Central Asia[10].

During the Fatimid period in 10th century AD the Egyptian merchants were famous as El Karemia who traded mostly in Indian spices. Very often these merchants stayed in India for long periods and often married with Indian women. They also played an important role in spreading Islam in India. These Egyptian spice merchants came to be known as Bohras (apparently from bahar-spices or bahar (outside). The Bohras still are a very important Indian trading community in Egypt – Cairo in the business as well as a link between the two countries. According to Sahar Abdel Aziz Salem, the Fatimid zeal to spread Islam in India indicates their desire to preside over the trade of the Indian Ocean. This strengthened the economy of the Fatimids while at the same time weaken that of the Abbasids (at Baghdad)[11]. He also argues that many Indian traders also visited Egypt as "Indian penetration into the Red Sea might have also taken place in the Fatimid period when relations between Egypt and India were very close and friendly, since they combined both commercial and spiritual interests". It appears Mohammed bin Tughluk Shah (who was known as the Sultan of India but also of Sind, Makran, Mogadishu and Sri Lanka) sent a ship to the Egyptian Mamluk Sultan Al Naser ibn Qalaun full of precious presents and diamonds, but it could not reach Cairo as the King of Yemen apparently looted it. This clearly reveals that Indian ships were famous in Red Sea, Aden and along the Arabian coast.

Thus, Egypt under the Fatimids flourished due to the brisk trade with India. The Fatimids encouraged trade as they needed customs duties Indian influence is seen in Egyptian mosques, especially design of the minaret as large number of Indian ships carried Moslems for Hajj and other Holy places. Since the entire Gulf region, Arabian Peninsula and North Africa including Egypt was undergoing rapid transformation under Islamic rulers this naturally affected the cultural relations as the Indian society was also undergoing similar changes in pockets of India under Muslim rulers both in North and South India. The Spanish Rabbi Benjamin of Tudela visited Alexandria in 1160 and found European merchants like Italians, Catalans, Frenchmen, English and Germans rubbing shoulders with merchants from all over the world. This is interesting in the background of fierce religious wars in Europe. In any case, Egypt continued to be the link to the extent possible between India and Europe and interaction with India was very lucrative especially in spice trade[12].

During 1170-1260 the Fatimids in Egypt were replaced by the Ayyubid rulers under whom the total volume of trade declined as the European traders began to take active interest and increase their share. Moreover the sea route to India became vulnerable to pirates and growing incidence of taxation. Some wealthy Egyptian merchants began to buy protection from rulers in the coastal regions to protect their ships from the menace of pirates. The role of Jewish merchants/agents (who could speak many languages) increased all along the routes from Alexandria, Jeddah, Aden, Muscat, Basra, and Bushier and to the Indian Coast. This may also have partly increased the European volume of trade with the East and hence partly contributed to decline in Indo-Egyptian trade. Egypt soon came to be ruled by the Mamluks (1260-1517) and the devastation of the region from Persia to Palestine and the downfall of the Abbasids in Baghdad (1258) due to the Mongol invasion enhanced the importance of Cairo in the trade through the Red Sea area. The crusade attacks and the prominent role of Saladin in defeating the Crusaders led him to contain the growing role of Frankish merchants from gaining direct access to the Red Sea and limited their interaction to the North African and Mediterranean ports.

Despite restrictions placed by the Pope on Christian traders for their purchases from Muslim countries, merchants from Geneo and Venetia did trade through Alexandria. The Egyptians conducted trade through "safe conduct passes"[13]. The Mamluk rulers assured security to merchants, property and goods etc. It appears during the fourteenth century Egypt and the surrounding areas went through a difficult period due to economic disruptions and consequent decline in trade mainly due to the Black Death in Egypt in 1347. Religion again came as a hindrance in Indo-Egyptian trade as in 1322, the Pope excommunicated many leading citizens of Venice for their dealings with Muslim rulers and for some time a papal ban prevailed which slowed trade with Egypt with its repercussion on trade with India. Under these circumstances trade simply passed into the hands of Armenian merchants from Turkey to Persia to India and the Armenian port of Lajazzo became the link for Europe reducing Egypt's importance. Despite restrictions placed by the Pope on Christian traders for their purchases from Muslim countries, some merchants from Geneo and Venetia did trade through Alexandria[14].

The **Black Death** in Egypt in 1347-8, [bubonic plague- Rattus rattus] which devastated agriculture and adversely affected the Egyptian population scared the foreign traders. This disease always started at the coast, and from there went up into the interior. Every freighter and galley shuttling from India to Egypt and from Alexandria to Byzantium was, potentially, a "death ship"[15]. According to one writer, "the exact relationship between these events and the rhythm of long distance trade through the Red Sea is not quite clear but the Cairo-Alexandria trade network however, remained open", although it did not see the brisk trade it was used to in earlier periods. It is interesting to know how an Egyptian scholar (historian) of the fifteenth century AD called Al-Qalqashandi appreciates India with these words. "India is a big and wide country having enormous wealth. The king lives with pomp and glory. Its ocean is full of pearls, its earth with gold and its mountains with rubies and emeralds. Its valleys have fragrance of sandal wood and camphor. The people are bestowed with wisdom. Peace and justice can be seen in the entire country". Another modern Egyptian scholar, Abu Zohra, in his book *Mohaderat Fi Muqarinat al Adyan* opines about ancient Indian religions and says: "Indians have a glorious history. They were possessed of civilization and culture in older days. The history of their civilization is so old that one remains unable to trace its origin"[16]. Soon the crucial areas through which trade between India and Egypt was to pass came under the Ottoman Empire and this led to disruption in commercial transactions due to political troubles especially in Egypt.

But the most significant development came in the Indian Ocean where the Portuguese under Vasco da Gamma with the help of an Arab pilot landed in Calicut, (May 21, 1498) Kerala. The arrival of Europeans in South India drastically changed the entire scene concerning trade, politics and control of colonies. The Portuguese met two stunned resident Tunisian merchants who spoke Genoese and Castilian. Da Gamma also met Italian merchants who had reached Calicut by land route. On March 8, 1500 Portuguese Admiral Pedro Alvares Cabral came to Calicut with 13 huge ships and a thousand strong crew. Soon Cabral demanded the expulsion of all Muslim merchants, [Arabs, Persians, Indian Muslim merchants]. When the ruler Zamorin refused, Cabral seized a large and heavily laden Arab ship preparing to sail to Egypt through the Red Sea. He also ordered two day heavy bombardment of Calicut destroying most ships and the port. "The Portuguese seized or sank all Muslim shipping they lay their hands on; Muslim merchants were hung from the rigging and burned alive in view of their families ashore...Calicut's fate was just a taste of things to come. In the years that followed, similar treatment was revisited on the city and other Malabar ports.... All to the strategic end of establishing a royal monopoly over trade in the Indian Ocean"[17]. The new rulers of the Indian Ocean henceforth ordered traders of all nations to require a permit to sail waters they had freely sailed for time immemorial. "The goal was nothing less than to make the Indian Ocean a Portuguese lake. All competition would be taxed or blown out of water"[18].

Soon the Portuguese began to take over the spice trade in the entire Indian Ocean region. The Portuguese King Mauuel crowned himself as "Lord of Guinea, and of the Conquest, the Navigation and Commerce of Ethiopia, Arabia, Persia and India". The new masters of seas now ordered Venetian merchants to buy spices at Lisbon. Soon there was drastic reduction in the supply of spices to Cairo and Alexandria the traditional markets to which Indian traders supplied via Aden and Red Sea. Since the Turks were also at war with major parts of Europe, this led to rise in the price of spices due to shortage of supply. All this greatly undermined the traditional Indo-Egyptian trade contacts and hence impacted on the cultural and other ties as well[19].

The Ottoman Sultans found them unable to control the growing Portuguese take over of vital trading areas in India, Gulf, and Red Sea and even in the Mediterranean areas (Ports). At this stage it is necessary to briefly assess the Ottoman Empire's position which was under mounting challenge from the European powers. After they took over Constantinople in 1453 and renamed it as Istanbul, the Ottoman's were undisputed naval power in the Mediterranean. They had achieved unprecedented growth mainly due to their skill in facilitating the transport of the products from the East after taking over the traditional silk routes in Central and West Asia, such as cotton, spices, silk and agricultural produce to Europe in exchange for weapons, ships and manufactured goods. The unprecedented and truly revolutionary geographical discoveries by the Portuguese, Spaniards, Dutch, French, British and others and the direct sea route especially to India led to importation of gold and silver from the new colonies and the almost takeover of Orient trade adversely affecting the Ottomans[20].

Soon the Ottomans were to suffer a terrible defeat in 1571 at the hands of Italians when they were defeated in a naval battle at Lepanto in East Mediterranean. This was seen as a "watershed in the history of East-West Relations." According to one writer: "Once the Ottomans were stopped at Leponto, the continued long-term autonomy of the Western Mediterranean would never again be in doubt. Leponto ensured that the growing Atlantic trade with the Americas would continue as Europeans not only became enticed by the New World treasure but found the Ottoman Empire increasingly irrelevant to their growing commercial interests in the Orient via routes around the Horn of Africa." Not only European control and hegemony over the Eastern Mediterranean was restored but with the rise of the Europeans, the Arab-Islamic lakes, as the Indian Ocean, Gulf, and Red Sea were known, came to be dominated first by the Portuguese, then by the Dutch, French and soon the British became undisputed masters over the area. The secret was due the fact that the Europeans possessed large number of sophisticated ships with powerful guns than the Ottomans. This also led to the shift in focus from the Mediterranean Sea to the Indian Ocean and the Atlantic. Clearly this marked a new era in which powerful guns, cannons with ships using sophisticated technology proved to be decisive and a real strategic shift. The Ottoman advantage with cavalry was now in changed circumstances not much of an asset compared to ships owned by small states like Portugal or Venice[21].

The Ottomans saw rapid drying of capital with the highly lucrative maritime trade carried by the Europeans with India and the East in general. In 1580 Emir Mehmet ibn Emir Es Su'udi wrote: "*The Europeans have discovered the secret of Oceanic travel. They are Lords of the new world and of the gates to India.... The people of Islam are without the latest information in the science of geography and do not understand the menace of the capture of the sea trade by the Europeans*". Also, Bernard Lewis quotes from Umar Talib, one of the Turkish elite, who complained in 1625 that: "*The Europeans have become acquainted with the whole world, sending their ships everywhere and seizing the harbors. The goods from India, Sind and China previously came to Suez and were distributed by the Muslims to the whole world. Now, however, these goods are transported by the Portuguese, the Dutch and the English to the Frankish countries, from whence they distribute them to the world. The goods that they don't need, they bring to Istanbul and the Islamic countries selling them at five times their value, thus reaping great profit. For the reason both gold and silver have become scarce in Islamic countries*"[22].

These momentous developments pioneered at sea by the Europeans sent the crucial spice trade shipping from Egyptian/Arab and Persian merchants as the price of spices went up due to war, scarcity of supplies and dislocation of the regular shipping between Malabar, Gulf and the Red Sea. Along with the Egyptian merchants, the Red Sea route was also busy with Persian traders from the Gulf and also the seafaring Omani Arabs. "After a few disrupted decades as the shock of the early Portuguese conquests reverberated back down the spice routes, Alexandria and Venice staged a comeback. In the 1560's, there were so many spices for sale at Alexandria that a Portuguese spy suggested that a Portuguese should abandon the Cape route altogether and ship their spices via the Levant in order to cut costs. So great was the flow of illicit spices through the Portuguese blockade that there was speculation that the Portuguese viceroy was in tacit revolt against the King"[23].

The religious bigotry and excessive violence earned the Portuguese many enemies. Other Europeans followed the Portuguese in their quest for spices, colonies, slaves and wealth. But Egypt regained its place as the prime intermediary between Europe, India and the Far East as prime supplier of spice. "By unknown means and ferried by unknown hands... spices arrived ...in the souks of Cairo and Alexandria and thence to the markets of Europe like so much cosmic driftwood. Arab dhows conveyed them across the Indian Ocean to the Persian Gulf or the Red Sea. At any one of a number of ancient ports-Basra, Jeddah, Muscat or Aqaba- the spices were transferred onto one of the huge caravans that fanned out across the deserts to the markets of Arabia and on to Alexandria and the Levant"[24].

Since Napoleon's invasion of Egypt in 1798, Britain took keen interest in the West Asian region as it was then establishing its grip over India and feared a French invasion by way of Egypt. It must be pointed out here that the south Indian ruler of Mysore, Tipu Sultan looked for French help against the British during the latter part of 18th century. After defeating Tipu in 1799 the British with the help of Indians took over much of the Arab world. In 1839 the British occupied Aden in Yemen and subsequently in 1882 they brought Egypt under their control basically to protect the communication lines between London and India. British desire to strengthen her grip over India was facilitated by her control over Egypt. The Suez Canal which is in Egyptian territory and opened for traffic in 1869 was an important link in the British Communication/transport lines. The Canal since then has proved to be a vital link between India and Egypt, although the British tried to reduce the relations between the two ancient civilizations.

As seen earlier, the discovery of direct sea route from Europe to India by the Portuguese sailor Vasco-da-Gama in 1498 (with the help of Ibn Majid an Arab Captain) at Calicut in Kerala and the subsequent European colonialism, however, had disrupted the close interaction India had with the Arabs. The British after dominating India (after defeating Tipu Sultan in 1799 who was the last Indian ruler to resist the British) used the Indian soldiers to dominate the Arab world. The Arabs saw Indians as collaborators with British imperialism. In fact the Mufti of Jerusalem accused the British of having a design to settle in Iraq "many million Hindus from British India". Many Indian soldiers died suppressing the Arabs who opposed British imperialism.

But soon the Indian National Congress [INC] declared India's struggle for independence as being part of the general worldwide struggle against colonialism and imperialism and hence supported the Arab struggle for freedom. The INC demanded withdrawal of Indian soldiers serving the British in the Arab world. Jawaharlal Nehru maintained close ties with Arab leaders. In fact he once said that India had "golden bonds with the Arabs in the past". Nehru supported Arab freedom movements from Morocco to Iraq and from Syria to Sudan. He was particularly moved by the sad plight of the Palestinian Arabs and held the British responsible for crushing the Palestinian national struggle for freedom. Hence he opposed the partition of Palestine by the UN in 1947 and favored a federal state in Palestine which would enable full participation of all citizens in the political system. He was also opposed to recognition of Israel until the last moment. With great reluctance and under all round pressure he decided to recognize the Jewish state on September 17, 1950 under certain conditions. After this Nehru refused to establish diplomatic ties with Israel. Maulana Abul Kalam Azad played a key role in bringing India and Egypt closer and also made Indo-Arab ties a cornerstone of India's West Asia policy[25].

Political Relations: The bonds between the peoples of the two countries were established on the basis of common anti-British struggle and common experiences in their nationalist fight for independence. This led to the launching of nationalist movements in both the countries almost simultaneously. In Egypt,

Saad Zaghlul Pasha, through the *Wafd* party worked for independence and in India Mahatma Gandhi, Jawaharlal Nehru, Maulana Azad and many others through the Indian National Congress, intensified the freedom struggle. The two parties and their leadership maintained continuous contact with each other. Nehru who took keen interest in India's foreign relations was anxious to relate the Indian struggle for freedom to a wider anti-colonial movement. In this connection he participated in the international Congress against imperialism held in Brussels in February 1927. During the interwar period, Nehru visited Egypt several times and maintained close ties with the Wafd Party leaders and invited them to attend INC annual sessions. During a meeting with the visiting Egyptian Wafd delegation to India, Nehru said: "Our peoples had much in common-close intercourse from the dawn of history, the exchange, even in remote ages past, of ideas and cultures and merchandise, and then, in the modern period of history a common struggle for freedom against a common imperialism[26]."

Soon after the Second World War both India and Egypt came to have similar views on the Palestine issue but both could not prevent the emergence of Israel in 1948. Once Turkey and Iran – two prominent Islamic states recognized Israel, India also did so in September 1950 even though the Egyptian government had urged postponement of recognition till such time that the issue of the Palestinian refugees was clarified. Despite the Indian decision on Israel, Nehru refused to establish diplomatic ties with Israel. Maulana Azad played a key role in bringing India and Egypt closer and also made Indo-Arab relations a cornerstone of India's foreign policy. He had started a journal called *Al-Hillal* from Calcutta (named after an Egyptian journal) and had visited Al Azhar in Egypt several times and had established close ties with prominent Egyptians. Due to this he advocated closer ties with Egypt. He also viewed Egypt to be the center of Arab-Islamic learning and the cultural capital of the Arabs. Addressing the Conference for Cultural Cooperation between India and Asian countries at New Delhi on August 21, 1949, Maulana Azad who was India's first education Minister said: "Political alliances are based on a spirit of bargaining while cultural contacts deepen mutual understanding[27]."

In July 1952 a fundamental change took place in Egypt with the overthrow of King Farook and the emergence of Gamal Abdel Nasser as the strongman of the new regime. This was an event of momentous significance for Egypt and a landmark in the history of the Arab world. It was to have far reaching consequences changing the very basic structure of the regions politics. Both India and Egypt began to move towards each other impelled by forces within each other, but also by external factors. In their desire to contain the USSR, the West pressurized the Arab states to join their military alliances like Middle East Command in 1951, the Middle East Defense Organization in 1953 and the Baghdad Pact in 1955. Nehru attacked the Baghdad Pact and said it "had in fact created in West Asia far greater tension and conflict than ever before. It has certainly put one country against another among countries that were friendly to one another"[28]. Both Nasser and Nehru came to have similar views on numerous world issues. Egypt came to follow non-aligned policy abroad and secular policy at home. Nehru sympathized with Arab nationalism represented by Nasser as the urge of the Arab people. Nehru described Nasser as "the most powerful symbol of Arab nationalism"[29]. Nehru was also impressed with Nasser's secular policies. Identity of views between the two leaders brought the two states politically, economically and culturally closer. Nehru was keen to have extensive cultural ties with Egypt to give substance to its political ties. In supporting Nasser's Arab nationalism, Nehru cemented the ties between India and Egypt. In fact, relations had become warmer as early as in 1953 when Nehru stopped in Cairo on his way to and back from the Commonwealth Prime Minister's conference. To Nehru this had been a consistent feature of his trips abroad even before 1947. Nehru made another trip to Cairo in February 1955. It is through these visits and meeting that the idea of non-alignment had a decisive impact upon Nasser. His talks with Nehru left a lasting impression about the numerous merits of following a non-aligned policy.

In this context, it would not be out of way to point out that soon after UK joined the Baghdad Pact, Egypt signed the Treaty of Friendship and Cooperation with India on April 5, 1955. Egypt signed the Treaty of Friendship and Cooperation with India on 5 April 1955, which said: "There shall be perpetual peace, friendship and brotherly relations between India and Egypt and between their respective peoples". Nehru attached great importance to his friendship with Egypt as he viewed Cairo to be the key to the success of India's policy towards the Islamic world and the Arab world in particular. He also saw this friendship as indication of India's claim as a secular country especially in the context of Pakistani offensive against India among the Arab/Islamic countries on the issue of Kashmir and treatment of Indian Muslims. Soon Egypt declared that Kashmir was an integral part of India and that "Suez was as dear to Egypt as Kashmir was to India. The Egyptian media blasted Pakistan and its close alliance with the US with an unprecedented anti-Pakistan campaign and branded the latter as the "number one enemy of Cairo and Arabs"[30]. The Pakistani press became very apprehensive of the close relations between India and Egypt. In an editorial Pakistani *Dawn* newspaper wrote: Nasser's hatred of Egypt and love of Bharat and its Nehru is an attitude of mind not warranted by facts but conditioned by intense bias and blind prejudice the source of which may well be examined by psychiatrist. It is nevertheless a matter of deep regret that in the views of this turbulent egoist not the blood of Islam should seem to flow but the turbid waters of Nile. Nasser will never be our friend; he will never think in terms of Islam[31]. At the 1964 NAM Cairo summit Nasser and India's new PM after Nehru's death in 1964, Lal Bahadur Shastri had established close rapport. During 1965 Indo-Pak war Nassser worked hard to see Arab League did not condemn India or declare it as an aggressor but the final communiqué expressed only "great disquiet" and urged the two South Asian States to end the war. Although Nehru and Nasser exchanged a good many official visits but Shastri was not driven by Nehru's passions and in fact some Arab progressives were not particularly fond of him. In fact, Heikal blamed Shastri for the cooling of relations between New Delhi and Cairo.

Many observers read too much into Mrs. Indira Gandhi's decision not to make a stop in Cairo on her first visit to USA as India's Prime Minister in early 1966. But during her state visit to Egypt in October 1967 she strongly condemned Israel's attack on Egypt and demanded Israeli withdrawal from Arab lands. She also asked for the reopening of the Suez Canal. She came down heavily on Israel which made the press in Cairo describe her as "one of the symbols of peace in the world"[32]. It is true that Nehru placed great emphasis on Nasser in the West Asian region and this largely continued until Nasser's death in September 1970 which made Indo-Egyptian ties appear as Indo-Arab relations. The emphasis on Indo-Egyptian ties perceptibly decreased in the wake of Nasser's disastrous defeat in the 1967 war and more especially after his death in 1970. Nasser's death many observers felt undoubtedly loosened the strong links that bound the two countries. Implicit in this perception, however, is the feeling that after the Nehru-Nasser era, relations between the two countries, although still characterized overall by friendship and warmth, were somewhat lacking the substance of the days of yore. Although this is largely taken to be the conventional wisdom, and a feeling shared by intellectuals and experts in both countries, this is perhaps too facile and a simplistic view of the relationship between the largest country in the Arab world and the second largest country in Asia.

The cordial relationship between the two countries continued in the initial period of President Anwar Sadat and Mrs. Indira Gandhi. In October 1970 India's External Affairs Minister Mr. Sardar Swaran Singh visited Egypt to offer condolences to the new leaders of Egypt. There seemed no reason for any change in the cordial and intimate relations between the two states. India had all along supported the Egyptian/Arab position on the issue of Israeli withdrawal from Arab lands and the restoration of legitimate rights of the Palestinians and this was reiterated during the 1973 October war when it said unless Israel withdrew from all Arab lands there could be no negotiations. Soon differences broke out between Egypt, Syria and other Arabs over the peace process. India's policy was not to take sides in intra-Arab disputes.

The so called lack of warmth in the Indo-Egyptian ties in 1970's was among others reasons due to the decline of issues like anti-colonialism, Sadat's preoccupation with the peace process with Israel and emphasis on domestic reconstruction. More significantly the 1973 oil price increase pushed India to focus its relations more on Gulf States due to India's energy needs, so crucial to the primary task of economic development. Under the Janata government (July 1977) led by Morarji Desai, A. B. Vajpayee, L. K. Advani and others there was fear that India may reorient its pro Arab policy and the secret visit of Israeli Foreign Minister Moshe Dayan to Delhi strengthened this, but soon the new government removed any apprehension in Arab countries about any shift in India's foreign policy. Egypt was sought to be expelled from NAM due to its peace treaty with Israel, but India opposed it at NAM summit in Havana, Cuba. Sadat's decision to sign peace treaty with Israel in 1979 led to Egypt's isolation and decline in its influence in the Arab world and this was reflected in the downward trend in Indo-Egyptian relations as well. It would be unrealistic to believe that bilateral relations can be insulated from the dynamics of a changing world. This applies not only to changes created by external impulses, but equally significantly to internal developments in each country over a period of time. The assassinations of Anwar Sadat in 1981 and Mrs. Indira Gandhi in 1984 drove many to conclude that an era of good Indo-Egyptian relations has come to an end.

But one should remember bilateral Indo-Egyptian relations are multi-faceted, healthy and rest on a solid foundation of historical and *strong cultural linkages*, shared national aspirations and commonalties in approach on most world issues of significance to both states. By mid 1980's the level of interaction between India and Egypt existed in virtually all fields of human activity which is sufficient enough ground for optimism. During President Hosni Mubarak relations considerably improved because India continued to accord a high place for Egypt in its foreign policy. Egypt has always been and will remain of great political significance to India. Both at the official and unofficial levels relations have undergone sea change.

Cultural Relations: Jawaharlal Nehru in his famous book *Glimpses of World History* wrote: "Egypt is, in many ways, very different from India, and Britain has been there for a comparatively short period and yet there are numerous parallels and common features in the two countries. The nationalist movements of India and Egypt have adopted different methods, but fundamentally the urge to national freedom is the same and the objective is to same. And the way imperialism functions in its efforts to suppress these nationalist movements is also much the same. So each of us can learn much from the others experience[33]." The INC and the Wafd party used the boycott of Royal Commissions as a vital weapon in the struggle for freedom. It was the Miler Commission in Egypt and the Simon Commission in India. Both India and Egypt were in contact through the Islamic reformers as well. Jamaluddin Afghani who stayed in Egypt for long years inspired the Egyptians for a great revival and prepared them to throw the imperialist yoke and also while on a visit to India he inspired the Indian Muslims to fight against British domination and conspiracies. Other Indian leaders who visited Egypt were Dwarkanath Tagore in 1845, the grandfather of Rabindranath Tagore. Rabindranath Tagore himself had passed several times through Egypt, and on one of his visits King Fuad of Egypt presented him valuable Arabic manuscripts for the Islamic Department of the Vishwa Bharthi University at Shantiniketan.

It must also be mentioned that many Indian students went to the Al Azhar University for studies and in 1937 Mahatma Gandhi while welcoming a delegation from Al Azhar said: "We should invite professors from Egypt and you should invite those from India, so that we may develop cultural contacts"[34]. India always used to emphasize that both India and Egypt are the inheritors of two glorious and ancient civilizations. Moreover India also highlighted that it has the third largest Muslim population in the world that have all the rights like other citizens. India's first Ambassador to Egypt was a Muslim who died in Egypt and who is buried in Cairo. It sent several distinguished Indians who were academics, historians as Ambassadors including Dr. AAA Fayzee who worked hard to strengthen Indo-Egyptian cultural ties. As Fayzee said: "Many Indians and Muslims are studying at Al Azhar and other institutions. This is evident proof of a cultural and religions rapprochement between our two peoples"[35].

Soon a cultural agreement was concluded which led to the flow of artists, writers, scholars, journalists, exchange of books, periodicals, films, music and dance groups, art shows, exhibitions and other types of cultural exchanges. Nawab Ali Yavar Jung, K.M. Pannikkar also served as Ambassadors among many others. Egypt's first Ambassador to India Ismail Kamel Bey, underlined the need for closer cooperation in the field of culture to supplement the close political and economic ties between the two states. Maulana Azad took the initiative for bringing out quarterly Arabic journal projecting Indian culture in the Arab world – *Thaqafatul Hind*. This helped India in building a favorable image in the Egyptian mind. Sheikh Mammon al Shinwa, Rector of Al Azhar and journalists like Dr. Mahmoud Azmi of *Al Ahram*, Hussein Abdu Fath, President of the Egyptian Press Syndicate visited India in early 1954 and wrote favorable articles on India in Egyptian papers. Two Indian press delegations visited Egypt one in 1950 and another in March 1955. Welcoming the first delegation the Rector of Al Azhar said. "Egypt and India are two old brotherly countries. Time will prove their brotherhood and friendship and further unite them. Muslims and Hindus must live together and work for the prosperity of India"[36].

In September 1952 India's Vice President Dr. S. Radhakrishnan visited Egypt and called for close cooperation in the field of cultural exchanges. Dr. Kalidas Nag who led a 3 man cultural delegation in 1949 gave a series of lectures in Egypt on India. More and more Indian and Egyptian students studied at each others universities. The September 1958 cultural agreement between the two states further intensified the ties. Dr. K.N. Raj was invited by the National Bank of Egypt to give series of lectures in 1955-56. In January 1953 a seminar was held at New Delhi on the "Contribution of Gandhian Outlook and techniques to the solution of tensions between and within Nation's'' in which Dr. Mohammed Hussein Heykal, former President of the Egyptian Senate and others participated. Delhi University conferred a honorary doctorate on Dr. Heykal. The famous Egyptian archaeologist Professor Abu Bakr was also given a D. Lit. by Delhi University in January 1964. Dr. C.D. Deshmukh, VC of Delhi University said. "By honoring Prof. – Abu Bakr we seek to remember the past in the context of the compulsions of the present day world, which are once again drawing India and Egypt together after the lapse of centuries of isolation"[37].

A number of art exhibitions depicting Indian and Egyptian Art have been held in both states. In 1952 the All India Fire Arts and Crafts Society organized an exhibition in Cairo. Inaugurating the exhibition Dr. Taha Hussein, Egypt's Education Minister and the author of *Future of Culture in Egypt* and a renowned Arab intellectual said: "The Indian forms of art are most appealing to the Egyptian mind and find a responsive chord in the Egyptian soul. I thank them for their initiative and I pray to God that the cultural bonds between India and Egypt may become stronger and more enduring"[38]. Music and Dance Groups especially Ballet troupes, folk dance groups have been regularly visiting each others cities. Indian films which are very popular in Egypt are shown at the film festivals which are regularly organized. Indian films often bag awards at the Cairo & Alexandria film festivals. Similarly Egyptian films with English subtitles take part in Indian film festivals and are awarded prizes. Many film personalities have visited Egypt like Shivaji Ganesan, M. G. Ramachandran, Shabana Azmi, Amitabh Bachhan, and others have received prestigious awards in Egypt. In 1953 an Indo Egyptian Foundation was established which is now known as Egypt-India Friendship Association which is actively working to strengthen

Indo-Egyptian ties. Nasser inaugurated the Indo-Egyptian friendship society in Delhi soon after the Bandung conference. Dr. Zakir Hussein was the first President of the society.

The first cultural agreement between India and Egypt which was signed on September 25, 1958 by Dr. Mahmud Fawzy, Egypt's foreign Minister and R.K. Nehru, India's Ambassador in Egypt is still the basis of cultural relations between the two states. This agreement has been improved upon and renewed several times. The Cultural Exchange Program [CEP] signed from time to time has over 65 articles covering the entire gamut of relations in the cultural field. This is one of the most extensive CEP India has signed with an Arab country. Although the cultural ties flourished between India and Egypt during Nehru-Nasser period but with the demise of Nehru in 1964, the Egyptian leader lost a close friend but Indo-Egyptian friendship was not the result only of the personal regards between Nehru and Nasser but it survived Nehru's death.

President Mubarak's visit to India during the NAM conference in 1983 and Rajiv Gandhi's visit to Cairo in 1985 gave a boost to Indo-Egyptian ties. Rajiv Gandhi during his visit had stated: "Along the passage of time this interaction between the *Egyptian* and *Indian Culture* has never ceased to exist, rather it has grown deeper and wider in recent and contemporary history"[39]. Just as great Indian and Egyptian minds have interacted and lofty ideas have flowed in the past, so also in the contemporary period close interaction is bound to succeed in various fields with the end of the cold war and with no major political problems between the two countries, Egypt and India as leaders of NAM should in line with the "sweeping changes" in international relations, focus more on economic cooperation among the countries of the South. In the aftermath of these visits the first meeting of the Indo-Egyptian Joint Commission was held in Delhi in November 1985.

Economic cooperation which had declined during the Sadat period has picked up considerably and India now exports a host of engineering goods to Egypt. Egypt has traditionally been one of

India's most important trading partners in Africa. India imports oil and oil products from Egypt. Egyptian diplomats although pleased with the growing political contacts, at the same time express dismay and emphasize the need for matching economic cooperation in order to genuinely strengthen bilateral ties. India has been having a favorable balance of trade for many years and Egypt is keen to have a more balanced trade with India. The total level of bilateral two-way trade is around US$ 500 US dollars. The selection of Dr. Boutros Boutros Ghali as the Secretary General of the UN was a clear indication of the success and rich harvest of Egyptian diplomacy. The appointment of Mr. Amre Moussa as Arab League Secretary General and award of Nobel Prize for Dr.Ahmed Zewail and appointment of Dr. Mohammed of Baradei as Head of IAEA all show the significance of Egypt in global scene. Egypt derives its strength mainly from its unique geographic location which undoubtedly makes it the focal point of international interaction. Geopolitically, Egypt sits at the gateway of three continents and the strategically important waterway, the Suez Canal.

In spite of the end of the cold war, the world remains a volatile place with regional conflicts that have global dimensions and repercussions. As an influential member of the world community, India looks to Egypt as a major force for peace and stability, directly through its central role in the Arab-Israeli Peace Process and as a keen advocate of principles which India shares in the global arena, especially at the UN, NAM, and G-15 and at WTO. Dr. Ghali an ardent admirer of India through his numerous visits to India has also contributed to the growing friendship between the two states. President Mubarak by sending such eminent diplomats to India like Dr. Nabil el Araby, Dr. Noaman Gallal, Dr. Mustafa El Fiki, Dr. Amre Moussa, Adel El Gazzar, Mahmoud Allam, Dr. Mohamed Khairuddin Abdel Latef and Dr.Mohammed Abdel Hamid Higazy as Ambassadors signified the importance he attached to New Delhi.

The new CEP was concluded during the visit of Egypt's Foreign Minister Ahmed Aboul Gheit on December 16, 2006 which provides for cultural exchange programs specifying concrete activities and exchanges from time to time. Hundreds of Indian students and experts have gone to Egypt and likewise Egyptians have come to India especially to universities, conferences so on. Under CEP many Egyptian students have acquired skills, degrees from Indian Universities and institutes. The Indian Technical and Economic Cooperation (ITEC) established in 1964 have also benefited Egypt. Since 1986 to 2004 more than 150 Egyptian candidates have imparted advanced technical skills from India[40].

Both the countries have decided on a number of measures to further strengthen the interaction between scholars, artists, intellectuals and others. The four day seminar in Cairo in September 1991 on Indo-Egyptian historical and cultural relations in Cairo was the continuation of this process which was initiated in 1958 formally. Among others, participants in the seminar included Dr. Najma Heptullah Deputy Chairperson of Rajya Sabha, Dr. M.C. Joshi of the Archaeological Survey of India, Dr. LP Sihare, former D.G. of National Museum and Professor MS Agwani, renowned expert on the area and Former Vice Chancellor of JNU, New Delhi. The papers were published in a book entitled "*India and Egypt: Influences and Interactions*" (1993)[41].

This was followed by the setting up of the Maulana Abul Kalam Azad Center for Indian Culture in Cairo on Republic Day in 1992 during the same month when India decided to establish diplomatic relations with Israel which according to some observers Egypt wanted India to postpone until a reasonable settlement was concluded between Israel and the Palestinians. MACIC was established to give a much wider exposure to the Indian Culture in Egypt. Since its inception MACIC has acquired a high reputation in the cultural and intellectual circles of Egypt. It has a well stocked library of more than 5000 books which are widely used by the Egyptians, including many research scholars from different Arab and Egyptian universities, institutes, journalists, in addition to members/students of the Indian community. The Center organizes regular Yoga classes and regular classes on Hindi and Urdu languages. The Center also organizes Indian cultural weeks which include film weeks, book exhibitions, painting competitions, seminars, lectures etc. In 2000 MACIC organized Indian Cultural Weeks all over Egypt (in the 26 Governorates) in which thousands of Egyptian students took part. This included film shows, book exhibitions and painting competition[42]. Certificates were distributed to all the participants, and prizes were given tb the winners. Every year MACIC organizes painting competition to school children during the birthdays of Mahatma Gandhi, Maulana Azad and Jawaharlal Nehru. The prizes are given to the winners on November 14, – Children's Day. This has become extremely popular over the years with a renowned Egyptian personality invited for the function along with many other dignitaries from Egypt, Indian Community and diplomats.

It also hosts the Egypt – India Friendship Association (EIFA) which organizes several programs. MACIC has an auditorium where Indian films are screened regularly which are popular. The Center is also the nodal agency for implementing the Indo-Egyptian Cultural Exchange Program which has been in existence since 1958. Until recently prominent intellectuals were appointed by ICCR as Directors of MACIC. Dr. (Ms.) Ismet Mehdi Latif (1992-95) of CIFL, Hyderabad was the first Director of MACIC followed by Dr. SA Rahman (1996-98) CAAS, SLLCS, JNU and Professor Aftab Kamal Pasha, (1999-2002) Chairman Center for West Asian and African Studies, and Director, Gulf Studies, School of International Studies, JNU New Delhi and briefly a journalist Mr. Kanchan Gupta. Now it is headed by Dr Basher Ahmed of CAAS, SLLCS, JNU. The annual budget of MACIC is Rs. 1.5 crore. In 1995 the Center for Asian Studies, Cairo University organized a seminar in Egypt wherein several scholars from India took part. The papers were published in a book entitled ''Egypt and India in the Post-Cold War World: Comparative Paradigms'' (Cairo: 1996)[43].

In 1996, CWAAS/SIS/JNUS organized the second Indo-

Egyptian conference in New Delhi in which numerous Egyptian scholars including the Director of the Center for Asian Studies Dr. Mohammed El Syed Selim participated. The papers were published in a book entitled "*Indo-Egyptian Perspectives: Global and Regional Concerns*" (New Delhi: 1999). The Indian Council of Social Science Research, New Delhi also organized an Indo-Egyptian Seminar at the prestigious India International Center at New Delhi on 10-11 September 1996 where three prominent Egyptian scholars participated. The papers have been published in a book entitled: "*The Role of India, Egypt and other Developing countries in the Emerging International Order*" (New Delhi: 1999)[44].

All these academic exchanges further strengthened Indo-Egyptian Cultural ties. Since then several Egyptian scholars have been regularly coming to India to participate in seminars organized by JNU, ICSSR, IDSA, Ford Foundation and others. A number of scholars have been coming to India from the Al Azhar as well. Indian scholars have also been visiting Egyptian institutes especially the Cairo University, American University in Cairo, Al Ahram Centre for Political and Strategic Studies, Centre for Middle Eastern Studies, Alexandria University, Ibn Khaldoun Centre for Development so on, thereby contributing to the strengthening of Indo-Egyptian cultural ties. A large number of Indian Scholars at JNU, AMU and other universities conduct research on different aspects of Egypt producing many books and research articles[45].

Mention must also be made of the contribution made by Dr. Mohammed Hassan El Zayyat, former foreign minister of Egypt to strengthen Indo-Egyptian ties. Dr. Zayyat was closely associated with Nehru and Indira Gandhi Memorial Trusts in India and was President of the Egypt-India Friendship Association. He delivered the 1983 Maulana Azad Memorial lecture in Delhi for ICCR on Indo-Egyptian Relations which is published by ICCR as "***India and Egypt: Modern Relations between two Ancient Nations***" (New Delhi: 1984). Prominent Egyptian intellectuals who have visited India include Dr. Abdel

Moneim al Nemir, former minister of Awaqaf; Mr. Ibrahim al Nafey, Editor of *Al Ahram*, Mohammed Odah, Dr. Abdel Moneim Said Aly, Director, Centre for Political and Strategic Studies, Al Ahram, Cairo, Editor of *Al Akhbar*, and many others. The India International Centre organized a two days seminar on "India and West Asia: History, Culture and Society", 1-2 March 2002 at New Delhi where a prominent Egyptian historian Dr. Mostafa el Abbadi participated. The papers have been published in a book "***History, Culture and Society in India and West Asia***" (New Delhi: 2003).

The ICCR invited Justice Mohamed Said Al Ashmawi to deliver the 1992 Maulana Azad Memorial lecture on "Religion and Politics". Similarly Dr. Boutros Boutrous Ghali was invited to deliver the 1993 Maulana Azad lecture on "Current World Challenges as reflected in the United Nations Today". Together with the 1983 lecture by Dr. Zayyat, Egypt is the only country from where three very distinguished scholars were invited by ICCR, reflecting the pride of place Egyptian intellectuals occupy in India. The visits by former Prime Ministers Narasimha Rao to Egypt in October 1995 as well as the visit of PM I.K. Gujral in October 1997 and the two visits by the Vice President of India Krishna Kant for the G-15 Summit in 1998 and 2000 in Cairo indicate the vibrant and active nature of Indo-Egyptian relations. This will provide a political impulse needed for expediting cooperation and bringing to fruition a whole host of proposals and initiatives that are already signed. Here one must note that the traffic from Egypt to India has been less than the other way round. Egypt's President Hosni Mubarak was awarded the Jawaharlal Nehru Award for International Understanding and Peace for the Year 1995. Although he has been promising to visit India, but this has not materialized despite best efforts by Indian diplomats and political leaders. It appears the Egyptian have some reservations like India spurning Egypt's attempt to mediate on Kashmir issue, the Babri Masjid demolition issue, BJP's policy toward Indian Muslims and growing strategic and military ties between India and Israel.

Although the Speaker of the People's Assembly Mr. Fathi Suroor visited India on the occasion of 50th anniversary of Indian Parliament in March 2003 and Dr. Najma Heptuallah as Deputy Chairperson of Rajya Sabha visited Egypt several times (in recent times) and other ministers from Egypt came to India on various official engagements, greater political thrust is needed to hasten and strengthen activities in all areas. Dr. Omar Abdullah, (2001)Minister of State for External Affairs visited Egypt, Jaswant Singh, External Affairs Minister (2001), Prof. Y.K. Alagh, (2002) former Vice Chancellor of JNU and Minister of State for Planning and Program Implementation, Prof. MS Agwani, (2002) Ex-Member National Minorities Commission, and former VC, JNU and many others visited Egypt including a large number of journalists, Members of Parliament and experts, but the potential for further Indo-Egyptian cultural cooperation exists. Mention should also be made of the need to open an Egyptian Cultural Center in India to which promises have been made by top Egyptian officials but is yet to take shape. A comprehensive framework for bilateral cultural cooperation already exists. What is needed on the one hand is a greater political impulse and a "delivery mechanism" to translate declarations of intent into action and to expedite action where this is slow. While existing Indo-Egyptian ties are mature but enormous possibilities exist which needs to be harnessed. Many other innovative ways could to be found to push through useful initiatives to widen and deepen Indo-Egyptian cultural relations[46].

Throughout the Arab world Indians like Rabindranath Tagore, Mahatma Gandhi, Jawaharlal Nehru, and Maulana Azad are well known. Indian music and dance groups are very popular, especially ballet troupes, folk dance groups. Indian Hindi films are very much liked by Arabs and often bag awards at film festivals. Many films personalities especially Amitabh Bachchan have visited the Arab world and have got warm welcome throughout the area. Amitabh received the prestigious Millennium award in the Egyptian Mediterranean coastal city of Alexandria in 2001. Cairo University has established the Center for Asian

Studies and likewise the Zagazig University has an Institute for Asian Studies where many Egyptian and Arab Scholars study on India. Arabs like Dr. Taha Hussein, Neguib Mahfuz, Yusuf Idris, Tawfik al Hakim and other Arab writers have become well known in India. Many seminars and conferences in India have attracted several Arab scholars.

Several books have been published on Indo Arab ties further enriching the cultural ties. The ICCR has invited several eminent Arab personalities to deliver the annual Maulana Azad Memorial lectures some of which have published. Diplomatic and commercial ties between India and the Arabs are good but it is the cultural ties which will prove to be more enduring. India as part of its cultural diplomacy has been giving awards like the Nehru Award for International understanding [to Egypt's Hosni Mubarak [1995] and Sultan Qaboos of Oman [2006] to prominent personalities in the region, working to send statutes or busts of Mahatma Gandhi and Jawaharlal Nehru, naming of roads and streets after Indian leaders so on. India has been inviting leaders from the area to the Republic Day parade in New Delhi which is now considered a measure of the importance India attaches to that country, apart from serving as an opportunity to showcase the country's military might as well as democratic and secular traditions. In recent times the Presidents of Algeria, Iran and the King of Saudi Arabia have been invited to the Republic Day. Over the last 50 years there has been an exponential increase in the number of scholars, exhibitions, film shows and other cultural contacts between India and the Arab world. After the establishment of diplomatic ties with Israel in 1992, Indo-Arab ties at the political level since then has seen some strains, but the steady growth in Indo-Arab cultural ties both directly and under the ICCR has sustained the relationship. Indian scholars, with Arabic knowledge have played a key role in strengthening India's cultural diplomacy with West Asia[47].

India's rapid economic growth, emerging middle class, English language advantage, expertise in IT, military capability, strong democratic structures with functioning democracy, influence in NAM, good relations with Russia, China, USA along with its growing soft power especially films [India produces more films in a year than the US [Hollywood] as Indian films offer stiff competition all over the world to films made by other countries are being gradually linked to promotion of India's national interest. Due to India's long history and vibrant civilization and rich culture and now as an emerging economic power more and more people are showing great interest in things Indian especially as Indian experiment as a multicultural, multilingual, and multilayered society is seen as a reasonably successful case.

Notes and References

1. Childe, *The Most Ancient East,* p.208, cited in Sudhansu Kumar Ray, *Prehistoric India and Ancient Egypt* (New Delhi: Cambridge Book and Stationary Store, 1956) p.39.

2. Shereen Ratnagar, *Encounters*: *The Westerly Trade of the Harappan Civilisation* (London: OUP, 1980)

3. Jack Turner, *The History of a Temptation* [New York: Vintage Books, 2005] pp.204

4. A. Murray, *The Splendour That was Egypt* (New Delhi: Cambridge Book and Stationary Store, 1956), p. xxi.

5. Maqbul Ahmad, *Indo-Arab Relation: An Account of India's Relations with the Arab World from Ancient up to Modern Times* (New Delhi : ICCR, 1969) ; Turner, n, 3, pp.238-9

6. Ray n.1, p.7-12; Shereen Ratnagar, *Under standing Harappa Civilisation in the Greater Indus Valley* (New Delhi: Tulika, 2001).

7. Mohammed Hasan el Zayyat, *India and Egypt: Modern Relations between two Ancient Nations* (New Delhi: ICCR, 1984) p.12; Turner, n.3, pp.147; Turner, n.3, pp. 147.

8. See also Abdulla el Madani, « Arabian Gulf during the British Era: The Impact of India », in NN Vohra ed, *History, Culture and Society in India and West Asia* [New Delhi : Shipra, IIC, 2003] p.109 ; Turner, n.3, pp.62.

9. Saryu Doshi, Influences and Interactions », in *India and Egypt : Influences and Interactions* (New Delhi: Marg Publications, ICCR, 1993) p.xiii ; and Sir George Watt, *The Commercial Products of India* (London : 1908); Turner, n.3.pp. 63-64.

10. Zayyat, n.4, p. 14;

11. Ray, n.1, p.38; Turner, n.3, pp.238-39.

12. Ibid., p.11 and 13; S. Maqbul Ahmad, *India and the Neighbouring Territoires* (Leiden: 1960); Turner, n.3, pp.82

13. SM el Mansouri, *Art and Culture of India and Egypt* [Calcutta: KL. Mukhopadhyay, 1959] p. 46.

14. Ibid., p.48; MA. Saleem Khan, *Early Muslim Perception of India and Hinduism* (New Delhi: South Asian Publishers, 1997); Turner, n.3, pp. 66.

15. Ibid., p.49; NA Faruqi, *Early Muslim Historiography: A Study of Early Transmitters of Arab History from the Rise of Islam to the end of Ummayyed Period, 612-750* (Delhi: 1979); Turner, n. pp. 96-7.

16. M.K. Dhavalikar, Early Contacts, in Doshi, n. 4, p.50. see also S. Maqbul Ahmad, *Indo-Arab Relations* (Bombay : Popular Prakashan, 1969).Turner, n. pp.104.

17. K.N. Chaudhuri, *Trade and Civilization in the Indian Occan : An Economic History from the Rise of Islam to 1750* (New Delhi : Munshi ram Manoharlal Publishers, 1985) p.59.

18. Doshi, n. 4, p.xiv ; see also Sahar Abdel Aziz Salem, « Commerce and one Faith », in Doshi, n.4, p.96.

19. Salem Khan, n.8, p.102 ; Tara Chand, *Influences of Islam on Indian Culture* (Allahabad : The Indian Press, 1965) ; Turner, n.3, pp.180-1.

20. Andre Wink, *Al Hind: The Making of the Indo-Islamic World vol. I* (New Delhi: OUP, 1999).

21. Chaudhuri, n.17, p.59-60 ; Turner, n.3, pp.20 ; Quoted from Bernard Lewis, "Some Reflections on the Decline of the Ottoman Empire", *Studies Islamica, 9,* 1959, p.118, see also K.N. Chaudhari, *Trade and Civilization in the Indian Ocean: An Economic History from the Rise of Islam to 1950* (Cambridge: 1985); see also Wrike Freitag and William G. Clarence Smith, Ed; *Hadhrami Traders, Scholars and Statesmen in the Indian Ocean, 1750's-1960's* (Leiden : EJ Brill, 1997); and AK Pasha, "Tipu and the Ottoman Empire", in B. Shiek Ali, Ed, *Tipu Sultan: A Great Martyr* (Bangalore: Prasaranga, 1993), pp.219-32; and AK Pasha, Ed; *Perspectives on India and the Gulf States* (New Delhi: 1999) pp. 1-23.

22. VD Hanson, *Carnage and Culture*, [New York: Anchor Books, 2002] pp. 265-269 ; Richard Hall, *Empires of the Monsoon: A History of the Indian Ocean and its Invaders*.[London: Harper Collins,1998] pp.195--224; Quoted from Bernard Lewis, « Some Reflections on the decline of the Ottoman Empire », *Studies Islamica*, 9, 1959, p.118 ; AK Pasha, *India and West Asia* : *Continuity and Change*, [Delhi : Gyan

Sagar, 1999] pp.7-15 ; Ibid., p.67 ; See also Mawlana Syed Sulaiman Nadwi, *Indo-Arab Relations*: *An English Rendering* (Hyderabad : The Institute of Indo-Middle East Cultural Studies, 1962). ; Turner, n.3, pp.22, 42, 45-47; For details see R C Majumdar et al. *An Advanced History of India* (Delhi: Macmillan, 1978), p. 346. See also MN Pearson, *Merchants and Rulers in Gujarat: The Response to the Portuguese in the 16th Century*, [New Delhi: Munshiram Manoharlal Publishers, 1976] pp.67-85; and J Chaube, *History of Gujarat Kingdom, 1458-1537* [New Delhi: Munshiram Manoharlal Publishers, 1975] pp.277.

23. *National Herald* (Delhi) 28 September 1992.

24. Riyaz Punjabi and A K Pasha, ed, *India and the Islamic World* (New Delhi : Radiant Publishers 1998) p.97 ; MS Agwani, « India and the Arab World », in BR Nanda, ed, *Indian Foreign Policy : The Nehru Years* (New Delhi : 1976), pp.72-3.

25. A K Pasha, "Indo-Egyptian Cultural Relations: Retrospect and Prospects", in Zohurul Bari, Ed, *Modern Egypt: Culture, Religion and Politics*, (New Delhi: Shipra Publications, 2003) pp.199; see also Saryu Doshi, Ed; *India and Egypt: Influences and Interactions* (New Delhi: Garg Publications, ICCR. 1993).

26. A K Pasha, "Nehru and the Crises in West Asia" *Détente*, Vol. IX, no. 1, May-June 1990, p.p. 4-9; AAA Fayzee, *Introducing the Middle East*, (Mysore, 1970).

27. MS Agwani, "Nehru and the Arab World", *Secular Democracy*, Nehru Number, 1976, p. 171; MS Agwani, "India and the Arab World" in B R Nanda, Ed; *India Foreign Policy: The Nehru Years*, (New Delhi: 1976) pp. 72-73; Hari Sharan Chhabra, Nehru and Resurgent Africa (New Delhi: Africa Publications, 1989).

28. A K Pasha, *Egypt's Relations with Soviet Union: The Nasser and Sadat Period* (Aligarh: CWAS AMU, 1986).

29. AK Pasha, *Egypt's Quest for Peace* (New Delhi: National Publishing House, 1994).

30. A K Pasha, "Indo-Egyptian Relations: Retrospect and Prospect,' *Third Word Impact*, Vol.11, no.23, November 1991, pp.23-27.

31. R K Srivastava, "*India's Relations with the Arab East, 1947-64*," Ph.D. Thesis, University of Kanpur, 1976.

32. AK Pasha, *Arab-Israeli Peace Process: An Indian Perspective* [New Delhi: Manas, Publications, 2000]

33. P R Mudiam, *India and the Middle East*, [London: British Academic Press), p. 56.

34. K R Singh, "India and WANA", in Bimal Prasad, Ed; *India's*

Foreign Policy: Studies in Continuity and Change (New Delhi: Vikas, pp. 247-59).

35. A K Pasha, *India and West Asia: Continuity and Change*, (Delhi: Gyan Sagar, 1999) pp. 43-46.

36. Ibid, pp.47-51 see also Richard J. Kozicki, "India and the Arab World after Indira Gandhi: Continuity in Foreign Policy", *Arab-American Affairs*, Fall, 1985, no. 14, pp.1-17.

37. A K Pasha, "Rediscovering old bonds with Egypt", *The Pioneer*, 23 December 1991; T.P. Bhat, "Indo-Egyptian Economic Relations: Perspectives and Perceptions", in G. Pant, Ed, *Indo-Egyptian Perspectives* (New Delhi: SIS, JNU, 1999) pp. 127-136.

38. Baher M. Allam, "Effects of Economic Reform Program on the Deficits of State Budget in Egypt", in Proceedings of the India-Egypt Seminar: "*The Role of India, Egypt and other Developing Countries in the Emerging International Order,"* (New Delhi: ICSSR, 1996) pp. 13-30

39. Boutros Ghali, *Egypt's Road to Jerusalem: A Diplomat's Story of the Struggle for Peace in the Middle East* (New York, Random House, 1997), pp. 80-81; 120, 214, 257, 278.

40. Salim, Mohammed El Sayed; Ed; *Egypt and India in the Post-Cold War World: Comparative Paradigms* (Cairo: CAS, Cairo University, 1996); Riyaz Punjabi and A K Pasha, Ed; *India and the Islamic World* (New Delhi: Radiant, 1998); A K Pasha, *The Arab-Israeli Peace Process: An Indian Perspective* (New Delhi: Manas 2000).

41. G. Pant, *Indo-Egyptian Perspectives* [New Delhi: SIS, JNU, 1999] pp. 127-136; Clement M. Henry, *The Mediterranean Debt Crescent* (Cairo: AUC, 1997) pp. 43-46; Pasha, n.24, p. 77-78; Pasha, n.16, p 207; Abdel Hamid Saba El Regal, Economic Cooperation between India and Egypt, RIS Discussion Papers No. 55/2003, New Delhi, June 2003; Bansidhar Pradhan, Changing Dynamics of India's West Asia Policy", *International Studies*, vol. 41, no.1, 2004, p.51; Why the US promotes India's great power ambitions, *Analytical Monthly Review*, Vol. 3, no. 12, March 2006, pp. 15-30.

42. A K Pasha, "Egypt's Search for food Security", *Détente,* vol. 7, no. 5, January 1989, pp. 10-15.

43. A K Pasha, *Egypt in a Changing World* (New Delhi: National Publishing House, 2003) pp. 242-260; P R K Swamy, "Mubarak in busy, please mail the Nehru award", *Asian Tribune*, 7-7-2007.

44. Egypt, 2004, Ministry of Foreign Trade; Egypt in Focus: 52nd National Day, New Delhi, Embassy of Egypt, 23 July 2004. Dr. Fathi

Abdel Fatah, "Egypt and India: Common Challenges and Ambitions", Ibid, p. 26.

45. *The Hindu*, 23 November 2005.

46. *Egypt News*, New Edition, vol.3, May 2006, p.2; Also see June-July Issue, Special Issue, Vol. IV, 2006.

47. Pavan K. Verma, "Culture as an instrument of Diplomacy" in Atish Sinha and Madhup Mohta ed., *Indian Foreign Policy: Challenges and Opportunities*, [New Delhi: Academic Foundation, 2007] pp.1135-1141; see also Arun Tandon, *India's Cultural Diplomacy,* M.Phil disst. SIS, JNU, 1979.

11

Globalisation and Indian Diaspora in West Asia and North Africa: Some Policy Implications

Prakash C. Jain

Globalisation and Diaspora

Globalisation can be defined as "the intensified and deepened cultural, economic, political and institutional interconnectedness and interdependency that has developed between corporations, communities and states, particularly since the 1970s" (Walton-Roberts 2004: 54). Globalisation implies that there is worldwide financial, economic, technological and ecological interdependence", and as such "goods, capital, knowledge, images, communication, crime, culture, pollutants, drugs, fashions and beliefs all readily flow across territorial boundaries" (Cohen 1999: 155). So much so that some scholars argue that globalisation is leading to the emergence of "the first global civilization" – a discrete world-order with shared values, processes and structures (Ibid).

There are observable and countertendencies to globalization that often manifest themselves in the form of nationalism and sub-nationalism, racism, religious fundamentalism, sexism etc. Thus both universal and parochial tendencies are at work in the process of globalization.

Before we further elaborate on this possible co-relationship between migration and diaspora it would be useful to define the term diaspora. A diaspora can be defined as an ethnic minority group of migrant origins residing and acting in host country but maintaining strong sentimental and material links with its homeland. Modern diasporas constitute trans-state triadic networks involving ethnic diasporas, their host countries and homelands, and as such they have significant ramifications for international relations and international politics, and other activities. The ties diasporic communities maintain through visits, marriages, trade networks, transfer of technology and skills and political lobbying for homelands are some other aspects of diasporic activities.

Within these broad parameters it can be argued that certain aspects of globalization are particularly relevant to the study of diasporas in terms of their emergence, survival and success. Following Cohen (1999: 157) these are discussed as follows:

- **A World Economy** with quicker and denser transactions between its sub-sectors due to better communications, cheaper transport, a new international division of labour, the activities of transnational corporations and the effects of liberal trade and capital-flow policies;
- **Forms of International Migration** that emphasize contractual relationships, family visits, intermittent stays abroad and sojourning, as opposed to permanent settlement and the exclusive adoption of the citizenship of a destination country;
- **The Development of "Global Cities"** in response to the intensification of transactions and interactions between the different segments of the world economy and their concentration in certain cities whose significance resides more in their global, rather than in their national, roles;
- **The creation of cosmopolitan and local cultures** promoting or reacting to globalization; and
- **A Deterritorialization of Social Identity** challenging the hegemonising nation-states' claim to make an exclusive citizenship a defining focus of allegiance and fidelity in favour of overlapping, permeable and multiple forms of identification. To sum up, globalisation has not only accelerated the processes of international migration and formation of Diasporas but also strengthened Diaspora-homeland linkages.

The Global Indian Diaspora

The modern Indian Diaspora is about 200 years old – largely a creation of British colonialism in India and some other countries of Asia, Africa, Oceania and the West Indies. Until the World War II Indians emigrated mainly as indentured labourers to British Guiana, Trinidad, Surinam (then a Dutch colony), South Africa, Fiji, Mauritius and Reunion Islands, and as kangani/maistry labourers to Burma, Malaysia, Singapore and Sri Lanka. Indians also emigrated as traders and government employees to the East and South African countries besides Fiji and South Africa.

Following the World War II Indian migration to the industrially advanced countries of Europe and North America, Australia, New Zealand etc. had also begun to gain momentum. The post-war economic expansion in these countries created heavy demand for skilled labour and professionals. Simultaneously, immigration laws were also relaxed in Canada and the US. This form of overseas Indian migration of skilled and educated personnels, popularly known as the "brain drain", thus resulted in the formation of sizeable Indian communities in Australia, Britain, Canada, New Zealand and the US. Since the early 1970s Indians have also been migrating in large numbers to the oil-rich West Asian countries. There are about 4.5 million non-resident Indians working/living in the Gulf countries. The total strength of the Indian Diaspora is presently estimated at 30 million.

Historically, five distinctive patterns of Indian emigration can be identified: (1) indentured labour emigration, (2) kangani/maisry labour emigration, (3) 'free' or 'passage' emigration to East Africa, South Africa, Fiji etc, (4) 'brain drain' or voluntary emigration to the metropolitan countries of Europe, North America and Oceania, and (5) manpower emigration to West Asia. Whereas the first three patterns are often categorized as colonial and the resultant diasporas as "old". The last two patterns are post-colonial giving rise to the "new" diasporas. The new Indian diaspora has clear linkages with the process of globalisation. It is with the last category that we are concerned here in this paper.

Indians in the Gulf Region

Trade and cultural contacts between India and West Asia go back to antiquity (Ahmad, 1969). These contacts were widespread extending up to the eastern Mediterranean and also covering large parts of Central Asia. Archaeological and literary evidence suggest that India and West Asia had trade relations since at least the days of the Indus Valley civilization.

In so far as the Gulf coast was concerned, a considerable number of Indians appear to have migrated there in pre-Islamic era "either to establish businesses, seek employment with Arab traders, or just to escape instability at home" (Ahmad, 1971). Apparently all these groups completely assimilated into the respective societies of their migration.

Seventh to Tenth century are said to be the "golden age" of Indo-Arab trade. This period began with the rise and spread of Islam and the founding of Baghdad in 762 A.D as the capital of the Arab World. It is very likely that a significant number of merchants and a variety of artisans and professionals from India must have migrated and settled down in this region.

Indian Merchant Diaspora in the Gulf

Medieval Arab sources provide the earliest evidence of the presence of colonies of Indian merchants in the Persian Gulf and Red Sea areas. "They reveal that Hindu merchants were present in the port of Shiraj on the Persian shore of the Gulf at least in the ninth century and that they also frequented the coasts of Oman, Socotra and Aden" (Gopal, 1998; Marcovits, 2000: 10). Sindhi and Gujarati merchants, both Hindu and Muslim played dominant role in maritime trade and finance across the Indian Ocean (Marcovits, 2000). During the later medieval period there was a considerable amount of exchange of Arab and Indian scholars and religious leaders.

Vasco da Gama noted the presence of Indians on the shores of

East Africa in 1498 and subsequently in the ports of the Red Sea and in the interior of the Arabian Peninsula (Gopal, 1992: 220). Port towns of Mocha and Aden and inland cities of Taif and Sanna were also inhabited by the Indians of Ormuz (Gopal, 1998). The ruins of a Hindu temple were found at Kalhat, the principal Omani port of the fifteenth century which further suggests a settlement of Indians in Oman (Miles 1966: 526).

In Iran besides Omuz, Indians in small numbers had settled down in Yezd, Shiraj, Isfahan, Tehran, Resht, Gilan, Khorasan and Mashad. Following the establishment of a new port of Gombroon or Bandar Abbas in the late 17th century Ormuz declined to insignificance and Indians shifted to the new city. In 1760 when Bandar Abbas was abandoned by the Persians, the Indians shifted to Abu Shehr, Bushahr, and to the Iraqi port of Basra. Towards the end of the 18th century Gujarati *Baniyas* were replaced by a new group of emigrants known as Shikarpuris who hailed from Sindh (Gopal, 1997).

In the 17th and 18th centuries Indians traveled via Iran to Central Asia, Caucasus region and Tzarist Russia. They were active as merchants as well as money-lenders in Bukhara, Samarkand, Taskent, Baku, Semakha, Derbent, Kokand etc. Scholars have also noted the existence of a Hindu temple in Iran and another at Baku "where a perpetual flame burnt and priest was always in attendance" (Gopal, 1998: 121). Outside India, Nepal and Tibet, the temple at Baku was a major centre of Hindu pilgrimage.

In contrast to the 17th and 18th centuries in which India's impact on the Persian Gulf region was sporadic confined mostly to trade, it was quite comprehensive in the later 19th and the first half of the 20th century. Indo-Gulf relations during this period were "varied and multi-faceted." For about a century or so India was not only a major partner in the Indo-Gulf trade and commerce, its impact on the Gulf countries in terms of initial modernization and cultural renaissance, reform movement and many other aspects of socio-cultural life such as cuisines, musical instruments, interior designing and architecture was also substantial (Elmadani, 2003). It was also during this period that a number of Indian merchant communities were more firmly established throughout the Gulf/Red Sea region. It hardly needs to be emphasized here that the Gulf region was virtually an extension of British India and that the Indians in the Gulf enjoyed privileges as British subject.

The British administration in the Gulf helped settle a number of Indian communities across the region. Among these the 19th century Muscat hosted three distinct Indian communities: *Thattai Sindhi Bhatias, Kutchhi Bhatias and Khojahs or Luwatiyyas.* Some of the prominent entrepreneurs from these communities still continue to flourish even today (Allen, Jr., 1981: 39-51). Besides Oman, Indian merchant communities also existed in Iran, Aden and the Trucial States (United Arab Emirates) (Al-Sayegh, 1998; Jain, 2004b).

Besides trading a wide variety of goods, Indians were also involved in pearl- fishing industry in some of the Gulf countries, namely Bahrain, Oman and United Arab Emirates. Pearl fishing was the mainstay of the Gulf economies in the 19th and early 20th centuries. Some idea of the nature and magnitude of this industry can be had from the fact that 18 per cent of the total Bahraini population was involved in this industry in the early 20th century. Corresponding figures for Kuwait, Trucial Coast emirates and Qatar were 25 per cent, 31 per cent and 48 per cent respectively (Zahlan, 1979: 22).

In the Red Sea region Yemen is one of the countries where Indians have been settled for a long time. Although Indo-Yemeni trade and cultural relations go back to antiquity, the evidence of the Indians' presence in Yemen is available since only the early seventeenth century. The Indians were found to reside in almost all the major towns of Yemen, including Mocha, Sana'a, Hodeida and Beital-Faqui. The Indians began to settle in the port town of Aden after its occupation by the British in 1839. By the time British left Aden in 1967 their population had risen to more than 20,000. Besides Aden, there must have been thousands of Indians in other towns of Yemen, but their history is sketchy. Today

Yemen hosts the largest permanently-settled Indian Diaspora in West Asia (Jain, 2003b).

With the decline of pearl industry in the 1920s and 1930s Indian merchants began to concentrate their attention on general trade, importing goods not only from India but also from Europe, America and Japan. These trends were further to strengthen after the World War II.

Indian Labour Diaspora

The Indian manpower presence in the region dates back to the early oil exploration days when a few Indians had been employed by the D'Arcy Exploration Company in 1902 (Seccombe and Lawless, 1986). Anglo-Persian Oil Company incorporated in 1909 employed more than 368 in December 1910, 158 Indians in January 1910 and in subsequent years this figure was to grow into several hundred and to a peak of 4,890 in 1925. The pattern was repeated in other oil companies in the 1930s and 1940s. Thus in spite of restrictive nationality clause the Gulf countries have relied on foreign manpower to perform various skilled, semi skilled and unskilled tasks (Seccombe and Lawless, 1986, pp. 548-74). A few thousand Indians worked in various Gulf oil companies. This situation more or less continued until the mid-1970s when following the hike in the oil prices during 1973-74, there was a substantial increase in the oil revenues of the oil producing and exporting Gulf countries.

The development programmes that were launched in the wake of the oil revenues included creation of amenities like schools, hospitals houses, improvement of transport and communication etc. were taken up. This resulted in a spurt in demand for not only highly skilled technical experts but also for semi-skilled and unskilled workers. Therefore, the major outflow of Indian migrant workers in the last three decades has been to the Gulf countries where a few million workers are estimated to have been employed. The largest number of Indian workers is in Saudi Arabia. Other major employers of Indian workers are UAE, Oman, Kuwait and Bahrain. The number of workers who were given emigration clearance for contractual employment abroad in the past three decades is mentioned in Table 11.1.

Table 11.1: Annual Labour Outflows from India to West Asia, 1976-2005

Year	Number of Workers	Year	Number of Workers
1976	4,200	1991	197,889
1977	22,900	1992	416,784
1978	69,000	1993	438,338
1979	171,800	1994	425,385
1980	268,200	1995	415,334
1981	272,000	1996	414,214
1982	224,257	1997	416,424
1983	217,971	1998	355,164
1984	198,520	1999	199,552
1985	160,520	2000	243,182
1986	109,234	2001	278,664
1987	121,812	2002	367,663
1988	165,924	2003	466,456
1989	125,786	2004	474,960
1990	143,565`	2005	549,000

Note: The figure given in the above tables do not include the persons who are running the business in partnership with foreign nationals; those who emigrated on visit visa and stayed on to get a job and those skilled workers and professionals (like doctors, engineers, chartered accountants computer specialist etc.) in whose case emigration clearance is not necessary.

Source: Annual Reports, Ministry of Labour, Government of India.

It must be pointed out here that India is not only the second most populous country in the world with surplus labour, it also has a vast reservoir of well trained and educated manpower. Therefore, as soon as the opportunities to earn better wages arose, Indians were the first among groups of immigrants to flock to the

Gulf countries. Moreover, as already pointed out there has been a tradition of out-migration from India to the various countries, including the Gulf region at least since the nineteenth century

Each year overwhelming majority of migrant workers have gone to West Asia, and particularly to the six G.C.C countries. In all, over six million contract workers have migrated to these countries during the past four decades or so. Besides these, during the same period at least six million Indians have gone to the Gulf countries that belong to the following categories: (i) workers in whose case Emigration clearance is not required such as supervisors, skilled workers, semi-skilled workers, drivers, cooks and clerical workers; (ii) businessmen, entrepreneurs, etc; (iii) illegal migrants (those who over-stayed visit visa and got employment.

Migration of Indian contract workers abroad has not been uniform. Fluctuation in migration figures can be explained in terms of a number of political economy factors: fluctuation in oil prices, law of labour demand and supply, Arablisation of labour policy and the changing profile of labour demand itself. Thus in 1999 there was a sharp decline in the number of persons migrating for employment to Saudi Arabia. This was primarily due to the determined efforts to enforce Saudisation. The situation has improved since then.

The majority of such workers are recruited in the four South Indian states of Kerala, Tamil Nadu, Andhra Pradesh and Karnakata *En block* the four South Indian States of Kerala, Tamil Nadu, Andhra Pradesh and Karnataka send about 70 per cent of migrants to the Gulf countries (Ministry of Labour and Employment, 2005). In this context, it would not be out of place to mention that channel of recruitment or migration plays and important role in the relative success of workers. A survey of 800 South Asian males employed in skilled or unskilled jobs in Kuwait showed that about 34 per cent moved through the network of friends and relatives and about 50 per cent through recruiting agents, and that those who went through friends/ relatives earned a higher salary, found the job to fit their expectations, and were happier than those who went through agents (Shah, 2000).

Table 11.2: Estimated Population of Overseas Indians in West Asia, 2001 and 2005

Country	PIOs (2001)	NRIs (2001)	Total (2001) Total (2005)
Saudi Arabia	.	1,500,000	1,500,000 1,600,000
United Arab Emirates	50,000	900,000	950,000 1,300,000
Oman	1,000	311,000	312,000 450,000
Kuwait	1,000	254,000	295,000 400,000
Bahrain	Nil	130,000	130,000 170,000
Qatar	1,000	130,000	131,000 180,000
Yemen	100,000	900	100,900 120,000
Israel	45,000	300	45,300 60,000
Egypt	40	1,350	1,390 1,500
Lebanon	25	11,000	11,025 20,000
Libya	400	12,000	12,400 40,000
Syria	1,800	-	1,800 2,000
Total	200,265	3,250,550	3,450,815 4,343,500

Source: High level Committee (2001). Figures for the year 2005 are author's own estimates.

Economic Profile

The Indian diaspora in the Persian Gulf region is in constant flux for two important reasons – continuous 'circulation' of migrants, and the upgradation of the skill composition of the workforce. Indian immigrants in the Gulf region constitute two major class segments (a) skilled, semi skilled and unskilled workers, and (b) professionals and entrepreneurs. The proportion of each class segment in the Gulf countries varies from country to country. Nevertheless it is widely believed that labour constitute about 60-70 per cent of the total migration outflow from India to the Middle East. This situation is sociologically akin to the earlier ones in South Africa, Fiji, Malaysia and Burma where indentured and/or *kangani* labour and petty bourgeoisie consisting of a variety of skilled personnel and traders migrated simultaneously and yet remained apart from one another (Jain 1990; 1999).

The available data on the occupational status of Indian workers in the Gulf countries suggest that until 1980s about 40 per cent of them were employed in the construction and transport industries. Utility and maintenance constituted another important category of employment followed by office and paramedical services.

Since the late 1980s there has been a gradual shift in the socio-economic profile of the Indian migrants to the Gulf. The preponderance of workers in the construction industry and other skilled and semi-skilled sectors has been slowly reversed. A recent demographic study done in the U.A.E. indicated that there has been an upward flow in white collar jobs. Indians have a stranglehold on textile, gold, electronics and construction industries. A sizable number also operate hotels and restaurants. According to the figures provided by the Indian Ministry of External Affairs skilled and unskilled workers accounted for about 70 per cent of the Indian migrants, white collar workers for about 20 per cent and professionals had a 10 per cent share in 1998. The study referred above had also found that in the early 1990s approximately 57 per cent of the Indian population in the UAE earned less than 5,000 Dirhams a month (3.6 Dirhams to a dollar) whilst those earning above 25,000 Dirhams a month was about 10 per cent. The rest figured in between these income brackets. In effect, more than three-fourths of the Indians in the U.A.E. earned less than 10,000 Dirhams a month. The real wages in the UAE appears to have decline since then. Thus in a sample survey of 361 Keralite workers in the UAE it was found that of the total sample about 48 per cent received monthly salary/wages of less than 1,500 Dirhams; about 42 per cent emigrants were getting between 1,500 and 5,000 Dirhams: only 9 per cent were receiving more than 5,000 Dirhams (Zachariah, Prakash and Rajan 2006). The survey was conducted in 2001.

A good number of Indian immigrants in the Gulf countries, particularly in the UAE, Oman and Kuwait are involved in a variety of business activities (Jain, 2004a; 2005b). Some of the business houses such as the Jashanmal in the UAE, Malhotras in Kuwait and Khimji Ramdas in Oman have since long been there. Many others are of more recent origin. Major Indian business houses have their operations all over the Gulf countries. Apart from individual entrepreneurs, a considerable number of Indian companies are also involved in joint ventures enterprises in the Gulf countries.

Another class segment of the Indian petty bourgeoisie in the region consists of professionals such as engineers, doctors, management executives, chartered accountants, bankers, architects, lawyers, teachers, etc. who constitute about 10 per cent of the Indian immigrant workforce. The professional migrants are drawn from all over the country.

The NRI remittances and investments have played an extremely important role in India's economic development. India's foreign exchange receipts from remittances have increased several-fold during the past three decades or so. According to one estimate whereas India's forex receipts totalled less than US$ 300 million in 1974-75, by 1984-85 this figure had increased to US$ 2,500 million. The West Asian share in the country's total receipts was 12 per cent in 1974-75 and 58 per cent in 1984-85. According to estimates made by Gulati and Mody, Kerala accounted for 42 per cent of the country's remittances receipts from West Asia in 1981-82. In 2005-06 India received US$ 21.7 billion as remittances from all over the world. Of this amount about US$ 10 billion is estimated to have come from West Asia.

NRI deposits have immensely helped India in averting its balance of payment crisis. A time series data compiled by the Department of Economic Analysis and Policy of the Reserve Bank of India on India's balance of payment trends since 1948-49 show that Non-Resident Indian Deposits (NRDs) have risen continuously since the mid-1970s. The data further suggest that the dependence on NRDs was negligible up to 1974-75. After touching US$ 40 million in 1974-75, these deposits rose steadily to US$ 1.04 billion in 1979-80. The dependence on NRDs grew substantially in the 1980s from US$ 1.8 billion in 1980-81 to US$ 10.4 billion in 1989-90 and US$ 10.6 billion in 1990-91, before falling for the first time in 1991-92 to US$ 7.8 billion. The reversal in the rising trend of NRDs was clearly linked to large-scale withdrawal of such deposits by Non-Resident Indians following the outbreak of Gulf War in late 1990. Since then the NRDs have picked up again and India's forex reserves, excluding gold and SDRs, were estimated to be US$ 10.2 billion by January 1994, US$ 34.0 billion by 1999, and over US$ 150.0 billion by 2005.

It goes without saying that Indian workers who generally migrate without their families for a number of reasons, save most of their earnings as they get free food, accommodation and transport during their stay in the Gulf countries. The remitted money is mostly spent on the up-keep and maintenance of the households, paying outstanding debts, purchasing land and building houses, and buying consumer durables. Lavish expenditures on marriage and other festive occasions have also been reported from the Gulf migration areas in Kerala and elsewhere. It appears that very little amount of remittances is used for economically productive purposes. As Nair (1989: 344) put it:

The available evidence suggests that migration and the

resultant receipt of remittances do not seem to have made any significant impact on economic growth rate of the state economies. Nor did they have substantial effect on employment rates, labour market conditions, agricultural development and industrialisation. It would appear that the major part of the remittances which flowed into Kerala seeped into other regions of India through the mechanism of trade in consumption goods and construction materials caused by the changes in consumption patterns and the boom in the house construction sector.

Although most of the Gulf workers send their remittances through official channels, a considerable number of them also send their money through *hawala* and other illegal channels. These channels usually offer some commission for every dollar. Moreover, *hawalas* are also fast and reliable channels of remitting money. Attempts to curb such transactions have not been successful in the past.

Regarding NRI investment in India it can be effectively argued that the desire on the part of the Gulf and other NRIs to invest in India and to retain their Indian citizenship should be seen not so much as an expression of their patriotism but as pure and simple economic calculations. If India provides competitive advantage in business operations for the NRIs they would be more than willing to invest in India; if not, they might go elsewhere. This was seen during the 1990-1991 Kuwaiti Crisis when Indian economy began to show the balance of payment crisis. The NRI investment in India had begun to decline and a considerable number of NRIs did not renew their FCNR deposits on maturity: instead they preferred to invest the money abroad. The successful subscription of the Resurgent India Bonds by the NRIs in 1998 which fetched US$ 4.16 billion was mainly due to the scheme's favourable price to the NRIs. It is significant to note that the West Asian/Gulf remittances accounted for about 40-50 per cent of the total receipts. Presently the Gulf remittances to India are estimated around ten billion US dollars. The ever increasing volume of Indian emigrants as well as the remittances to India clearly suggests that the policy of indigenization of employment opportunities in the Gulf countries have not been working in expected directions.

In recent years extortion has emerged as another "industry" for some Gulf-based Indian "entrepreneurs". This enterprise is thriving in some metropolitan cities of India, especially in Mumbai. Its conspicuous presence has been particularly noted in the Bollywood – the Mumbai film industry which annually produces about 800 films. "It is well-known that the Abu Salem faction of the Dawood Ibrahim gang has been behind extortion threats to film personalities for the past five years. Film producers admit that extortion threats are common and that most of them pay up quietly after a bit of haggling over the sum". Between January 1995 and January 2000, ten well-known film personalities were gunned down or shot at by extortionists.

Apart from extortion, some Dubai-based gangsters have also infiltrated the Mumbai film industry. Globalisation of the entertainment industry, competition from cable television, piracy through the influx of DVDs and VCDs in the market, and unlawful private screening of films – have all given a blow to the Indian film industry. It is against this backdrop that the infiltration of the underworld black money has occurred in the film industry.

The Mafia is not only interested in producing films but also in grabbing distribution rights of films in the blossoming overseas market. The overseas market, which until recently, was a "mere pocket money" option for Hindi film makers is now emerging as the big factor. Not surprisingly, "the overseas territory started becoming a favorite demand of extortionists". It gives "the gangsters an added advantage. Using a dummy distributor as a front, he can launder the money under the guise of bringing in forex. This white money is used to finance his benami but legitimate businesses in the construction, transport and hotel industries".

If Dubai provides a safe haven for a variety of criminals, the pilgrimage cities of Mecca and Madina, have emerged as child beggars' paradise. Estimatedly, about 1,000 to 1,500 Indian children (both boys and girls) are annually involved in this begging racket, especially during the Hajj time. About 400 of them are sent from Murshidabad district of West Bengal alone. Estimates suggest that the mafia running this racket earn about Rupees Five lakh per child annually (after deducting the expenditure). Depending on the number of children involved in the racket, the economics of begging in Saudi Arabia by the Indian children run into multi-crore rupees business

Social Organisation

The layman notion of social organisation among overseas Indian communities is represented in the Rabindranath Tagore's analogy of the Banyan tree. Tagore held the view that Indian settlement abroad is akin to the spread of grand old Banyan tree. Implicit in this analogy is the assumption that Indian culture as well as social organisational patterns scan be transplanted overseas. This view obviously does not correspond with the reality. The nature and patterns of social organisation among overseas Indian communities have varyingly been affected by numerous local factors. Perhaps the most generic among them was the nature and conditions of employment.

The kind of initial employment (e.g. indentured or wage labour, trade or profession, etc), and the socio-political conditions in the colonial/metropolitan societies under which such employment was taken up constitute the broad parameters of the evolution of varying social organisation and community life among overseas Indians. Changes in such social organisational elements as caste, kinship and family, religion, etc. have occured due to these conditions in different places. Hypothetically, it would seem that the degree of freedom of immigrant Indians in various colonial societies was a major factor in transforming the indigenous patterns of social organisation among the overseas Indians. Thus overseas Indian communities in the West Indies, Mauritius and Fiji which were primarily formed due to the slavery-like indentured labour migration exhibit more radical transformation in their social organisational aspects than the less coercive *Kangani/Maistry*-recruited overseas Indian communities in Burma, Malaysia, Singapore and Sri Lanka.

To countries where Indians migrated more freely under "passage" or "free" migration system (e.g. Kenya, Uganda, Tanzania), social organisation among them shows least transformation. Similar argument can be advanced in relation to the more recent 'brain drain' emigres and their communities in Britain, Canada and the US. This remains an empirical issue whether the above mentioned hypothesis is also applicable to the Indians in West Asia. The purpose of this brief discussion is to show that compared to the "Banyan Tree" view of the overseas Indians, it is far more fruitful to study the emerging patterns of social organisation among them from the political economy perspective.

The banyan tree view presumes that transplantation of socio-cultural patterns abroad is an unhindered exercise. This however, has never been the case. The migration process itself sets the limits on this presumption in terms of selectivity of migrants, their motivation and destination of migration, etc. The working and living conditions of Indians in the Persian Gulf region amply demonstrate this. To begin with Indian migration to West Asia is a male-dominated migration. A great majority of Indian migrants to the Gulf either cannot afford or do not want to take along with them their wives, with the result that there is an extreme sex imbalance in the diaspora, particular among the workers. This seriously hampers the formation of Indian "community" in the Gulf countries. Middle class comprising professionals and entrepreneurs are an exception but even here all family members are not there for a variety of reasons. Grown up children seldom live with their parents as most of the time they are in India or abroad for their higher education which is expensive or lacking in most Gulf countries.

Short-term stay and inevitability of returning home is the hallmark of the Indian migration to the Persian Gulf region. A recent study in Bihar found that about two-thirds of the working class migrants to the Gulf stayed between 2 to 6 years, and 85 per cent between 2 to 8 years. The same study also found a high degree of circularity among the migrants: 25 per cent were once migrants, 42 per cent twice migrants, 21 per cent thrice migrants and 12 per cent had migrated four times or more (Rahman 2003). We do not have comparable data about the middle classes. Thus short-term stay and circularity - both these factors keep the "community" in a flux.

The attitude of the host society is another factor in any consideration of a community life among the immigrants. The Gulf countries are absolutely clear on this count. As Weiner (1982) put it, Migrants are incorporated into the economic structure, but are excluded from the social structure. Separation, not integration or assimilation, is the goal... Social contacts between Arabs and expatriates are minimized... An increasing number of migrants stay for extended periods, and some may remain legally 'temporary' resident, with little notice they can be asked by the government to leave.

The above quotation underlines a number of pertinent issues regarding the attitude of the host countries of West Asia. Legally, there is no question of permanent resident status, naturalisation and citizenship for the Indian migrants. Politically, the Gulf regimes are authoritarian – no political or trade union rights. Economically, market forces and a bit of anarchy (split labour market in wage structure, coercion in domestic service sector etc) is the norm. Socially, the Gulf societies are patriarchal in ethos and practise. There is a certain social duality in terms of Arab vs non-Arab in the Gulf countries. Fortunately, there is no racism in the Gulf region but ethnic articulations such as *watni* vs. *non-watni* (native *vs* non-native), and Muslim *vs* non-Muslim are rather strong. Finally, Islam is the state religion in all the Gulf countries and any criticism – direct or indirect – is absolutely prohibited and can be severely punished.

The above discussion suggests that for a majority of Indian immigrants, particularly the working class, there is no organised community life in the Persian Gulf countries. Some degree of community life can be said to exist among the middle classes. To what extent this community life is based on traditional Indian social structure and institutions such as caste system, family and kinship, village and caste panchayats (agencies of social control), religion and festivals, regional-linguistic ties, etc is difficult to tell for lack of any study on the subject. In fact we do not know even the social origins of the contemporary professionals, traders and other entrepreneurial groups working and living in the Persian Gulf region. However, newspaper reports and knowledgeable people about the region suggest that regional-linguistic ties are particularly strong among the immigrants in the Gulf. These ties probably supercede religious ties. Thus community life appears to be organized in the form of regional/linguistic associations. It would not be out of place to suggest that the reproduction of the "community" among the Gulf Indians is perhaps done more through fresh immigration and less through procreation.

The vast majority of Indian immigrants in the Gulf countries continue to hold the more or less the same identities and patterns of cultural consumption as in India. Perhaps it would not be an exaggeration to say that for all practical purposes the Gulf countries are an extension of India. Most migrants to the Gulf return to India within two to six years and the non-labour migrants who visit India for attending marriage of relatives and for doing business, pilgrimage and sight seeing do so more often than any other groups of NRIs. There is also an impression that must Gulf NRIs seek spouses in India itself which further extend and strengthen the bonds of family and kinship across the Arabia Sea.

Social life of Indians in most of the Gulf countries is highly segmented. They are required in most cases to live away from the areas of native Arabs in the camp sites where the workers have to live a regimented life. There is therefore little scope for building a "community" among the working class Indian immigrants in the Gulf countries. However, many middle class Indian migrants who expect to remain in the Gulf for many years live with their families and have begun to evolve a network of socio-cultural associations which cater to their needs. These include schools, sports clubs, art centres, ladies associations, etc.

In Oman land was given by the Sultan in 1974 to enable the

Indians to build a social center. "There are now several schools for Indian children, a Roman Catholic Church, a few Protestant churches, and several temples, including a Gurudwara for the Sikh community" (Weiner, 1982). Similarly, Bahrain and Dubai also have one temple each; the Bahrainian temple being over 100-year old. Elsewhere "Hindus must observe their festivals in less conspicuous locations, or in private." Non-Muslim Indian immigrants in Saudi Arabia are not allowed to take along with them any religious books or idols. Any negative reference to Islam – even if mild or indirect – is considered blasphemy. Thus in 1992, a Sharjah court had awarded six-year jail-term to eleven Indian theatre activists (all from Kerala) for staging a play "The Ants That Feast on Corpses".

Thanks to globalisation, the Indian entertainment industry which includes film, musical concerts, fashion shows, theatres, etc has expanded tremendously in the 1990s. The Middle East connection through underworld and/or otherwise is well known. Regular shows of films, music concerts and plays are organized in major cities of the region to packed houses. The audience includes not only the non-resident Indians but also the Arab masses. Perhaps this has something to do with cultural and civilizational affinity between India and the Middle East.

Sports and particularly cricket is another Indian industry which has been expanded and extended to the Gulf region. Although the favourite sport of Arabs is football, cricket matches are particularly popular in the region, particularly in the UAE. The World cup hosted at Sharjah has acquired considerable prestige and popularity. Similarly, Indian food, fashion and jewellery are some items which are gaining ground in the Middle East in a big way. As Professor Jain (1998) put it in the wider context, "the diasporic Indians display a dogged attachment to religious, linguistic, culinary and performative aspects of Indianness." Additionally, in the Arab/Islamic context the Indian expressive and performing arts serve as complementary items to art forms which cannot develop due to religious sanctions.

Policy Implications

The emergence and consolidation of the global Indian diaspora during the past few decades and its multi-layered home connection had significant implications for the policy makers in India. One major outcome in this context was the *High Level Committee Report on the Indian Diaspora* (2001) that was aimed at "informing the Indian public of the achievements of the Indian Diaspora, sensitizing it to their problems and their expectations from their mother country, proposing a new policy framework for creating a more conducive environment in India to leverage these invaluable human resources – and thus forging stronger ties between the Indian Diaspora and India." The committee made a number of recommendations to facilitate greater economic and socio-cultural interaction between India and Indian Diaspora. Some of these will be discussed shortly in relation to Indian Diaspora in the WANA region.

The committee not only recognized the importance of Indian Diaspora for India's development and its international relations but also appears to suggest that manpower export or even so-called "brain drain" is no longer an undesirable phenomenon, and that Overseas Indians deserve all the help they need from India. This is in line with observations/recommendations from other think tanks. Just to name one, the study by AnnLee Saxenian found that "brain drain (in the case of Chinese and Indian professionals it surveyed) was replaced by "brain circulation", meaning a variety of two-way flows of highly skilled workers between the technologically advanced countries were they reside and the less-developed countries such as India where they were born" (Thandi, 2006: 5).

Besides professionals a considerable number of Indian entrepreneurs and traders and a wide variety of labour – skilled, semi-skilled and unskilled – have been migrating in a large numbers to different parts of the world and particularly to the Gulf countries – a piggyback ride on the globalization, as it were.

As already pointed out in the WANA region consists of two kinds of Indian Diaspora: trader and labour. Indian entrepreneurs and professionals can also be considered a part of the former whose demographic strength is about one-fourth to one-third of the total WANA Indian diasporic population. The two components of the Indian Diaspora in WANA have separate policy implications.

Policy implications in case of traders/professionals in WANA region emerge from certain problems faced by them in India as well as abroad. These mostly relate to bureaucracy, red-tapism, corruption, license raj, higher rate of customs duties and other taxes, lack of adequate banking facilities and overall apathetic attitude of the Indian Government and the public (Buxani, 2003). Fortunately many of these grievances have already been taken care of by the Indian Government's economic liberalization policies.

The Indian expatriate labour in the WANA region is one the most exploited segments of the Indian Diaspora there. They are thoroughly exploited at home and abroad. In India most offences pertaining to potential emigrants are related to recruitment agencies which need to be regulated. Clearly the existing Emigration Act, 1983 has become outdated and needs urgent amendments. Newspaper reports suggest that the Ministry of Overseas Indian Affairs (MOIA) has been working on the draft amendment Bill. Stringent condition for recruiting agencies, severe punishment for touts, smuggling people abroad, heavy penalties for violators and constitution of special courts for speedy trial are some of the provisions of the proposed new Emigration Act.

Reportedly, in the new Bill the bank guarantee for the recruiting agencies has been increased from Rs. 1,00,000 to Rs. 25 lakh. Penalty for violation of the Act has been enhanced to 5 years' imprisonment instead of two. Further, the fine will be Rs. 2,00,000, not Rs. 2,000. A new section has been introduced for the touts and recruiting agencies who misuse visit visas for employment purposes. Such offences will fall under the category of human smuggling, for which seven years' imprisonment and a fine of Rs.5 lakh have been provided. Special courts for speedy trials of such offences will be set up (Das, 2006).

Apart from enacting the appropriate legal framework the government of India needs to initiate a wide variety of programmes as part of its manpower export policy. These should include awareness campaign among the potential emigrants through orientation courses, training and skill upgradation for second-time potential migrants and bilateral labour agreements with the Gulf countries. Workers are required to be aware of the changing Gulf market conditions, rules and regulations pertaining to employment and visa procurement. Local trade unions and NGOs in India and NRI associations in the Gulf can play constructive roles in regard to some of these measures.

Indo-Gulf relations have been asymmetrical since the British colonial days. The Gulf countries were dominated and administered by the British India. The asymmetrical relations of the bygone era have drastically changed since the oil boom of the early 1970s when the surplus petrodollars gave the monarchies unprecedented political clout. Today Indian expatriates are at the mercy of the Gulf regimes. The policy of indigenisation of labour (not so successful so far) coupled with the human rights violations of expatriates is very much part of this asymmetrical relations syndrome that is in favour of the Gulf regimes.

Concluding Remarks

India's trade ties and cultural relations with the Persian Gulf region date back to antiquity, but the evidence of Indian settlement in the region dates back only to the sixteenth century. Small communities of Indian traders called *baniyans* existed in present day Iraq, Iran, Oman, Yemen and Saudi Arabia in the seventeenth and eighteenth centuries. When the region came under the British influence in the 19th century, Indian merchant communities flourished in a number of towns in the Gulf countries. The Indians served as bankers, importers and exporters customs farmers, agents for local merchants, government contractors, financiers etc.

The emergence of the Gulf countries as oil-producing and

exporting economies and the consequent demand for labour changed the size and complexion of the Indian and other expatriate communities in the region. With the increase in oil prices in the mid-seventies Indians began to migrate in large numbers to the Gulf countries for a variety of jobs, and this trend has been continuing since then. Currently, there are about 4.5 million Indian expatriates in the six GCC countries and Yemen. Indians constitute about one-third of the total expatriate population and ten per cent of the total GCC population. The largest number of Indians live in Saudi Arabia (1.6 million) followed by the UAE (1.3 million), Oman (4,50,000) and Kuwait (4,00,000). Overwhelming majority of these Indians in the Gulf are Indian passport holders and stay there for not more than three to five years. A considerable number of them again migrate to the countries. Contrary to this situation the majority of Indians in Yemen are Yemeni citizens. Thanks to the colonial legacy, the Indian Diaspora suffers from a number of disabilities in the Gulf societies/states which are essentially rentier and patriarchal in nature.

Globalisation has significant bearing on the formation of the Indian diaspora. "In the case of India, a significant cause and effect of globalisation are the million of emigrants, both temporary and permanent, that work beyond India's borders" (Walton-Roberts, 2004: 54). In spite of the variable and at times contradictory effects of globalisation processes – the movement of people, capital and ideas – India has been successful in exploiting them to its economic advantage. Not only an ever-increasing number of Indians are migrating abroad, particularly to the Gulf countries, the quatum of remittances, investment and trade networking has also grown significantly. The bond between India and its diaspora has given a new meaning and form to Indianess that is increasingly global. One alarming aspect of the Indian diaspora in the Gulf countries however is the fact that relatively very little research has been done on the subject.

References

Ahmad, Maqbool S., 1969, *Indo-Gulf Relations,* Popular Prakashan,

Bombay.

Ahmad, Maqbool S., 1971, "Indians in West Asia", in Aniruddha Gupta (ed), *Indians Abroad: Asia and Africa,* Orient Longmann, Delhi.

Al-Sayegh, Fatma, 1998, "Merchants' Role in a Changing Society: The Case of Dubai, 1900-90", *Middle Eastern Studies,* 34 (1), pp. 87-102.

Allen, Jr., Calvin, 1981, "The Indian Merchant Community of Masqat", *Bulletin of the School of Oriental and African Studies,* 44 (1), pp. 39-51.

Buxani, Ram, 2003, *Taking the High Road,* Motivate Publishers, Dubai.

Chaudhri, K.N. 1986, *Trade and Civilization in the Indian Ocean: An Economic History from the Rise of Islam to 1950,* Cambridge University Press.

Cohen, Robin, 2001, *Global Diasporas: An Introduction*, Abingdon, Oxon: Routledge.

Das, Arun Kumar, "New Act to Protect Emigrants", *Sunday Times of India,* New Delhi, September 24, 2006.

Das Gupta, Ashin, "Gujrati Merchants and the Red Sea Trade, 1700-1726", Blair B. Kling and M.N. Pearson (eds*) The Age of Partnership,* Honolulu, pp. 123-158.

Elmadani, Abdulla, 2003, "Arabia Gulf during the British Era: The Impact of India", in N. N. Vohra (ed), *History, Culture and Society in India and West Asia,* Shipra Publications, Delhi, pp.109-124.

Foster, William, 1985, *Early Travels in India,* New Delhi.

Gopal, Surendra, 1997, "Indians in Iran in the 17th & 18th Centuries", *Journal of Indian Ocean Studies*, 4 (2), pp. 160-70.

Gopal, Surendra, 1998, "Indian Diaspora in West, Central Asia and Russia in Medieval Times", *Journal of Indian Ocean Studies,* 5 (2), pp. 116-28.

High Level Committee, 2001, *High Level Committee, Report on the Indian Diaspora,* Indian Council of World Affairs, New Delhi.

Jain, Prakash C., 1990, *Racial Discrimination against Overseas Indians: A Class Analysis,* Concept Publishing Company, New Delhi.

Jain, Prakash C., 1999, *Indians in South Africa: Political Economy of Race Relations,* Kalinga Publications, Delhi.

Jain, Prakash C., 2003a, "Culture and Economy in an "Incipient" Diaspora: Indians in the Persian Gulf Region", in Bhikhu Parekh, Gurharpal Singh and S. Vertovec (eds.), *Culture and Economy in the Indian Diaspora.* Routledge, London, pp. 102-124.

Jain, Prakash C., 2003b, "Indian Diaspora in Yemen", *Journal of Indian*

Ocean Studies, 11 (1), pp. 99-111.

Jain, Prakash C., 2003c, "Indians in Bahrain", *Journal of Indian Ocean Studies*, 11 (3), pp. 437-46.

Jain, Prakash C., 2003d, "Indians in Oman", Working Paper, Gulf Studies Programme, Centre for West Asian and African Studies, School of International Studies, Jawaharlal Nehru University, New Delhi.

Jain, Prakash C., 2004a, "Indians in Kuwait", *Journal of Indian Ocean Studies*, 12 (3), pp. 440-50.

Jain, Prakash C., 2004b, "Indians in the United Arab Emirates", Gulf Studies Programme, Centre for West Asian and African Studies, School of International Studies, Jawaharlal Nehru University, New Delhi.

Jain, Prakash C., 2005a, "Indian Labour Migration to the Gulf Countries: Past and Present", *India Quarterly*, 61 (2), pp. 50-81.

Jain, Prakash C., 2005b, "Indians in Qatar", *Journal of Indian Ocean Studies*, 13 (2), pp. 215-25.

Jain, Prakash C., 2005c, "Indian Entrepreneurs in the Gulf Countries: Some Case Studies", *India Quarterly*, LXI (4), pp. 123-42.

Jain, Ravindra K., 1998, "Indian Diaspora, Globalization and Multi-Culturalism: A Cultural Analysis", *Contributions to Indian Sociology* (n. s.) 32 (2), pp. 337-6

Latch, Donald, 1965, *Asia in the Making of Europe*, Chicago.

Markovits, Claude, 2000, *The Global world of Indian Merchants, 1950-1947: Traders of Sind from Bukhara to Panama*, Cambridge University Press, Cambridge.

Miles, S. B., 1966, *Countries and Tribes of the Persian Gulf* Second Edition, London.

Ministry of Labour, Government of India, 2005, *Annual Report*, Chapter. 14.

Ministry of Labour and Employment, Government of India, 2005, *Annual Repor.*

Rahman, Anisur, 2003, *Indian Migration to West Asia*, Rajat Publications, Delhi.

Ratnagar, Shireen, 2003, "Cultural Implications of Trade between South Asia, the Gulf and Mesopotamia in the Bronze Age", in N. N. Vohra (ed) *History, Culture and Society in India and West Asia*, Shipra Publications, Delhi, pp.102-108.

Rawlinson, H. G., 1926, *Intercourse between India and Western World.* Cambridge University Press, Cambridge.

Ray, Himnshu Prabha, 2003, "Enduring Relationship: Maritime Contacts in the Western Indian Ocean, in N.N. Vohra (ed), *History, Culture and Society in India and West Asia,* Shipra Publications, Delhi, pp.77-101.

Seccombe, I.J and R.L. Lawless, 1986, Foreign Workers Dependence in the Gulf and the International Oil Companies 1910-50", *International Migration Review,* 20 (3), pp. 548-74.

Shah, Nasra M., 2000, "Relative Success of Male workers in the Gulf Country, Kuwait: Does the Channel of Migration Matter?", *International Migration Review*, 34 (1), pp. 59-78.

Thandi, Shinder S. 2006, Indian *Diaspora – Homeland Linkages*, (mimeographed).

Walton-Roberts, Margaret, 2004, "Globalization, National Autonomy and Non-Resident Indians", *Contemporary South Asia*, 13 (1): 52-69.

Weiner, Myron, 1982, "International Migration and Development: Indians in the Persian Gulf Region", *International Migration Review,* 8 (1), pp. 1-36.

Weiner, Myron, 1986, "Labor Migrations as Incipicnt Diasporas", in Gabriel Sheffer (ed) *Modern Diaspora in International Politics,* Croom Helm, London.

Wink, A., 1990, *Al Hind: The Making of Indo-Islamic World,* vol.1, *Early Medieval India and the Expansion of Islam*, 7-11th Centuries, Leiden.

Zachariah, K. C., B. A. Prakash and S. Irudaya Rajan, 2006, "Aspects of Indian Labour Diaspora in the United Arab Emirates", in Prakash C. Jain (ed) *Indian Diaspora in West Asia,* Manohar Books, New Delhi (forthcoming).

Zahlan, Rosemarrie Said, 1979, *The Creation of Qatar*, Crrom Helm, London.

12

The Changing Dimensions of India's Image in the Arab World

El Sayed Mekkawi

Introduction

The perception of an individual shapes his attitude towards other individuals. In the same way, the collective perception of a nation shapes the nature of its relations with other nations. Moreover, this perception of a nation towards "other nation" will decide in a way to what extent the interests of the "other nation" are secured or not inside the territories of the perceiving nation or through its policies. A clear example of that is the case of USA in West Asia. USA was perceived positively till 1956 but later USA policies in the region undermined its positive image. The American President Woodrow Wilson was the first to apply self-determination to the modern international relations context in his Fourteen Points of January 1918, in which he set out a blueprint for a just and lasting peace in Europe after the First World War. The Wilsonian approach influenced the idealist tradition in International Relations, which has at times supported military intervention in support of self-determination[1]. The Wilsonian Declaration was seen favorably in the region that suffered from European imperialism. USA was seen as a supporter of the freedom of other nations. Arabs saw USA as a trusted friend and not as an imperial power. USA invaded Lebanon in 1958 and supported the Israeli aggression against Arab countries in 1967.

Therefore, the way Arabs perceived USA was changing drastically from a savior and liberator to a new colonial power. Now, American administration is seen in the region as an enemy for the Arab people. This happened because Arabs consider USA policies responsible for many tragedies at the region. They saw

American policies in the region as Anti-Arabs. People used to make fun by comparing how USA managed to liberate Kuwait soon after its occupation but not the Palestinian territories or Golan Heights of Syria, which has been occupied for decades. Arabs do remember how USA forced Israel in 1957 to end its occupation and withdraw within weeks from Sinai Peninsula of Egypt. This perception was not limited for the region but it has been transferred to other regions where West Asia has close cultural and religious connections. The Result is that USA succeeded to be the most hated country in the Islamic world, including Muslim communities in the non-Muslim countries.

It is the hatred perception against USA that generates and sustains violent militants and inspires their acts. The tragedy of September 11 did not convince USA to reevaluate its polices and solve the problem (terrorism) from the roots, instead USA launched two aggressive wars against Afghanistan and Iraq and supported another aggression against Lebanon in 2006 .The level of hatred against USA has been only increasing as a result. There was a debate inside USA on "why they hate us?" and the answer came from another debate on "why not to hate us?" Officially, the only reaction that USA did was to launch public relations campaign (PRC) in West Asia to reduce the hatred against it and improve its image. These efforts met no success because USA insisted in pursuing the same old policies that generated hatred for the Americans. According to Carl Weiser:

"The Bush administration spends US$ 1 billion a year trying to polish the United States' image around the world, yet polls show anti-Americanism rising to record levels, especially in Muslim and Arab nations where the government is concentrating its efforts...Public diplomacy spending has risen 9 per cent in the two years since the September 11 attacks — and more than 50 per cent in the Middle East and South Asia. But a comprehensive poll in foreign countries this spring showed that in Muslim nations from Morocco to Indonesia the United States has never been more loathed. In many places Osama bin Laden gets more favorable ratings than President Bush"[2].

However, American politicians may think or like to think always that there is some thing wrong with the public relations techniques which has been followed in these PRC. As Sen. Richard Lugar, Republican, who chairs the Senate Foreign Relations Committee, put it once:

"Americans are brilliant at communication. Why in the world we are all thumbs in this particular area just strikes me as one of the anomalies of history. But it's an important one to solve pretty fast"[3].

This American way of neglecting the facts has been perfectly reflected in Egyptian proverb that says "Much washing does not make the chark white"[4]. Therefore, the side effects of what is seen in the region as unjust American policies could not be treated with public relations campaigns.

The new tilt of India's foreign policy towards USA foreign policy in West Asia has its implications for Indian interests in the region. It started changing harmfully the colors of India's traditional image in the region. This paper will try to draft the shift in India's image in the Arab world that took place after 1992 by comparing between the image of India in the Arab world before 1992 and its image after 1992. The paper will also highlight the implications of the new image for both India's security and interests in West Asia.

Masses and Elite Perceptions

Today, there are two perceptions of India in the Arab world; one is how the masses in the region perceive India and the second is how the Arab elite perceive India. For the masses, India is what has been presented at the Bollywood movies; these include the India of Maharajas, spices, Sari and Amitabbachan.

The Popular image for India in the Arab countries is very similar. India is seen in Arab world as the land of spices, silk, Taj Mahal, Maharajas, spices, Sari and Amitabbachan.

Bollywood movies are so popular in many Arab countries and usually screened by some national TVs in special occasions. It is also accessible in the market for private use. Bollywood is the major source to enlighten Arab masses about India since 1950s and Indian movies are so widespread across the Arab world. Many Arab visitors will be surprised to see the differences between the India of Bollywood and India as it exists in realities. There are few Indian figures that are so famous in the Arab world, especially among old generations and elite i.e. Mahatma Gandhi, Jawaharlal Nehru, Indira Gandhi and Rajiv[5].

India's Image before 1992

The image of India in the Arab world before 1947 was that of a comrade in the common battle against colonialism. During this period, there were personal friendship between the Arab leadership and Indian leadership, Mahatma Gandhi was a close friend to Saad Zaghlul Pasha, the Egyptian national leader of 1919 revolution; and Jawaharlal Nehru was a close friend for both Nahas Pasha (Egypt) and Kamil El Chadirchi (Iraq) . Two examples could be given to highlight the image of India at this period; one example is the Egyptian reaction for the passing of Mahatma Gandhi in Suez Canal in his way to London for participating at the Second Round Table Conference in 1931. A Wafdist delegation visited Mahatma Gandhi aboard the ship S.S. Rajputana to express the good wishes of Egyptians for his success in his struggle against British colonialism[6].

The Indian leader also received telegrams welcoming him to Egypt from the leader of the Wafd Party Mustafa El- Nahhas and Safiyya Zaghlul, wife of the late Egyptian nationalist leader Zaghlul Pasha. Gandhi was received warmly by Egyptian committee. According to Al Ahram newspaper, "The gifts the Egyptian reception committee presented to the Indian leader were most unusual for what was tantamount to a state visit. One was a vessel of honey inscribed with the Qur'anic verse: "From their bellies comes variegated coloured syrup that contains a curative for people." A second gift was a large, grey, camel-wool shawl "to protect the leader from the cold during his stay in the British capital". Finally, Gandhi was presented with 20 liters of goat milk and a large quantity of dates Egyptian, not imported. Among these, a special package was prepared of the famous Egyptian red dates, known as Zaghlul, "because of the significance of the name"[7].

In his message to Egyptian people, Mahatma Gandhi encouraged Egyptians to carry out their struggle for freedom. He pointed out the strong link between the destiny of both India and Egypt. The Mahatma addressed Egyptians through Al Ahram newspaper,

"You, like us, are an ancient people. I pray that you do not blindly imitate everything Western. If I have properly understood what has happened to your country you must persist in your endeavours to realize true freedom. And, if I may hazard a modest opinion, it is that Egypt will attain its liberty very quickly if India obtains its true freedom within the next 12 months. I firmly believe that if India gains its freedom through sincere perseverance and without violence this will have a great effect on the world and certainly for all the nations of the East"[8].

In mid-December, Gandhi embarked on his return trip to India. It was hoped that when he arrived in Port Said he would make a brief trip to Cairo, towards which end Mustafa El-Nahas Pasha delegated a senior Wafd aide, Mahmoud Fahmi El-Nuqrashi, later both of them became Prime Ministers for Egypt, to meet the Indian leader and escort him to the Cairo. A detailed programme was also drawn up for the visit but British authorities prevented the visit to take place as it was going to empower Egyptian national struggle movement against them[9].

Another example is the letter of Kamil El Chadirchi to Nehru on December 13, 1938 where the Iraqi nationalist leader expressed the feelings of Arab nationalists towards India and its nationalist leadership. El Chadirchi wrote,

"Your country has been truly great from time immemorial, nature having given it inexhaustible resources. Though, from the dawn of civilization, India has not been as great as today when its intellectual seeds burst into bloom of such men as the country is in need of, more especially since a personality as unique as your own appeared on the horizon of the orient filling my imagination and that of my brethren ...we whole heartedly appreciate your struggle and wish we had the opportunity to share in it though in a small measure, for we both in the same boat. True endeavour in the campaign against imperialism and exploitation must not be considered in separate units, but rather that neither geographical frontiers nor political obstacles can suppress it"[10].

In the post-colonial era, India continued to be seen in Arab world as anti-imperial power. Furthermore, it was seen as a leader of the Non-Alignment Movement and strong supporter of the rights of Afro-Asian peoples to get their independence, especially the Palestinian people. India opposed the imperial projects and acts such as Baghdad Pact, Israeli-Anglo-French aggression on Egypt, and the American intervention in Lebanon in 1958. It also supported the liberation movement in Morocco, Tunisia and Algeria during this period. India's image was so popular and its policies in the international arena were highly appreciated by Arabs. India's first Prime Minister Jawaharlal Nehru was called in Arab world as the prophet of peace[11] and the wise man of India and the giant of the East[12]. India was seen in Arab world as a secular country and a promising democracy[13]. Arabs saw India as a place for religious tolerance. They saw Indian as a state committed for minorities' rights. The Sheikh of "Al Azhar" Dr. Abdel Halim Mahmoud visited India to attend the Islamic conference in Lucknow in 1970s. He was impressed of religious freedom that Indian Muslims enjoyed. While he was receiving the President of India Fakhruddin Ali Ahmed on his visit to the thousand year-old prestigious university of Al Azhar in 1975, the Sheikh stated that in India "all places of Islamic culture were well preserved and that the Muslims enjoyed complete freedom in the performance of the ritual of Islam and the propagation of its principles"[14]. India was also seen as a close friend for Arabs because it supported Arab causes, especially Palestine.

Image of India among the Arab Elite

As for Arab elites, India has multi-images one that has been obtained by reading both medieval and modern Arab literatures and poems that describe India as the land of civilization, sciences, religions and beauty[15]. Many Arab poets admired India and wrote about it for example the Prince of Arab poems Ahmed Shawqi wrote his "the virgin of India"[16] and Khalil Motran described India in his poems as Paradise and the land of romance. Other poets and writers like Shawqi, Abdel Aziz Bioli, Khalil Girges, Mahmoud Bairm Al Tunsi, Amal Al Shami praised different Indian figures such as Mahatma Ghandi and Jawaharlal Nehru for their struggle against British colonialism where both of them were considered as heroes and sincere in sacrificing their lives for the cause like prophets do. Tagore's writing was so popular in the Arab world and the great poet was himself received by the prince of Arab poets Ahmed Shawqi and his mates at Cairo in 1928[17].

The other face of this multi-faceted image that prevail among Arab elite is seeing India as a growing economic power and advanced nation due to its successful educational system, especially in information technology and the ability of Indian elite to speak English. They do criticize India for allowing the conflicting coexistence of both caste and democratic systems at the same time. Some Arab intellectuals argue that India's role in Non-Alignment Movement is declining and gradually replaced by realignment policy. This disappointed many of them as India was assumed to be one of the leading countries in the Third world. Some of them argue that India's non-alignment was motivated by its own interests such as countering Pakistan and continuing its nuclear programme. India is also praised for being a productive country and self-sufficient, which enjoys good infrastructure and high-quality educational system[18].

Indian Miracle

One of the main features which Arab nationalists will appreciate in India is the success of Indian nationalism which brought different cultural, linguistic and ethnic, castes and religious groups into one united Indian state. For many Arabs, this is an Indian miracle comparing with the Arab failure to be united in one Arab state; in spite of having common language and culture and the majority of Arab populations are Muslims[19]. There are also religious minorities but they are not minorities in terms of culture or language or race. They are an integral part of the matrix of the Arab society. They are living in harmony with the Muslims majority. It was only the western attempts to play the minorities' card which jeopardize the religious relations in the region to serve their imperial agenda[20].

Image of India after 1992

In the years after 1992, the image of India in the Arab world has changed dramatically in its political dimensions, especially the classical Indo-Arab friendship that was a feature of the politics of post-colonial era. This change was the result of complex factors. These factors are the rise of Hindutava as an active political power inside the Indian politics. This resulted in a serious development in both internal and external politics. Internally, there were two communal acts; one against the history by destroying the Babri Masijid; and the second was the communal riots of Gujarat. Externally, India's policy in West Asia was changing. India, a classical ally of Arabs, decided to have close relations with Israel, especially in the areas of security, defense and strategic affairs. Furthermore, India seemed in harmony with USA policies in the region. Many of these policies were seen as anti-Arabs. India, under BJP, was even prepared to send forces to Iraq to support Americans but Indian opposition blocked the project.

Gujarat Factor

The rise of Hindu fundamentalism was seen in the Arab world as India's abandonment of Nehru and Gandhi principles of secularism[21]. Gujarat has been cited often as a case that damaged the traditional image of India internationally. According to Al Ahram Weekly,

"One thing is clear. In the aftermath of the Gujarat events, India has lost its moral high ground. The international goodwill that the country gained from the December 13, terrorist attack on its parliament has been erased by Gujarat's communal savagery. The sectarian violence has also blunted India's diplomatic offensive against Pakistan. Recently Delhi has launched a PR campaign through its diplomatic missions and circulated an express advisory that puts its version of events across – detailing the circumstances leading to the violence and the steps being taken to rehabilitate riot victims and bringing the culprits to justice"[22].

New Delhi became sensitive about Arab media commentators drawing parallels between violence against Indian Muslims in India and the Israeli crackdown on the Palestinian Intifada[23]. The media reports cited also Kashmir as an example of violence against Indian Muslims. This angered India's ambassador in Cairo. He told Al Ahram weekly that, "Comparing Kashmir with Palestine is the biggest disservice to the Palestinian cause ...As pointed out by none other than President Hosni Mubarak himself; there is no parallel between Kashmir and Palestine. It is surprising that there are opinion-makers in Egypt who wish to continue supporting terrorist elements by making such statements, even when Egypt itself, like India, has suffered from terrorism for so long ...Unlike Palestinians, whose land is occupied by Israel, and many of them have been expelled from their homes, most Kashmiris are living in the land of their forefathers. They have full opportunities to use their language, to promote their culture, to practice their religion and to run their own administrative and economic affairs"[24].

The Saudi daily Arab News newspaper observed the changes in the image of Gujarat which was remembered as the land of Mahatma Gandhi and turned into a place for communal violence. The newspaper described the then ongoing situation as the "reign of terror". According to the Arab News, "Gujarat was once famous as the seat of the world's best-known peace activist and the biggest proponent of Hindu-Muslim amity, Mohandas Karamchand Gandhi. Sadly, today the name brings to mind images of charred bodies, burned mosques and wailing people. The communal flare-up which began on Wednesday has already taken over 800 lives; left thousands injured and caused property damage amounting to millions of dollars"[25].

This harm for India's image has been even acknowledged inside India, according to Asia Times, "Gujarat's pogrom politics are destroying India's carefully cultivated image of a secular democracy in the community of nations"[26].

After three years, the tragedy of Gujarat was still alive in the memory of Arab elite. Mohamed Ouda, who is known as the friend of India, while welcoming the coming back of Congress to power, he wrote an article on "India correct history and get her shining face back" , called what happened in Gujarat as massacre and an attempt from the side of BJP to destroy the heritage of Mahatma Gandhi[27].

Realignment of India

Another factor was the realignment of India in the post-cold war era. India faced a strategic dilemma after the disintegration of Soviet Union, which was the main ally for India and an important tool to contain Chinese. India was searching for an alternative strategic ally. USA was left as the only super-power in the new global disorder. Meanwhile, Americans were trying hard to win India in their own camp. This will serve their purpose in encircling both China and Russia. This will also make it difficult for India to join both Russia and China in making a new equation of power that may change and / or end the American uni- polarity of global politics. However, India's tilt towards USA proved to be practically harmful for Arab interests. Today, there are many in the Arab world started to feel that the growth of India relations with both USA and Israel might be on the expenses of the Arab causes. Unfortunately, the West is acting as if it is in a de-facto war against the Arab and Islamic world. This made it easy for many Arabs to doubt every Western move. Moreover, they doubted every country get closer to USA and vice-versa. This will explain why Russia's Putin is getting its popularity and influence in the region back and why India is losing its traditional image. Al Zawahri of Al Qaeda spoke soon after the visit of Sharon to

New Delhi about "the American –Jewish-Indian alliance against Muslims". Confusingly, Sir John Thomson, a former British High Commissioner to India spoke a similar language to this of Zawahri. According to Thomson,

"The geographical definition of South Asia has expanded. If we had any doubt before, September 11 [2001] has made it clear that we have to take into account Afghanistan and its neighbors: Iran to the west; all the former Soviet republics to the north; and China to the east. The geographical context for South Asia may be even wider. We in the West say—sincerely, I believe—that we are not against Islam, but many Muslims do not believe it. So, to a greater or lesser extent, our relations with Arab countries can be connected with our South Asian policies. And this potential extension of our area of concern is being reinforced, unfortunately, by the spiraling disaster in Israel-Palestine"[28].

Kashmir and Palestine: The Diplomatic Equation

Both the destruction of Babri Masijid and the Gujarat riots activated the Kashmir factor.

The Kashmir issue was latent for long in affecting Indo-Arab relations and shaping India's image. Officially, many Arab countries favored the resolution of the problem through peaceful bilateral resolutions and according to Shimla agreement. The issue was confined only for conferences and diplomatic forums in the Arab world. But now, the collective Arab mind started to refresh its memory on Kashmir. For decades, Kashmir and the conflict with Pakistan was the main negative factor which disturb Indo-Arab friendship. A clear example of that is the diplomatic crisis that took place between India and Egypt as a result of some controversial statements on Kashmir by Egyptian ambassador in Pakistan during the years 1950/1951.The crisis ended when Egypt asserted its complete neutrality in the conflict between India and Pakistan over Kashmir[29]. Yet, Kashmir continued to be the biggest challenge for Indian diplomacy in West Asia. According to Jagdish Sharma,

"Despite repeated efforts by hostile states to break the bonds of friendship, India, with the help of friendly nations of West Asia and North Africa like Nasser's Egypt and Arafat's Palestine, successfully countered such moves, each coming to the help of the other in times of crisis. The success of Indian diplomacy during Suez crisis was offset by the problems of the Kashmir issue. Kashmir was an important facet of Indian national interests and the protection of national goals is a determining factor of any country's foreign policy"[30].

Kashmir is still a problem for Arabs also because it prevents them from expanding their relations freely with the two conflicting neighbors. Pakistan insisted on raising the issue of Kashmir in the OIC meetings which discomfort not only Indians but Arabs too as an Arab diplomat put it, "This has made it very difficult for us. We are being asked to stand up and be counted"[31]. It seems that Arabs have an interest to Kashmiri problem being solved. This will explain why many Arab leaders used to offer mediation between India and Pakistan to solve the problem. The negative impact of Kashmir problem on Indo-Arab relation was eliminated by India's support for Palestinian rights in their land and state. Additionally, India secured also the friendship of Arabs. Palestine was the heart of Arab politics and diplomacy. According to Abu-Jaber, "Palestine has been one of, if not the focal point of Arab international diplomacy since and even before 1947...India voted against the United Nations Resolution for the partition of Palestine when it was voted upon on November 29, 1947. India has also voted consistently with the Arabs in the United Nations when the Palestine question and its various aspects were discussed in the various councils of the United Nations"[32].

India's support for the Palestinian cause was in complete harmony with India's spirit in struggling against colonialism. It was a just cause which deserves to be morally supported. Moreover, this Indian support served the national interests by securing the neutrality of Arab countries in the continuing conflict between India and Pakistan because Arabs felt indebted for India for its pro-Arab policy. Moreover, it secured the goodwill of Arabs towards India. The reaction of Arabs for India's decision to accord full diplomatic status to the PLO was a clear evidence of the centrality of Palestine factor (Iraq could be considered another one) in Indo-Arab relations. According to the report of Ministry of External Affairs of India for the year 1980-81, "A perceptible new warmth characterized India's relations with the Arab world. The Governments in West Asia and North Africa responded enthusiastically to the initiative taken by the new Government to foster closer political and economic relations with countries in this region. The decision of the Government of India to accord full diplomatic status to the PLO was warmly welcomed. This was a clear demonstration of India's consistent, steadfast and sincere support to the Palestine people. The Chairman of [the] Palestine Liberation Organization, Mr. Yasser Arafat, visited Delhi and had extensive discussions with the Prime Minister and the Minister of External Affairs. The visit of Arafat to India produced very favorable reactions among the Arab countries and several Arab Heads of State personally expressed their appreciation for India's gesture"

India's support for Palestinian cause was the core of its strategy to counter Pakistan politically and diplomatically in West Asia. India's Palestinian policy aimed to win the hearts and minds of Arabs and to also prevent them of getting so close to Pakistan[33]. Therefore, many Arab states were always trying to balance their relations with both India and Pakistan. This strategy was a reaction of Pakistan's attempt to isolate India in West Asia. Pakistani attempts were recognized by Nehru, who explained that, "There is undoubtedly a certain pan-Islamic tendency drawing the Islamic countries of the Middle East towards each other. At the same time, there is a completely different tendency which may be said to be pro-Asian as against Europe and America.... This latter tendency bases itself more on nationalism just as the former bases itself on religion. The nationalistic tendency is more confined to the intellectuals who can see a little farther. They try to play down to certain extent Islamic sentiment as such because they realize that while it is the cementing factor for certain Islamic countries, it comes in the way of a larger cooperation with other Asian countries"[34].

This motivated India to race with Pakistan in supporting Arab causes, especially Palestinian cause. It was clear that India used to observe closely the implications of Pakistan's diplomacy in West Asia. This was evident from the cable, that Nehru sent on March 30, 1948 to his sister, Vijayalakshmi Pandit, he wrote: "I have been considering whether we should try for one of the seats in the Security Council which will fall vacant at the end of this year. I have been officially informed that Iran is proposing to stand for election and I would not be at all surprised if Pakistan were also to enter the field, supported by the Arab states who feel grateful to her for Zafrullah's advocacy of the Arab cause during the debates on Palestine ...Our position in Asia makes our claim a very strong one and there seems no reason why a seat should go year after year to a Muslim country[35]."

The success of this Indian strategy in securing the goodwill of Arab public and reducing to far extent the impact of Pakistani propaganda over Kashmir on the Arab mind was so clear when Pakistani Dawn criticized the good relations between the symbol of Arab nationalism during the Suez crisis, 1956 that, "Nasser's hatred of Pakistan and love of Baharat and its Nehru is an attitude of mind not warranted by facts but conditioned by intense bias and blind prejudice the source of which may well be examined by psychiatrists"[36].

Risking the Assets and Winning the Liabilities

Today, India is risking "the love of Baharat" to be lost in the Arab world as a result of the growing Indo-Israeli relations that contradict with what MEA called in 1981 "India's consistent, steadfast and sincere support to the Palestine people". The love of Baharat is explained in the flow of Arab energy to India, seven million Indians work in the Arab Gulf, the Arab market offers a plenty of projects for Indian investment. Strategically, the Arab world is the first defense line for India from Westward. The failure or success of the West in its quest for dominating completely over West Asia will affect drastically the economic and political future of India. Many Arabs could not imagine thinking about India's support for the struggle of the indigenous people of South Africa against the Apartheid regime while India had close relations with the same Apartheid regime.

They argue that India established diplomatic relations with Israel on the context of peace process, and with the hope that it will enable India to put pressures on Israel to end its occupation for the Arab land. When Arafat was asked about the visit of Sharon to India, his reply was that the opening of Indo-Israeli relations was the result of the beginning of peace process and he expected India to pressurize Sharon for joining peace talks again. Arafat also warned that Sharon's visit will further escalate tension between India and Pakistan[37]. Arafat who was a very sensitive friend for India did not want to say frankly that the justification (peace) for the close relations between India and Israel is not more there. Mousa Ragheb, a Palestinian writer, considered the visit of Sharon evidence that Arabs lost India as a classical ally .He blamed Arabs for such results because they did not care to keep their friendship with India and other friends[38].

Asharq Alarabi, An Arabic newspaper based in UK, saw Sharon's visit as, "India's shift from the camp that support Arab right to the camp that support the Zionist aggression. This is a part of international equation, which is sponsored by USA and Israel in the context of clash of civilizations. The Arab regime did not care enough for such equation. This recent Zionist move is a step in the broader American-Zionist strategy to contain Islam and the Arab world"[39].

A Kuwaiti writer feared that Arabs are the only loser due to the growing Indo-Israeli relations because, "The support of India for Arab cause will be changed gradually. India will tend to adopt the Israeli position inside the international forums. At the best scenarios, India will be neutral which will be a loss for Arabs anyhow. The linkage of Indo-Israeli relations will keep Arabs as the biggest loser militarily and politically in this new equation"[40].

This view has been accepted by Dr Mohamed No'man Galal, an Arab strategic and diplomatic expert, who argued that, "The decade of 1990's saw an important shift in India's position vis-à-vis Arab causes, especially the question of Palestine and the question of making the Middle East a free nuclear zone. No doubt that the great cooperation between India and Israel, since establishing diplomatic relations between them in 1992, was the main motive behind this shift, which India denies its happening. This shift is an established fact that could be noted by anyone who observes developments in the Middle East and India's reactions for it. We can give two examples of this shift; one example is India's support for a resolution that will cancel a resolution that considered Zionism as a feature of racism. This was the resolution which has been supported by India in 1975 and India has supported canceling it in 1992, to be in harmony with the stream of international politics and its shifting sands. The second example is India's vote in 2000, object to the sixth paragraph of the resolution to make the Middle East a nuclear-weapons-free zone, and free of weapons of mass destruction. The sixth paragraph calls upon Israel to accede to the NPT as the only country in the region is not acceding to the Convention, and that this in under the concept of the universality of the treaty. Before 2000, India used to vote by abstaining on that paragraph for special considerations to its nuclear arsenal. Apart from the fading voice of Indian objection to the repressive policies of Israel in the Palestinian territories, these policies have culminated in the siege of Yasser Arafat in Ramallah and the destruction of villages and cities and massacres in Jenin, Nablus, Tulkarem and other Palestinian cities"[41].

Ibrahim Arafat, an Egyptian political scientist, wrote an article titled "what to do with India" where he argued that Arabs need to get rid of three illusions in their understanding of Indo-Arab relations: the illusions of history, ideology and unlimited oppression, before

"They can think confidently what to do with India; the whole issue could be summarized in utilizing the balance of Arab interests successfully and exploiting what Arabs have in their hands carefully. India needs Arab countries in many ways .It needs Arab energy for its industrial development; Arab market for its skilled workers and goods. India also needs not to lose Arab countries in the International forums, especially when it comes to its relations with Pakistan. India also needs not to see the coldness of its relations with Arab world angering its Muslim citizens. Moreover, India's relations with Israel will not anger only the Arab world but also other peoples in South Asia. India could not neglect the latter as it is trying to assert its leadership in the region. All these cards seems like showing stick which might not work with a big country like India unless some carrots will be offered such as more Arab investments in India, channeling Indian exports to European and African markets via Arab countries, encouraging India to rethink joining the OIC after Russia requested also to join the OIC and signing an Arab treaty with India for countering terrorism. The problem with Arabs is not the lack of enough sticks in their hands but in knowing what India's stomach is hungry for"[42].

The growing Indo-Israeli strategic and defense ties continued to raise a controversial debate among Arab military and strategic circles on the implications of these relations for Arab national security. Some argues that Arabs could not deny New Delhi rights to have such relations while some Arab countries have diplomatic relations with Israel. However, it is still widely believed that India can not compare itself to these countries as their cases are different. The voices of national security circles are the most influential when it comes to Indo-Israeli relations. The views of these circles are well represented by General Talat Mesalm, according to him,

"Any cooperation between Israel and another country is considered a threat for Arab and Islamic world as this will strengthen Israel to exercise more aggression against Arab and Islamic rights; and will end the isolation of Israel in the region where many Arab countries realize the dangers of Israel. Therefore, the development of relations between India and Israel represent a danger against Arab and Islamic countries. This danger could be seen in the security and strategic relations that allow Israel to use Indian Ocean, in cooperation with Indian Navy. This is an immediate threat for the South East of Arab world, especially Arab countries in Gulf region, Iraq, Iran and Pakistan. This is a threat for the self-existence of these countries. The Israel sales of arms for India increase the capabilities of Israeli in developing its military industries, which will increase its threat for Arab and Islamic world. This will help Israel in facing the economic dangers, resulting of Palestinian Intifada and therefore the continuation of Israeli in threatening Palestinian people and neighboring Arab countries[43]." Other scholars saw much strategic implication for Indo-Israeli relations. According to Medhat Ayub,

"The growth of the Indian-Israeli relations and India being convinced that Israel is the gateway to the market and USA, and that the Arab countries would not be serious in its reactions to affect Indian interests in the region, especially access to oil and trade with the Arab world and Indian expatriates in the Arab countries, this growth in Indo-Israeli relations, particularly, in both its military and security aspects would strengthen Israel, and will disrupt the military and strategic balance in favor of Israel. Also, this cooperation between the two countries will lead to the revitalization of the Indian-Pakistani conflict, which will neutralize the Pakistani factor in the Arab-Israeli conflict, and will also neutralize the Iranian power that will be preoccupied with the threat coming from India"[44].

Despite the collapse of the peace process between Arabs and Israel, Indo-Israeli relations was still improving, in particular, under the BJP rule as the Indian support for Palestinian became a verbal exercise[45]. Other aspect of Indo-Israeli relations is the "Joint Counter-terrorism" between Israel and India. This was interpreted by Arabs as Indian acceptance of Israel's definition of terrorism which considers the legal Palestinian resistance as terrorism. The continuation of Kashmir dispute is creating negative reaction towards India in the Arab world due to religious affinity and what has been seen in the Arab world as heavy-handed military handling of the problem, and also media reports suggest Israeli role in suppressing Kashmiris or Israeli advice to change the demography of Kashmir[46]. Some Islamic websites consider Kashmir as one of the tragedies which the Islamic Ummah (nation) is facing[47]. There were some incidents when few oriented religious young Arabs were inspired by such readings to join militant groups in Kashmir. Kashmir is still remembered among Arabs as a place where Muslims are suffering in the hands of Indian army[48]. The informed understanding of the problem is just limited to the academicians who study about India and intellectuals who are aware of the historical context of the problem and the role of British in dividing India.

Changing Images: Bright and Dark Colours

There is a huge gap between the colors of traditional image and the colors of the new image of India in the Arab world. Some pictures will make this gap clear. The old image has positive bright colors. For example, one picture shows Palestinians in Gaza demonstrating to welcome the arrival of Indian peace forces there during Suez crisis, 1956. They carried the photos of Nasser and Nehru and shouted "Live Nasser Live Nehru"[49]. Other picture from Cairo showed Krishna Menon while surrounded with Egyptian masses that discovered him in the middle of Cairo. He was in a walk with India's ambassador in Egypt. Egyptians gathered to celebrate seeing Menon and to welcome him and show their affection for India's support. He was hardly able to leave these friendly masses. This happened in 1957 when Menon was the diplomatic star of Suez crisis.

The new image has some dark colors. One example of that happened after Babri Masjid's demolition in 1992 when A Kuwaiti cooperative society in the Gulf tried to dismiss its Hindu employees but the government stopped them. Another dark color was that, when a group of people gathered and threw some stones on a Hindu temple in UAE but the police controlled the situation[50]. There was even a silent agreement among many businessmen in the Gulf to stop recruiting non-Muslims as a way of protesting against the destruction of Babri Masjid[51]. Further more, Another dark color was the picture of Sharon while shaking hands with the former PM of India Atal Bihari in September 2003, which shocked the Arab masses who always remember seeing Nasser with Nehru and Arafat with Indira Gandhi and Rajiv. Many European countries refused to receive Sharon who stands responsible for many massacres against Palestinians.

Arabs fail to understand why India, as a leader of NAM and developing countries did not take any initiative to stop the Israeli aggression on Lebanon. Arabs used to compare between India's reaction vis-à-vis Suez crisis in 1956 and its response to the aggression on Iraq (2003) and Lebanon (2006). The gap seems so wide. In 1956, India supported Egypt after its realization of the severity of the situation on its national security. India considered that the Israeli Anglo French invasion is an attempt from the western Imperialism to return to Asia and destroy the bloc of neutralism. Nehru wrote to Nasser during the crisis that: "If colonialism succeeds in coming back to Egypt, it will reverse the entire course of history and return to every other country from which it had been forced to go. Therefore ...colonialism should not be allowed to succeed in Egypt. Otherwise it will signal a new and long fight for the whole of Asia and Africa."

The Indian efforts to support Egypt varied from the beginning of the crisis to its end. India played the role of the mediator in the conflict and explained the dimensions of the Egyptian situation, showing the inflexibility of the west. India tried to pressure upon the aggressors and their allies through a withdrawal-Threat from the commonwealth, and forming an international world public opinion front that includes Afro-Asian countries, and the communist bloc and the U.S.A, and thus pursuing the invaders inside and outside lounges of the U.N. India concluded its role with its contribution in the United Nations Emergency Force (UNEF). New Delhi accepted to participate in UNEF according to the Egyptian conditions. UNEF supervised the withdrawal of the attacking troops and was helpful factor in maintaining peace till 1967. The moral influence of India and its size in the strategic balance of the divided world gave its attitude towards Suez crisis a heavy weight, this weight helped Egypt in winning its battle against the west. India took inactive position to prevent or end the occupation of both Iraq and Lebanon. The Statement of Ministry of External Affairs Spokesperson on the commencement of military action in Iraq came on March 20, 2003 to state that "The military action begun today ... lacks justification"[52] where there is no any identification to this action if it is illegal or aggression. Moreover, BJP wanted to send forces to Iraq but the Indian opposition stopped it. Foreign forces in Iraq, regardless of their nationalities, are seen as occupying powers by not only Iraqis but also Arab public. The Indian reaction for Israeli aggression against Lebanon came so late and did not call it "aggression" or question its legality and morality. The Israeli aggression started in July 12, 2006 and India commented on July 30, 2006 when the Ministry of External affairs stated that,

"India strongly condemns the continued irresponsible and indiscriminate bombing of Lebanon by the Israeli military, ignoring calls for restraint. Particularly outrageous is the bombing this morning of a building in Qana in south Lebanon, which has resulted in the deaths of dozens of innocent civilians, mostly women, children and old people who had taken shelter there. India expresses its deep condolences to the Government and people of Lebanon over this tragic incident[53]."

One can wonder if Indian diplomacy will be enough to neutralize the side effects (the decline of India's image as a close friend for Arabs) of the new trends in India's foreign policy regarding WANA. In this context, Pakistan will be able probably to cultivate its image as a good friend in the Arab world as it did not recognize Israel till today. This may put much pressure on Indian Muslims and lead to much polarization inside the Indian society.

India needs to rethink its close association with Israel in defense and strategic arena and to avoid being identified as approving or supporting the USA polices in the region in order to preserve its traditional image in the Arab world. Continuing of American policies in the region will increase only its instability.

This will empower religious militants and endanger the energy security of the countries depending on its needs on the Gulf.

If India's Image in the Arab region continues to deteriorate, India may lose completely the goodwill of Arab masses and secure a place for itself in the agenda of Al Qaeda or any other fundamental organizations, with serious implications for Indian security. In this regard, one should remember the reaction of Al Qaeda for the visit of Sharon in September 2003 , according to Al Jazeera TV that broadcasted his video tape after the visit of Sharon to New Delhi, Al Zawahri, the second man on the leadership of Al Qaeda, condemned the agreements that India signed with Israel and considered it as a "a drop of the flood of the American – Jewish-Indian alliance against Muslims". Zawahri called "Muslims to provide their support for Mujahidins in both Afghanistan and Kashmir"[54].

Concluding Remarks

The destruction of Babri Masjid, the growing Indo-Israeli relations and the communal riots in Gujarat, 2002, accumulated negative reactions among Arab masses towards these developments and contributed to changing the traditional image of India by adding some new dark colors. The new image of India in the Arab world has two main trends. One of these trends is the feeling among Arabs that Indian secularism is endangered by the rise of Hindutava, and that this might affect negatively the position of Muslims in India. The other trend among Arabs assumes that India's friendship for Arabs is doubted today as a result of growing Indo-Israeli relations.

The bottom line is that the dynamics of India's internal politics and foreign policy redraw the image of India in the Arab world with negative flavor. India needs to address this issue, before it is too late, to avoid its long-term implications for both Indian security and Indian interests in West Asia. India is in no need to repeat the mistakes of USA by losing the goodwill of Arabs or to share Americans in paying the price of their mistakes/policies. It is the goodwill of Arabs that excluded India from the oil embargo of 1973, and made Egypt preventing the passing of Portuguese warship in Suez Canal while Indian army was invading Goa, Diu and Daman to liberate it from Portuguese occupation. It is the goodwill of Arabs that made the Arab Gulf a home for 7 million Indians expatriates and its lack which made the result of enforcing 5 millions Jews upon Arabs on Palestine many wars and ongoing conflict.

Notes

1. Self-determination, March 16, 2007, Wikipedia Encyclopedia,<http://en.wikipedia.org/wiki/Self-determination .>

2. Carl Weiser, US$ 1 billion international image campaign isn't enough to buy U.S. love, 14-9-2003, USA Today ,<http://www.usatoday.com/news/washington/2003-09-14-rawar-gns_x.htm >

3. Ibid.

4. < http://amthal.m3loma.com/gamal.htm>

5. The data in this paper is based mainly on interviews which have been conducted with nationals from different Arab countries in the months between October 2006 and February 2007. These Arab countries include Egypt, Sudan, Jordan, Tunisia, Palestine, Syria, Yemen and Saudi Arabia. Their names are not disclosed on their own request. Sudanese people will appreciate the quality of Indian education and Tunisians will admire that Indian elite can speak English fluently, which is not easy for many in the Tunisian elite who speak mainly French. The researcher has the feeling that the subject of this paper should be carried out as a research project by a joint research group of scholars from India and different Arab countries as it needs a lot of field work and access for literature written in Arabic in different Arab countries.

6. G. S. Bhargava, India-U.A.R. Relations, an Assessment, People's Publishing House, New Delhi, 4-6.

7. Al Ahram Weekly, 19-25 December 2002.

8. Ibid.

9. Ibid.

10. Najma Heptulla, Indo-West Asian relations, the Nehru era, Allied Publishers, New Delhi, 1991, p.102; Ajay N. Jha, Indo-Iraqi relations: 1947-86: need for fresh initiatives, in Verinder Grover (ed.), West Asia and India's foreign policy, Deep & Deep Publications, 1992, p.441.

11. He was even called the prophet of peace during his visit to Saudi Arabia in 1956, Aasharq Alawsat (London), January 31, 2006.

12. Anwar El Sadat, who became the president of Egypt (1970-1981), called Nehru in his articles that appeared in Al Goumhouryia newspaper (Cairo) the wise man of India and the giant of East during the crisis of 1956, Anwar El Sadat, A Tycoon and A Dwarf, Al Gomhuria (Cairo), 10-8-1956.

13. Mohamed El Said , an expert of strategic affairs called Egypt to copy the Indian model of election committee, Mohamed El Sayed El Said, For Indian Committee, Arab and International Analysis, Center for Strategic and Political Studies, Al Ahram,

<http://www.ahram.org.eg/acpss/ahram/2001/1/1/ANAL614.HTM>

Nasser Yahia wrote an article titled "a lesson from the land of Sind : This is how Indians fight corruption!" on the website of "Islah" , the Islamic movement of Yemen , where he appreciated Indian democracy and called the biggest democracy in the world, 11-3-2007, <http://www.alsahwayemen.net/view_news.asp?sub_no=2_2007_03_11_55080>, Other Arab writer saw the Indian model of democracy as the only solution of the Iraqi crisis, Hadi Hassan Elewi , Al Sabah newspaper (Baghdad), 17 March, 2007,

14. Jagdish P. Sharma , Indo-Egyptian relations, the Kashmir factor, in Riyaz Punjabi and AK Pasha, India and the Islamic world, Radiant Publishers, New Delhi,1998,P.108.

15. Habiballah Khan, Alhend wal henod fe Al adab Al Arabi [Indian and Indians in Arab literature], Thaqafat-ul-Hind,Vol.49,No.1,1998,pp.96-106; S.Ahmed Al Siddiqi, Al Asateer wa al athar Al Hindyia fe Al sher Al Arabi Al hadith [Myths and Indian Monuments in Modern Arab poems], Thaqafat-ul-Hind,Vol.49, No.1,1998,pp.107-117; Kafil Ahmed Qasimi, Al Hind Wa Al Hinod fe Nazaar Al Masodi [India and Indians on the eyes of Masodi], Thaqafat-ul-Hind,Vol.52,No.2,2001,pp.16-27.

16. The novel has been published in 1897. It has a political dimension where history was used in the novel to reflect Ahmed Shawki's political views of the British occupation of Egypt, which was a blow for Egyptian pride. The story spoke of Ramses II who led his armada to conquer India. His son Achim helped him in leading the campaign. Dahnsh "the virgin of India" is the daughter of India's king of kings. She is the key character of the story with Achim who fall in love with her. This love became a tragedy as Achim died in unknown way and Achim throw her self in the river and passed away; see Al

Hayat (London), January 24, 2006.

17. Mohamed Aslam Islahi, Al Hind wa A'lam al Hind Fe'aion Sho'raa Mesr Al Goded [India and its figures in the eyes of modern Egyptian poets, Thaqafat-ul-Hind,Vol.45,no.1,1994,pp.195-216.

18. See 5.

19. See 5.

20. A discussion with my Indian friend Ginu Zacharia, who carry out currently a research on this idea, late 2006; interestingly, Fawaz Traboulsi, a Lebanese historian , argued that minorities politics was not a new phenomena in West Asia. It is an imperial invention that has been played in the region since late 19th century, Fawaz Traboulsi. "War and Imperialism in Lebanon, View from the Resistance Movement" JNUSU-SIS, JNU, New Delhi. March 17, 2007.

21. See 5.

22. Al-Ahram Weekly (Cairo), 9 - 15 May 2002.

23. Al-Ahram Weekly, 7 - 13 March 2002.

24. Ibid.

25. Arab News (Jeddah), 5 March, 2002, the newspaper gave a detailed accounts of the developments of communal riots at Gujarat on regular basis. some of its reports has been quoted in other magazines in Arabic such as Al Mujtamaa (Riyadh) which gave a lengthy report of the problem in the issue of July 5, 2002 . The magazine compared what happened in Gujarat with The Spanish model of eliminating Muslims from Spain in Medieval times.

26. "Asia Times, April 26, 2002.

27. Ouda called also Egyptian opposition to cooperate with Congress party and suggested sending a delegate from Egyptian opposition parties to congratulate the Congress for its victory in the election, Al Arabi (Cairo), May 30, 2005.

28. Sir John Thomson, "Policy Paths in South Asia: Intersections Between Global and Local," Michael R. Chambers, ed., *South Asia in 2020: Future Strategic Balances and Alliances*, Carlisle Barracks, PA: Strategic Studies Institute, U.S. Army War College, 2002, p. 17, cited in Stephen J. Blank, Natural Allies? Regional security in Asia and Prospects for Indo-American Strategic, Strategic Studies Institute (SSI) monographs, Carlisle Barracks, PA: Strategic Studies Institute, U.S. Army War College, September 2005.

29. El Sayed Mekkawi, Misr Wa Kashmir: Dirasa Tarikhyia Fe Diplomaciat Al Azamat (1950-51), [Egypt and Kashmir: A Historical Study in The Diplomacy of Crises (1950-1951)], The Proceedings of

The 5th Annual International Conference of The Management of Crises and Catastrophes, vol.4, (Cairo: Ain Shames University, 2000), pp.193-225.

30. Jagdish P Sharma, Indo- Egyptian Relations: The Kashmir Factor, in Riyaz Punjabi and AK Pasha (ed.), India and Islamic World, Radiant Publishers, 1998, p.104.

31. AK Pasha ,India and West Asia: Continuity and Change, (Delhi: Gyan Sagar. 1999 p.115; see also Kalim Bahadur, Pakistan as a factor in India-OIC relations ; and also S.K. Singh , India,Pakistan and the OIC: some personal reflections , in Riyaz Punjabi and AK Pasha (ed.), India and Islamic World , Radiant Publishers,1998,pp.19-26 , 27-33.

32. Faiz Abu-Jaber, The Development of Indo-Egyptian Relations, Indian Political Science Review, vol.4, no.2, April-September 1970, pp.157-70.

33. See 28.

34. G. Parthasarthy, ed., Jawaharlal Nehru, Letters to Chief Ministers, Vol. I, 1947-49, J. Nehru Memorial Fund, Oxford University Press, 1987, p.165, quoted in Najma Heptulla, Indo-West Asian relations, the Nehru era, Allied Publishers, New Delhi, 1991, p.161.

35. Selected works of Jawaharlal Nehru, Second Series, J. Nehru Memorial Fund, Oxford University Press, 1987, p.509, quoted in Najma Heptulla, pp.161-162.

36. Dawn (Karachi), December 1, 1956, quoted in Jagdish P Sharma, p.107.

37. Arabic news item appeared on this link < http://www.arabiyat.com/forums/showthread.php?t=67877 > and it was based on an exclusive interview to Vikram Sura for the The Hindu, the relevant parts of the interview for our discussion is here:

"**Vikram:** Prime Minister Sharon is to make a `historic' visit to India in September. On the agenda is the `war on terror'. Israel is expected to assist India in border control practices, some of which are followed at the borders of Gaza, West Bank and also with Lebanon. How do you feel about this?

Arafat: This is silly talk. Because he can't offer anything for this programme. Don't forget you are speaking to Arafat; the Shimla agreement, they say, is an Arafat agreement. You forget this, what I have done between two friendly, brotherly countries? And I am ready to play a role again if there is a misunderstanding. But what he [Mr. Sharon] is saying is to escalate the situation and war between Pakistan and India.

Vikram: Do you welcome this relationship between Israel and

India?

Arafat: Look, when we signed the agreement with my partner Rabin, the doors were opened to my partner Rabin from China to Indonesia and to Senegal and in between, you remember? More than 64 countries opened their doors to him. What is the meaning of `the peace of the brave,' which we have signed with my partner Rabin? But we hope that this visit will be a pressure for him [Mr. Sharon] to make real peace with your brothers, the Palestinians." The Hindu, August 3, 2003<http://www.hinduonnet.com/2003/08/03/stories/2003080300231400.htm >

38. <http://arab.moheet.com/asp/show_f2.asp?do=1107567>

39. Asharq Alarabi (London), September 9, 2003;http://www.asharqalarabi.org.uk/paper/s-ruiah-zi1.htm

40. <http://www.arabgate.com >

41. Mohamed Noaman Galal, Indo-Arab relations from rapprochement to neutrality, 17-5-2006, Special Files, Al Ma'refa, Al Jazeera TV website, http://www.aljazeera.net/NR/exeres/46D0825F-F848-4DB0-9AE0-CCDF450255EE.htm

42. Raya (Qatar), September 16, 2003.

43. General Talat Mesalm , Indo-Israeli Relations and its dangers, 17/5/2006, Analyses, Al Ma'refa, Al Jazeera TV website, <http://www.aljazeera.net/NR/exeres/8C98DE8E-2722-44F2-B9A6-37BBC69B7D8D.htm>

44. Medhat Ayub, the future of Indo-Israeli alliance, 17/5/2006, Special Files, Al Ma'refa, Al Jazeera TV website, <http://www.aljazeera.net/NR/exeres/0FBE1967-2160-4465-946C-47D920D64AEB.htm>

45. See 5; some Indians submit to the same view. During the meeting of the PM Dr Manmohan Singh with the Arab delegate at the International Conference of Indo-Arab Relations - Partnership and Development, on November 13, 2006, I told him that Arab people is looking for an active role for India to end the sufferings of Palestinian people .PM asserted that India supports the Palestinian rights . I replied that Indian support for Palestinian struggle is welcomed by Arabs but still the Arab people are looking for active pro-Palestinian role that will stop the sufferings of Palestinians. PM commented that "the suffering of Palestinians is a shame on humanity", Prime Minister Office website, Photogallery, 13-11-2006, <http://pmindia.nic.in/photogallery.htm>

46. Medhat Ayub, see 44.

47. India was counted responsible for three masscres and crimes out

of 22 in the whole world and the same information were shared among many websites, see for example: Mahdi Qadi , Read and cry blood for the massacres of our Umma at the modern times (a survey for the massacres during the last century).. When?, <http://saaid.net/Minute/m7.htm>

48. The argument over Indian and Pakistani position was controversial for decades where some Arabs may agree with India or Pakistan but as a result of the long ongoing conflict and Kashmiris are suffering most; there is emerging trend among some elements of the elite and informed people that Kashmir should go now independent. See 5

49. Al Goumhoria (Cairo), March 14, 1957.

50. See Aftab Khaled ,Indo-Kuwait Relations since 1961 ,M.phil thesis, JNU,1999; Rashida M. Sofia, Indo- Kuwait Relations: The Post-War II Phase, M.Phil thesis,JNU, 2000.

51. See 5.

52. Statement by Official Spokesperson of Ministry of External Affairs, New Delhi, on the commencement of military action in Iraq, March 20, 2 003 < http://meaindia.nic.in/speech/2003/03/20spc01.htm>

53. Statement by Official Spokesperson of Ministry of External Affairs, New Delhi on the situation in Lebanon, 30/07/2006 < http://meaindia.nic.in/searchhome.htm > path: search Lebanon in Press Releases.

54. Associated Press , CIA analysing new 'al-Qaida' tape, Guardian Unlimited, 29 September, 2003, < http://www.guardian.co.uk/alqaida/story/0,,1052028,00.html>; On a tape broadcasted by Al Jazeera: Al Zawahri calls for toppling the Pakistani President , 28/9/2003 , Al Jazeera TV website, <http://www.aljazeera.net/News/archive/archive?ArchiveId=61115 >

Part VI: Globalisation, India and North Africa: Bilateral Dimensions

13

Fostering Ties with the Arab-African World

Jagdish P. Sharma

The end of the cold war and the growing importance of the economic aspect in bilateral relations is changing many old concepts. India's emergence as an economic and technological power gives it a great opportunity to fashion its ties with countries of the Arab African region in the modern context. In the way the global polity is evolving relations with one nation or another need not inhabit the development of bilateral relations of countries. In the post cold –war period the US has emerged as the sole super power. We can not neglect our relations with the US or with neighbouring countries particularly Pakistan and China. But these are independent factors which should not come in the way of our developing bilateral relations with countries of Arab-Africa. It is rather simplistic to say that since we are friendly to the US we are bound to be pro-Israel in our Arab world policy. The two are not inter-dependent.

Long dominated by colonial and Imperial regimes the Arab-African world faces the challenges of change posed by a variety of internal factors. In the recent years, significant degrees of political, economic and social reforms have been evident in a number of Arab-African States. This region is of great economic significance because of its abundant natural resources, especially petroleum, gas and energy and of strategic significance, being the underbelly of Mediterranean Europe.

Traditionally, this Arab-African region constituted an important component of the Mediterranean basin. It's ethnic and cultural roots can be traced to the Phoenician, Roman and Greek Civilisations. The beautifully preserved ruins of this heritage are scattered throughout this region, from Egypt to Morocco. The

Mediterranean culture of Arab-Africa, owed its growth to the maritime contacts that bound the northern, southern and eastern shores of the Mediterranean and thus, linked three continents Africa, Asia and Europe.

On the eve of World War I, the old political map of Arab-Africa seemed destined for change. Nationalist ideas spread to the Arab-African region in the second half of the nineteenth century for several reasons. First, the opening of modern schools, particularly in Egypt, Lebanon and Syria, helped disseminate new ideas. Second, the introduction of printing press extended knowledge of political affairs and encouraged a cultural-literacy revival. Third, as the old empires began to break up, the idea of self-determination for national groups took root. The anti-colonial movement *ipso facto* led to the search for national identity different from the Europeans. In the inter-war period, European liberal thoughts and subsequently socialism also influenced the growth of the nationalist movement.

With the outbreak of war in 1914, Egypt was proclaimed a British protectorate but it won independence in 1936. The Italians were the last to gain colonial territory and the first to lose it. The conquest of Libya by Italy was not complete until 1932. In 1939, the Italians were driven out of Libya as part of Allied campaign in North Africa. Libya became independent in 1951. Morocco and Tunisia became independent in 1956 after 44 years and 75 years of French rule. Algeria's path to independence was much less straight forward because the French saw Algeria as part of France. France, put up a strong fight to retain Algeria in the face of one of the most determined struggles for national independence by any colonized people. After eight years of bitter struggle, Algeria achieved independence in 1962. The political map of Arab-Africa still had in 2006, one major area of uncertainty in Western Sahara, formerly Spanish Sahara. Following Spain's withdrawal from Spanish Sahara in 1976, the territory was partitioned between Morocco in the north and Mauritania in the South. In 1978, Mauritania withdrew from the Southern part of Western Sahara, leaving Morocco to claim the whole territory. However, as we see today, majority of the territory's 90,000 inhabitants are still fighting for independence from Moroccan occupation[1].

The position in Western Sahara in 2006 seems to be positive in the sense that the Polisario Front of Western Saharawi people and Morocco had agreed in principle to a referendum under the auspices of the United Nations Secretary General Mr. Kofi Annan. The recent developments there show that the problem is in the process of getting solved with goodwill on all sides including Morocco, which is one of the major contestants. A permanent peace in Arab Africa is possible only through a just resolution of the Western Sahara problem. The decade, following the end of World War II, saw the demise of the colonial powers in Arab Africa. But the post Second World War history of emerging nations of Arab-Africa has been marked by the struggle for self-government. During the post war period, all the states, Algeria, Egypt, Libya, Morocco, Sudan and Tunisia except Western Sahara have emerged from foreign domination. In terms of international politics, this emergence has taken the form of a struggle for independence. But in terms of domestic politics and economy, it has meant transition from dependence to self-government[2].

Each Arab-African state has approached the problem of political independence, legitimacy and the concepts of equality and liberty in its own way. To a large extent, their approaches have been conditioned by the methods by which they gained independence; in all countries there are elites of different sizes that are governing national affairs. But in no country was populace in a position to rule itself directly. The obstacles to direct participation of people in Arab-Africa lie essentially in the nature of the people, the nature of the leadership and the relationship between the two, in fact, the very lack of modern experiences kept the masses from being able to directly participate in government. Nonetheless, despite the obstacles, the Arab-African states have paid attention to democratic ideals in recent times.

Arab Africa is on the move. Many already see the signs of an

African Renaissance. Far reaching political, economic and social changes have reshaped the Arab-Africa of Post-Cold War era and laid the foundation for a better future.

India's Ties with Arab-Africa

India recently (November, 2006) called for expanding the existing areas of trade and investment with North Africa and to finding new areas of cooperation between the two regions.

Historically India has had a long-tradition of friendly relations with all the countries in the Afro-Arab and Asian World. India has survived through the ages because she represents a synthesis of various cultures, civilization, races and religions of mankind. The geographical position of India enables her to act as sort of a bridge between the Afro-Arab and Asian World and the West. India is part of Asia, but, its geographical, spiritual and cultural location makes it an important centre of civilizational interaction. Soon after Independence, India took a principled stand on Arab-African issues in the United Nations. Steering a middle course between partition and a unitary state in Palestine, India proposed a Federal State with an Arab majority in charge of the Federal State but with autonomy for the other region, that is, the Jewish region. Later while India recognized Israel's right to exist within secure borders, it condemned Israel's aggressive tactics against its Arab Palestinian neighbours and its efforts to keep the territory occupied through aggression. India has also consistently supported the legitimate rights of the people of Palestine, South Africa, Namibia and Western Sahara for independent state in their respective homeland.

India's support for the independence of the countries in the Arab African World and its efforts in the UN are noteworthy. India continued to extend support to the Liberation Movements struggling against the remaining vestiges of Colonial rule in Southern Africa. India has extended economic, educational and technological assistance to the independent countries of Arab-Africa both on a bilateral basis and through multilateral arrangements like the Special Commonwealth African Assistance

Programme (SCAAP) and the Africa fund created by the Late Prime Minister Rajiv Gandhi. Through her participation in the UN and association with the non-aligned countries India has played her rightful role in world affairs. The fight against imperialism gave birth to freedom movements in both the regions and spawned nationalist leaders who gave new hope and direction to their people. The similarity of the plight of their countries and the common goal of independence from foreign rule brought together the nationalist leaders from Afro-Arab and Asian region.

The Post-cold War era has witnessed a profound transformation in the international environment, throwing up fresh challenges to the foreign and economic policies of India and Afro-Arab-Asian World. India has sought to respond optimally to the dynamic, emerging situation, and to safeguard and promote the national interest in relation to the outside world. A major focus in India's Arab-African foreign policy since the 1990's was to create an atmosphere of mutual trust and economic cooperation[3]. During the Nehru era and the Post-Nehru era, India was helping the Arab-African region in conducting elections, setting up Constitutions and democratic institutions wherever the climate was congenial. India and Arab-Africa can set up joint projects in different sectors. This can be expanded. Indian diplomatic representation in various countries should be strong enough to tell the areas of opportunity, investment and cooperation in India and the various commodities to be exported to the Arab-African region. They need to ensure a remunerative and decent price for various commodities. One can have regional commodity export councils. Today we have national export councils. Arab and African countries like other developing nations are going through various developmental programmes, including programmes related to economic development, technical and infrastructural collaboration and educational, health and academic advancement.

India can provide the services of specialists like academics, taxation experts, agricultural experts and scientists, election observers and organizers, and parliamentary officials. Development of primary healthcare centres in the shape of doctors, nurses, medical specialists and other consultants will be beneficial.

India has always believed that Afro-Arab and Asian cooperation is a powerful instrument to strengthen solidarity among developing countries. Indian Political leadership from Jawaharlal Nehru to Dr. Manmohan Singh[4] have consistently advocated the cause of Africa's liberation and development particularly through various international forums like The United Nations, the Commonwealth, the Non-Aligned movement, the Group of 77, the WTO, The Group of 20 etc.

India has played a salutary role in the economic and social development of the Third World countries liberated from the colonial yoke. India endeavored to deepen and broaden its multifaceted interaction with countries of the North African region through exchange of high-level visits. India continues to be keenly interested in the peace, development, stability and economic and social prosperity of the region[5]. The relationship with the countries of the region was further strengthened by economic and commercial linkages. India's trade with the region registered steady growth. Besides joint venture projects in Algeria, Morocco, Sudan and Jordan, negotiations are continuing on joint venture in Tunisia, Libya and Egypt. Bulk of India's sourcing of phosphate is done from countries of this region[6]. India has acquired a 25 per cent equity stake in a Sudan oil field from which it will get about three million tones of crude oil annually. The acquisition has been made at a cost of US$ 699 million recently[7] India has, so far, invested over US$ 700 million in exploration efforts in Sudan. Till date ONGC Videsh limited has invested US$ 3.5 billion globally and one billion dollars in Sudan alone. The Gujarat State Petroleum Corporation (GSPC) is in negotiation with Oman, Qatar, Algeria and Egypt to import liquefied natural gas[8]. Egypt also agreed to import wheat from India, opening up its seven million-ton a year market to Indian exporters. The breakthrough came after Egyptian quarantine authority approved the Indian wheat quality for imports.

Moreover, India has a strong image in the region from the

decolonization period and through its peacekeeping operations. The United Nations operations in Congo from 1960-63 after its independence from Belgium had the largest Indian participation in peacekeeping operations. India was part of the UN Transition Assistance Group in Namibia and other UN operations in Rwanda, Mozambique, Somalia, Liberia, Angola, Lebanon, Western Sahara and Sierra Leone. Lebanon Rwanda, Somalia and Western Sahara have actively sought cooperation from India because they feel the Indian experience is more compatible with their needs. India is one of the few Developing Countries which has not only considerable expertise and experience in the technological and management fields but also is in a position to help other Developing and Under Developed Countries in the process of their economic development in a variety of sectors such as agriculture, industry, trade, joint ventures and consultancy services[9].

Both India and the Arab-African World are facing daunting challenges in the economic, social, political, cultural and strategic spheres including removal of poverty and unemployment, globalisation, food security, communicable diseases and environmental hazards along with the task of tackling regional ethnic, religious and cross border terrorist threats. The challenge before them today is to make the transition to the Post-Cold War era more smooth and orderly and responsive to the needs of Afro-Arab and Asian people. They feel that the United Nations should be "equitable" and "represent a just world order". On the West Asian Peace, India and the Arab and African states have reiterated their support to the existence of two states, a Palestinian and Israeli state, living side by side in secure and internationally recognized borders. The lingering crisis in Iraq including the recent verdict against President Saddam Husain of Iraq has implications for the whole world. The transition in Iraq has not broken the long cycle of violence and instability there. Both India and Arab-African states have much to offer to each other for their mutual benefit. Our image in the region is that of a helpful non-aligned power which has commonality of interest and shared values with people of the region.

Notes

1. Alasdiar Drysdale and Gerald H. Blake, *The Middle East and North Africa: A Political Geography* (New York, Oxford University Press, 1985, p. 70).

2. William Zartman, *Government and Politics in Northern Africa* (London: Methuen & Co. Ltd., 1964, p. 3).

3. Jagdish P. Sharma, *Afro-Asia and Contemporary Politics* (Delhi: Anamika Publishers, 2003, preface).

4. See *National Herald* 20th October, 2006.

5. For details see Jagdish P. Sharma, *Foreign Policy Challenges: India and Afro-Arab World*, (Delhi: Anamika Publishers, 2003.)

6. *Annual Report 2000-2001*, Ministry of External Affairs, Government of India, p.42.

7. *The Hindu*, 14 March, 2003. Also see Sudanow (Khartoum) April 2003, p. 7.

8. *The Financial Express* 28th October, 2006.

9. V. Saran, "South-South Cooperation: An Analysis of India's Economic Assistance Programme" *Foreign Trade Review*, Quoted in K. Mathews, "A Multi-faceted Relationship: A synoptic view" *Africa Quarterly*, vol. 37 Nos. 1&2, 1997, p.14.

14

The Ongoing Struggle for Independence: Saharawi Arab Democratic Republic and Indo-Algerian Ties

John Cherian

Introduction

The Issue of Western Sahara: Since the 1970's, the Popular Front for the Liberation of Saqiat al Hamra and Rio de Oro (Polisario) and the Kingdom of Morocco, have been locked in a bitter dispute over the territory known as Western Sahara. The 260,000 square km territory, though sparsely populated, is resource rich. Western Sahara was a Spanish colony till 1975. After the precipitate withdrawal of the Spanish colonial power, Morocco which claims historical rights to the territory, sent in 3,50,000 of its citizens into Western Sahara. The Polisario Front launched an armed struggle against Morocco in 1976. It set up the Sahrawi Arab Democratic Republic (SADR) and launched a guerilla war against Morocco. The SADR is a full fledged member of the African Union (AU) and continues to be recognized as a state by many countries all over the world. The fighting with Morocco ended in 1991, after a cease fire was signed under the auspices of the United Nations.

The dispute is the longest running territorial dispute on the African continent. Most of the Sahrawis have been forced to stay in refugee camps. In all more than 1,60,000 refugees are scattered in five remote desert camps near the Algerian border. Algeria is the main backer of the Polisario Front. The World Food Program (WFP) has said that the refugees are living in squalid conditions, experiencing severe shortages of essentials like food and medicine. With the prospects of a peaceful solution not very encouraging, the Polisario Front has threatened to re-start its armed struggle. The Western Sahara issue continues to be an emotive one. Western Sahara is viewed by many states, especially those states which have won their independence by waging liberation struggles, as the last remaining colony. The issue continues to figure prominently in international forums like the Non Alignment Movement (NAM). This is one reason why many countries friendly to India were taken aback when in 2000 India withdrew diplomatic recognition it had accorded to SADR.

Algeria, especially had reasons to be aggrieved as it has been the main backer of the Sahrawi cause. Besides, Algeria and Morocco have been traditional rivals in the Maghreb. The Indian move also came at a time when Algeria was emerging out of the virtual decade long civil war that had erupted after the Algerian military prevented the Islamic Salvation Front (FIS) from taking power, despite the party having won at the ballot box. In the nineties, the Algerian state was more preoccupied with matters relating to internal security than with international diplomacy. The Sahrawi cause in a way became receded to the backround as the secularists battled Islamists for supremacy in Algeria. Coupled with this was the economic meltdown the Algerian state temporarily experienced throughout the nineties. In comparison, Morocco remained stable. Its diplomats worked overtime in countries like India to make them reverse their decisions regarding the recognition of the SADR. Countries like Iran were not convinced. But India's de-recognition was the icing on the cake for Moroccan diplomacy. India after all was a big player in NAM and had considerable clout in the developing world.

India-Algeria Relations: The Western Sahara Factor

India and Algeria have enjoyed cordial relations since 1962 the year in which the North African country gained independence. Both the countries had broadly similar foreign policy objectives until the eighties. The end of the Cold War saw both the countries re-orienting their foreign policies. Until the late eighties, both the countries were leading players in the non-aligned movement.

They continue to be active in NAM but it has been obvious for some time that they do not give the grouping the kind of importance they had accorded it in the past. Both the countries are also active participants in the G-15 and G-77.

Jawaharlal Nehru was all praise for the ideals the Algerian revolution had enshrined in its constitution after independence. Nehru had observed that the goals of social justice, secularism and non-discrimination on the basis of race, religion and creed espoused in the Algerian constitution are similar to the ones enshrined in the Indian Constitution. "We therefore look upon Algeria as partners in common endeavours", he had said at the time of Algerian independence. However, Algeria's revolution markedly differed from India's struggle for independence. It was inspired more by the armed anti-colonial and anti-imperialist struggle waged in Indo-China and other parts of the world from the early fifties. The National Liberation Front (FLN) was inspired by the anti-French struggle waged in Indo-China. The FLN was formed a few months after the historic victory of the Vietnamese over the French in the landmark battle of Dienbienphu in 1954. That battle had marked the demise of French colonialism in Indo-China. It was an inspiration for those struggling for freedom in other parts of the world. Algeria's independence had come at a great cost. More than a million Algerians lost their lives in the bloody struggle for independence.

It was therefore no surprise that after independence Algeria followed a radical foreign policy in comparison to that adopted by Nehru for India. Algeria was among those countries, which considered the Soviet Union a "natural ally of NAM". Algeria was very liberal in providing material and logistical support to the liberation struggles that were going on all over the developing world from the sixties. Algerian support was important for liberation movements like the ANC, the PLO, and the MPLA in Angola and the FRELIMO in Mozambique. At that time, support from countries like India to the liberation movements was mostly confined to political support. Countries like Algeria provided arms, sanctuary and training. On key international issues, India and Algeria have invariably been on the same side. Jawaharlal Nehru and Indira Gandhi were iconic figures for Algerians, identified as they were with NAM and other projects meant to unify the South. Relations between the two countries peaked in the mid-eighties when Rajiv Gandhi was the Indian Prime Minister. Rajiv Gandhi was the first Indian Prime Minister to visit Algeria. In the course of his 1985 visit, Rajiv Gandhi had pledged Indian help in modernizing the Algerian economy. Rajiv Gandhi was also the statesman who took the decision to recognize the Sahrawi Arab Democratic Republic (SADR) in the same year.

The SADR was the name of the new state that had sprung up after the Spanish abandoned their colony of Western Sahara in 1974. The Polisario Front, a grouping encompassing almost all the political parties in the sparsely populated but resources rich colony, had been waging a guerilla war against the Spanish colonizers. After the collapse of the fascist Franco dictatorship in Spain, the government in Madrid unilaterally withdrew from its colony without transferring power to the Sahrawis. Neighbouring Morocco and Mauritania immediately sent troops and settlers to the territory and apportioned the territory into two parts. Both these countries occupied the territory citing historic claims to the region. The Polisario resumed its guerilla struggle while at the same time bringing its case into the international arena. The biggest backer of the SADR continues to be Algeria, which shares a long border with the former Spanish colony. The Polisario guerillas waged a successful war, forcing the Mauritanians to completely withdraw from the territory they had occupied. The Mauritanians sued for peace and eventually recognized the SADR. The Moroccan army had to beat a strategic retreat and confine itself behind a high-tech wall that encompassed the most productive part of Western Sahara, consisting of its phosphate deposits and marine wealth. The Sahrawi issue for the Moroccans is an emotive issue. All the political parties in the Kingdom are united on the issue, insisting that Western Sahara is an integral part of the country. The Moroccan position is that the Polisario Front is a creation of Algeria and that the SADR is being propped up Algiers.

At least on the African continent, the Moroccan argument did not elicit much support. The SADR was given a seat as a full-fledged member in the Organization of African Unity (OAU), now known as the African Union (AU) in 1984. Morocco had staged a noisy walkout from the OAU to protest the move. Though Morocco can claim strong diplomatic support from Paris and Washington, the international community has so far not recognized the annexation of Western Sahara. The unresolved issue has stymied political and economic integration in the Maghreb region. The Arab Maghreb Union (AMU) established in 1989 with Algeria, Morocco, Tunisia and Libya as members has failed to take off. The initial goal of the AMU was economic integration in the region. The Libyan leader, Muammar Gaddafi, openly conceded four years ago that the Western Sahara issue "was blocking the process of Maghrebian integration". Because of the dispute over Western Sahara, the AMU summit has not been held since 1994. India's recognition of SADR was a big diplomatic victory for the Polisario Front. India's decision to recognize SADR had come in the wake of a NAM resolution in 1983 in support of the decolonization process. Morocco immediately withdrew its ambassador from Delhi in protest against India's move. India along with Iran was the only two major countries in Asia to accord recognition for the SADR. New Delhi had joined the so-called radical grouping in NAM like Cuba in recognizing SADR. At the time, the Indian government's decision to recognize SADR seems to have come as a surprise to the mandarins of South Block.

The contention of the Indian External Affairs Ministry officials at the time was that they were not kept in the loop about the surprise decision. The argument being advanced in the corridors of South Block was that New Delhi was interfering in what was basically a face-off between Algeria and Morocco, the two major powers in the Maghreb region have been traditional rivals since the early sixties. The radical foreign policy that Algeria followed till the late eighties was in marked contrast to the pro-western posture of the Kingdom of Morocco. The late King Hassan was the closest ally of Washington and Paris in the region. Morocco was among the first Arab countries to allow Israeli security services to operate from its territory.

The SADR enjoyed full diplomatic representation in India for more than a decade. At the same time New Delhi did not go out of its way to propagate the Sahrawi cause in international forums like NAM or help the tens of thousands of Sahrawis languishing in refugee camps on the border with Algeria. It looked the other way when reports of human rights abuses came out of the occupied parts of Western Sahara. In retrospect, the assassination of Rajiv Gandhi in 1991 left them without a friend at the top most echelons of the Indian government. P.V. Narasimha Rao of the Congress Party, who had taken over as Prime Minister, was more focused on improving relations with the West, particularly with Washington. The collapse of the Soviet Union, New Delhi's traditional ally in the international arena, had made the Indian elite insecure. Moscow's support for India on Kashmir for instance was almost taken for granted. After the end of the cold war, New Delhi felt that it had to look for new friends and alliances. Countries like Morocco, which were members of groupings like the Organization of Islamic Conference (OIC) started giving assurances that they would help to keep contentious issues like Kashmir on the backburner if India made some reciprocal moves on issues like Western Sahara.

International Backing for the Holding of a Referendum in Western Sahara

New Delhi's decision may have influenced the United Nations to accept the Sahrawi demand for a referendum on the independence issue in principle. According to the documents signed in 1991 which led to a cease fire, it was conceded that the Western Sahara dispute was basically an issue of decolonization. But the Moroccans with the help of their traditional western allies like France and the United States have been successful in stalling the referendum on some pretext or the other. The UN Security

Council Resolution 690 (April 29, 1991) established the United Nations Mission for the Organization of a Referendum in the Western Sahara (MINURSO). It called for a referendum to offer a choice between independence and integration with Morocco. The referendum was supposed to be originally held under UN auspices in 1992.

The UN had drawn up a list of 86,361 voters. This list was disputed by Morocco, which wanted to add the names of those Moroccans who had settled in the territory after the Spanish had left. The Kingdom had actively encouraged Moroccans to settle in the disputed territory since the time the Spanish colonialists left. On March, 1997, the then UN Secretary General, Kofi Annan named the former US secretary of state, James Baker, as his personal envoy. Initially the UN was toying with the idea of partition. This idea was rejected by all the parties involved in the conflict. Finally, in 2003, Baker finally came out with a plan to end the impasse. According to the Baker Plan, there would be a trial autonomy period to be followed by a referendum in which the Sahrawis would be able to vote on their final status. Baker had stated that his "compromise formula does not require the consent of both parties at each and every stage". The Moroccan government rejected the plan questioning the priority given to the referendum in the Baker plan. Rabat also expressed its indignation at the use of the word "independence" as an option for the Sahrawis in the Baker proposals. Algeria and Polisario had Okayed the Baker Plan. Baker resigned as the UN Secretary General's personal envoy on June, 2004. His successor as special envoy, Peter van Walsum, almost immediately came to the conclusion that only "direct talks" between Morocco and the Sahrawis was the only way to end the deadlock. Valsum also made the observation that the Western Sahara issue is not high on the international political agenda as most countries continue to seek good relations with both Morocco and Algeria. UN Security Council Resolution 1675 of April, 2006, noted the responsibility of both the parties with respect to achieving a political solution.

"What is the difference between East Timor, Namibia and

Western Sahara? If the UN is unable to make one of the parties accept the results of a referendum, then it should not have kept the Sahrawis waiting for so long", a senior Sahrawi official was quoted as saying. By the beginning of this decade, the UN had spent more than US$ 600 million in trying to organize a referendum in Western Sahara. The UN mission in Western Sahara continues despite the consistent stonewalling from the Moroccan side. Since the late nineties, the Moroccan government has signaled that it would never allow the holding of a fair and free referendum. The government in Rabat has shown by words as well as deeds that the maximum the Saharawi people can hope for is for "substantial autonomy". However, the Moroccan government has repeatedly emphasized that under no circumstances will an "autonomous" Sahrawi state be allowed to have its own foreign or defense policies. A Report by the US Congressional Research Services on Western Sahara notes that while the United States "supports" UN efforts it "wants a solution that would not destabilize its ally". The ally in question is Morocco although Washington has come closer to Algeria also in recent years. The US-Algerian Trans Saharan Counter-Terrorism Initiative is an illustration. There is close cooperation between the two countries in the energy sector.

India's Withdrawal of Recognition of SADR

The way the BJP led NDA government in Delhi chose to do a "volte face" on the Western Sahara issue gave Indian diplomacy a bad name, especially on the African continent. The NDA government in mid-2000 suddenly made the announcement regarding the withdrawal of recognition for the SADR. No prior warning, formal or informal was given either to the Sahrawi officials or to the Algerian government. The Moroccan Prime Minister at that time, Abderrahmanne Youssufi, was in India before the decision was taken. There was speculation that his visit was timed with the express intent of persuading New Delhi to withdraw recognition. In response to a query in Parliament, the then Minister of State for external affairs, Ajit Panja, had assured the House that there was no question of withdrawing recognition of SADR. A few months later, the decision was taken to withdraw recognition. The Algerian authorities were not even informally sounded about the impending decision, though there was a joint commission meeting between the two countries a month before.

Mystery still surrounds the circumstances under which the decision to derecognise the SADR was taken by the Indian government. Moroccan officials had been unofficially drawing parallels between the Kashmir and Sahara issues. The media in India reported that after the withdrawal of the recognition of SADR, a multi-million dollar "phosphate mining" contract was signed between a leading Indian company and Morocco. The Indian tourism industry has also invested millions of dollars in Morocco's tourism industry. India is one of the biggest importers of phosphates from Morocco. The decision to de-recognize SADR from available indications seems to have been taken in a hurry and in stealth. The decision came as a shock to the Sahrawis and the states that have been whole-heartedly backing their liberation struggle. "The wise and pondered decision—made by the government of a major country, founding father of the non-aligned movement and outstanding actor in international relations-crowns similar decisions made by several other governments, especially in Africa and Latin America", said Mohammad Benaissa, the Moroccan Foreign Minister at the time. The minister had urged other countries to follow the "new position" taken by the Indian government. Since King Mohammed VI took power in 1999, Morocco changed its diplomatic strategy in its dispute with Algeria and the SADR. The strategy included persuading nations that had recognized SADR to reconsider their position. Morocco promised handsome economic and political rewards in lieu for withdrawal of recognition. Several African countries now back Morocco's position on the Sahara issue. Among Rabat's prominent backers in the continent are Senegal and Sudan.

The NDA government however moved fast to assuage the hurt feelings of Algeria. The Algerian President, Abdel Aziz Bouteflika was invited to be the chief guest at the 2001 Republic

Day celebrations. Though New Delhi's abrupt decision on Western Sahara still undoubtedly rankles, Algerian diplomats prefer to concentrate more on economic issues. "The Partnership Document" signed during the Bouteflika visit outlined the general framework of bilateral relations as well as strategic cooperation in different fields. The two countries are known to have exchanged information on terrorism related issues. Algeria was wracked by an Islamist insurgency that claimed tens of thousands of lives in the nineties. Algeria like India has been lending a helping hand to the US in its "war on terror" by sharing information. Bilateral trade between the two countries has gone up to US$ 256 million in 2004. India was invited as an observer for the first time during the Arab League summit held in Algiers in 2005. The nineties have been a bad decade for Algeria due to domestic upheavals. The country has now slowly limped back to normalcy and is registering a steady economic growth. Algeria's vast hydrocarbon reserves have made it Africa's second largest economy after South Africa. Indian oil and gas companies are doing good business in Algeria.

Algiers continues to remain committed to the Sahrawis in their quest for statehood. But the preoccupation of the Algerian government with its home grown Islamic militancy since the early nineties has made it focus more on domestic issues. The collapse of the Soviet Union had made both New Delhi and Algiers radically alter their foreign policies. The fight against terrorism in Algeria had the support of the West. Algeria on its part has also become a key ally of the US in its so called "war on terror". In the process, Algiers and Washington have become diplomatically much closer. Algerian diplomacy may have played a part in influencing key policy makers in the US. In June 2004, The US Congress had supported the idea of a referendum in Western Sahara in recent years. On June 30, 2005, the Congress while passing the Foreign Operations Appropriation Act, 2006, requested the Secretary of State to report on steps being taken to ensure that a referendum will be held in Western Sahara.

The withdrawal of Indian recognition to the SADR did not go

down well with many AU members, especially those countries that had waged long liberation wars against their colonizers. Diplomats from these countries were perplexed by the action coming from a country that had supported them wholeheartedly during their quest for independence. The issue of Western Sahara has been described as the last unresolved colonial problem. The Algerian President in his address to the UN General Assembly this year said that "there is no other lasting solution to the issue of Western Sahara than its lasting decolonization in line with international legality, a task that should by undertaken by the Organization as an irrevocable responsibility and through the exercise of an exclusive authority".

Western Sahara: Recent Developments

The Western Sahara issue had figured prominently on the sidelines in the recently concluded NAM summit in Havana. Some countries, including India helped in watering down the resolution on Western Sahara so that a consensus could be achieved. South Africa is the latest country to extend recognition to the SADR and is now one of its strongest supporters in international forums. Meanwhile in New Delhi, there are no indications of a rethink on the issue. Interestingly, the Left Parties have not yet brought up the issue with the government though they have links with the Polisario Front. The Left was very vociferous in condemning the NDA government's decision to withdraw recognition from the SADR.

In April, 2007, the UN has come forward with yet another initiative to find a lasting solution to the Western Sahara issue. The UN Security Council in a unanimous resolution urged Polisario and the Kingdom of Morocco to talk without any preconditions. Both the parties have agreed to do so. The UN has also renewed the mandate for its peacekeeping force in the region. The Security Council's move came after Morocco and Polisario had both submitted rival plans for the future of the territory. Morocco had once again re-stated its position that talks should be confined to self-rule for the territory and not independence. The

Polisario restated its position that a referendum should be held at the earliest with full independence as an option.

The UN Security Council Resolution "calls upon the parties to enter into negotiations without preconditions and in good faith---with a view of achieving a just, lasting and mutually acceptable political solution, which will provide for self-determination for the people of Western Sahara". The UN resolution had gone to the extent of hailing the new Moroccan proposal of granting substantive autonomy to the Sahrawis as "serious and credible efforts" to end the long drawn out crisis. The Security Council merely took note of the Polisario proposals that talked about meaningful independence for the Sahrawi people. The Polisario Front despite initial misgivings about the wording of the UNSC Resolution has backed the new initiative. There is also a noticeable mellowing of its rhetoric towards Rabat. Polisario in one of its recent statement has indicated that an independent state of Western Sahara will not be averse to sharing its resources, including its huge fishing resources and offshore oil, with Morocco. However Morocco remains inflexible on the demand that a free and fair internationally supervised referendum on statehood for the Sahrawis be held.

Rabat is insisting that the proposed talks with the Polisario will be only confined to the subject of autonomy. The Moroccan government had in a statement said that the proposed autonomy referendum only envisages giving Sahrawis "control over their affairs through legislative, executive and judicial institutions under Moroccan sovereignty. Morocco called for "negotiations for a political solution acceptable to all parties". Polisario, on the other hand wants the Sahrawis to choose between full independence, autonomy or integration with Morocco. The 1991 ceasefire had only promised a referendum. The recent development therefore can be therefore construed as a diplomatic triumph of sorts for the Moroccan government. According to media reports in the region, the Moroccan plan has strong backing from Washington and Paris. US officials have been saying that the political stalemate in the region is not helping the so called war against terrorism. Islamists groups have staged big attacks in Algeria and Morocco in the first half of 2007. The US Undersecretary of State, Nicholas Burns, released a statement hailing the "Western Sahara initiative", describing it as "a serious and credible proposal that would lead to real autonomy for the Western Sahara". The US President, George W. Bush, has openly backed the Moroccan position on Western Sahara in the past. On December, 2003, the American President had in a message to the Moroccan King, expressed understanding of the "Moroccan people's sensitivity over the Sahara issue" and said that the US does not seek to impose a solution.

Algeria has welcomed the new UN resolution. The statement issued by the Algerian government in the last week of April said that the resolution which was unanimously passed reaffirmed the right of the people of the region to opt for self-determination. New Delhi seems to have detached itself from the Sahrawi cause. Algerian diplomacy has let the Sahrawi issue be put on the backburner in so far as bilateral ties with India are concerned. New Delhi has said that it is closely following the situation in the region. New Delhi has expressed its support for the UN settlement plan. But with some forward movement on the issue, New Delhi and the international community may be forced to take a stand. In the third week of May, the international media reported that the Moroccan authorities came down with a heavy hand on Sahrawi activists in Laayoune, the capital of the occupied territory and on Moroccan University campuses. Prominent Sahrawi human rights activists have been arrested. Sahrawis in Laayoune had been staging demonstrations calling for independence. These developments do not augur well for the holding of a vote to freely determine the future of the territory.

The UN has indicated that it would not like to remain deeply involved in resolving the issue. It has made clear to both parties- Morocco and the Sahrawis that the responsibility to find a solution to the dispute now rests with them. The UN Secretary General however has said that any solution must be found within the framework or under the auspices of the UN. The Personal

Envoy of the UN Secretary General to the region has suggested more Algerian involvement so that the latest round of negotiations has better chances of success. The newly appointed UN Secretary General, Ban Ki-Moon, in his statement has also mentioned the 1975 ruling of the International Court of Justice which had concluded that the rules of decolonization and self-determination should apply to Western Sahara. The Secretary General's view is that a solution to the impasse on Western Sahara can only be achieved if the concerned parties worked to achieve a mutually acceptable compromise based on the principles of international law and "current realities".

15

Social Development, State and Globalisation: A Comparative Study of Egypt and India

Sebastian N

Introduction

The question of the retreat of state from social sector has been a matter of concern for social scientists ever since the mid-eighties with the process of globalisation picking up momentum. Though there is no single accepted definition of globalisation, it is generally identified as the process which integrates economies and societies through cross country flows of information, ideas, technologies, goods, services, capital, finance and people. The major societal features of the process of globalisation in the late 20th century are the high government spending with low priorities to social development, the absence of any linkage between the revised trade policies and social development plans like health care poverty alleviation and the failure of state of convert economic growth into total welfare of the people. However, the social implications of the process of globalisation are to a large extent linked to the policies and programs adopted at the national level.

The origin of globalisation is linked to the growth and spread of capitalist relations of production from its developed centers. It refers the complex and complicated process of world wide economic, social, cultural and political expansion and integration. It has enabled the transnational flow of capital, production, finance, trade, ideas, images, people and their organizations across regions, nation states and cultures[1]. It projects the dynamic and intensifying networks of global consciousness, system, interdependence human interaction and societal changes with far reaching consequences[2].

The historic failure of the socialist project and the expansion of capitalist economic system were the two major developments, which intensified the process of globalisation. It strengthened the role of non-state actors in national and international sphere. Many new agencies have entered into the sphere of social development in order to fill the vacuum, which was created by the retreat of state from social sector. Internationalization of capital and the new paradigm of market-led development have reduced the role of state in economic and social sector. The erosion of the autonomy of the state was the result of increasing involvement of the non-territorial capitalist forces in the economy of nation states[3]. The role of state is changed from the major player in the economy to 'a partner, catalyst and facilitator'[4] of globalisation and market economy. It is accused that the new role of state promotes world wide unequal development by supporting privatization insensitively[5].

This paper undertakes a comparative study of the impact of globalisation on the role of state in social development in contemporary Egypt and India. They follow totally different political systems and have different political development patterns. Hence, the study compares the performance of alternative regimes in India and Egypt coping up with the project of globalisation. The paper intends to explore whether the systemic differentiation in political structures influences the pattern of social development.

On the basis of the social development experience of Egypt and India, the paper analyses how the political structure of a country regulates and mediates the pace of globlisation, taking into consideration its social impact. In the case of Third World, the weakness (or absence) of effective civil society institutions and the inefficient and underdeveloped political institutions have historically enhanced the domination of state/ruling elites in the socio-political and economic domains of the society. The state maintained its character as progressive nationalist[6]. Since the hegemonic role of state put itself in a place above and outside the society, the sudden retreat of state from social sector has reflected in the society in the form of social tensions and deprivation of a huge population who stay at the lower strata of the society. The concepts like social capital was popularized by the prophets of market economy/world capitalism as a viable alternative to state in the social sector which has failed to address the fundamental structural issues under lined in the societies of Third World.

An attempt is made to analyse the concept 'social capital', its origin and development as an alternative to state in the new context of trade liberalism with a special emphasis on the problems and significance of the concept in the socio-economic and political realm of these two states. It is a concept developed by Robert Putnam et al, and a major theme in the development package proposed by the World Bank in the last decade of 20th century. This underscores the creation of networks and relationships, social interactions and certain other features of social organization to facilitate the coordination and cooperation among people and within societies for mutual benefits and peoples' participation in socio-political arena through village committees and development associations which promotes social development.

Egypt and India had introduced independent development program in the same period, early 1950s, with an extremely interventionist role of state. The economic and social policies introduced by these states were more close to socialism – Etetisme in Egypt and mixed economy in India – and the states tried to ensure basic social services to people. An ideological shift was started roughly in the same period-during mid-1970s in Egypt and late 1970s in India – that became rigorous by 199s with substantial changes in the economic policies and developmental orientations of these two states[7]. The process of economic reforms culminated by the introduction of Structural Adjustment Programme (SAP) agreement signed with IMF and World Bank in the year 1991.

On the whole, the paper explores the problems and prospects

of the new development pattern proposed by international economic institutions as part of the present globalisation process and its impact in the social sector of Egypt and India. Socio-economic indicators like literacy, health, gender disparities, unemployment, social security, and the level of poverty and income inequality are used as variables in the study.

Globalisation and Social Development: Contemporary Debates

Globalisation has become an increasingly dominant theme in the contemporary socio-political, economic and cultural debate. The current globalisation can be considered as a product of technological revolution and the global restructuring of capitalism. The globalisation is coupled with the growth and spread of capitalist relations of production to the periphery states of world capitalist system. As the result of globalisation, more countries are getting incorporated into the global economy through the cross border expansion of trade and free transnational flow of capital, information and the advances in communication technologies.

Globalisation projects certain highly complex and contradictory set of institutions and social relations which intensity the infinite flow of goods, services, ideas, technologies, cultural forms and people across the borders[8]. It is a general understanding that the financial globalisation and the expansion of transnational flow of capital have redefined the role of nation states in social development[9].

Scholarly opinion differs on the impact of globalisation on human societies, particularly on Third World countries. Some of them emphasize on the progressive and liberating features of globalisation, other underline the discrepancy and uncertainty. Critics of globalisation argue that the process of globalisation marginalized the role of nation state in the developmental process. The capacity of national actors and policy makers to act independently is largely restricted. Thus, globalisation weakens the sovereignty of nation-states, particularly their role in economic decision-making. The control over capital and the conditional ties of global economic institutions have expanded the hegemony of the 'haves' over the 'have-notes' and increased the level of inequality in the distribution of world's resources between states. Precisely, according to the critics, the economic aspect of globalisation was merely the continuation and broadening of the logic of capital that was subjugated by the corporate and commercial interests of the world economy.

On the other side, the supporters of globalisation argue that globalisation is a natural phenomenon and the gradual outcome of the dynamics of global economy, technology and the redefined social relations in a largely integrated world. It is a force of progress, which enhances the process of modernization, human freedom, wealth and happiness by creating large-scale fresh economic opportunities, global citizenship, governance and by the elimination of borders and barriers between states[10]. They defend the logic of capital, competition and free market, which only can strengthen the national economics and build up social development in the developing countries. Since the states are not individual actors in the international system, no state can turn down to globalisation process. The relevance of interdependence in a highly integrated global economy virtually makes impossible for any country to keep itself away from the process globalisation. Globalisation is a fact, not an opinion, it is an inevitable process that goes beyond human control and developing countries have either to learn to take in it or simply drawn in the global crosscurrents.

In the era of globalisation, market forces gained upper hand in coordination and the control of the process of social development in the global context. Market forces emphasizes on sovereignty of free market, limited government intervention, individual autonomy and economic self-interest. The sudden entry of market forces has created a crisis in the social sector of most of the third world countries and it reflected in the form of increasing inequality against the marginalized sections of the society. This has reflected in India and Egypt in the form of ever-increasing inequality in the distribution of wealth/income and increasing real poverty, unemployment and ever deteriorating conditions of women and other marginalized sections[11]. The decrease in the social sector expenditure/subsidies and gradual withdrawal of state from social welfare policies is the direct fallout of globalisation in both states. It is important to note that the imbalance between economic growth and social development has remained unchanged.

The economic reforms aimed at financial consolidation and economic growth such as controlling of money supply and devaluation proposed by globalisation rarely address/include social issues. It remains as the major hindrance of social development, despite displaying high economic growth in these countries. The high government spending with low priorities to social development and the failure of state to convert economic growth into total welfare of the people were two major issues in the social development in developing countries during 1980s. The cut in the social spending of state is one of the major policy shifts, which badly affected the social development. Provisions of social safety nets were substantially reduced/removed from the state policies as a result of structural adjustment programme. The new rules in investment and the trade facilitation diluted the possibilities of more private investment in the social sector. Thus, the ground rules of market capitalism – competence, instability and inequality – had a perceptibly negative impact on the social structure and social development of most of the third world countries.

Both in Egypt and in India, the state-led development strategies came under increasing criticism by early eighties due to inefficiency, corruption and lack of cohesiveness. The increase of external debt and the unfavorable conditions in the balance of payment created a major crisis in the public sector. The regimes of these countries pursued World Bank instructions in order to overcome the crisis. This led to a fundamental change in the economic and development policies of these states during 1990-91. Egypt and India introduced many new programmes and policy reforms as part of the Structural Adjustment Programme such as decentralization of economy, intensification of market mechanisms, liberalization of foreign trade, activation of capital markets, deregulation, cutbacks in welfare programmes, privatization of public sector enterprises, devaluation of currency[12]. Those were the primary steps of the integration of national economy with the global market system.

The intensification of globalisation process in Egypt and India has led to the formalisation of the relation of the state with world market. It has rewritten the association between international financial institutions and private markets with states and domestic economy in the regional level. It has also created imbalances between regions and different social classes in the domestic level as well as international level. The role of state was redefined from the builder of economy to the facilitator of favorable conditions for the penetration of foreign capital and for the participation of private sector in the development process. It ultimately led to the gradual withdrawal of state as the sole agent of economic activities in these countries. As a result, the social sector, wherein the state intervention was very significant compared to the private sector was badly affected. The subsidy cuts and the sudden decline in the public spending eventually led to the decline of the standard of living of a huge chunk of the population.

State Structure, Social Development and Globalisation: An Overview

The social impact of globalisation is more connected with national policies and strategies. The systemic differentiation – the difference in the political system/political structure – and its impact on social development are the major concerns in the era of globalisation. Political structure of any country regulates and mediates the rates and flow of globalisation and its impacts on society. In most of the developing states historically, state is the major influential force and key player in reform process. The predominantly democratic structure in India allows participation of people in political process to a large extent where as the authoritarian regime in Egypt tightly controls/limits the citizen participation in state affairs. The nationalist populist regime in the post independence Egypt characterized as a bureaucratic polity where decision-making power concentrated exclusively at the top brass office corps and civilian bureaucrats like managers and technocrats[13]. It restricted any meaningful political participation or the development of effective and autonomous civil society organizations in the state. The exclusion of people from the political system has raised questions on legitimacy of the regime.

In India political freedom, which is guaranteed through the timely and open elections and the participation of people in the political process provide legitimacy to the system. Though the economic reforms were implemented within the frontier of democracy in India, the political and bureaucratic elites continued as the decision makers as it is in the case of Egypt in India, the regime could not capitalize the inherent advantages of a democratic system through incorporating the people into the system and ensuring their effective political participation. It is obvious that the large size and population of India and the heterogeneous character of society has raised obstacles in the effective implementation of development policies.

The experience of Egypt challenges the popular notion that 'economic liberalization will lead to democratization of the polity' in authoritarian regimes. The introduction of multi-partyism (1976) soon after the introduction of *infitah* (Open door policy) did not open the polity to a democratic space in the state[14]. The absence of a powerful social force from below that could promote democratization was observed as the major cause of this. The elections, easing of media censorship and invigoration of associational activity – that represents political relation – did not make any impact in the case of democratization. On the other hand, liberalization process continued through privatization, currency devaluation, rejuvenation of capital markets and reduction of subsidies on basic consumer goods[15]. The government controlled political party – National Democratic Party

– miserably failed in interest articulation, interest aggregation and political socialization of the masses. Instead it simply strengthened the ruling elites by strengthening status quo.

The Structural Adjustment Programme (SAP), which is the core component of globalisatoin, is extremely important in the social development debates. Both Egypt and India had followed state capitalism based on rapid industrialization and rigid control over foreign capital as the development policy before entering into the era of globalisation. The leading role of state in economic planning was the major feature of this pattern of development. But the SAP ruled out the possibilities of economic and social management by the state to a large extent by various types of deregulation, forcing the withdrawal of state from marketing and social distribution of resources, getting rid of process controls, elimination of investment controls, fiscal compression, cutbacks of public provisions for social services etc. It has ever since reduced the economic and social role of the state by targeting the states' arena of responsibility by targeting on public services and social security.

Egypt and India signed the paper with IMF in 1991, setting out policies to reduce public expenditure as a way of limiting the budget deficit, which had risen to an undesirable level by that time. Though it was the continuation of the ongoing reform process which started in 1970s itself, it was a more rigorous one. Many contractionary fiscal and monetary measures were taken to handle the situation. The negotiation with IMF not only ruled out the chances of more allocation for social sector but also reduced the government spending in social welfare. As a consequence of this, the share of subsidies in total government expenditure in Egypt went down from 31 per cent in 1985 to 25 per cent in 1997[16]. Similarly, in India it had gone down from 44 per cent to 38 per cent in the same period. Such a decrease has affected the level of social development in these states.

Egypt finished the first stage of SAP in 1993-94 with the introduction of some immediate policies to stabilize the economy, such as minimizing inflation, reduction of budget deficit, and control over balance of payment crisis. The privatization of public sector enterprises was started. The policies were successful in attaining macroeconomic gains. The budget deficit was reduced from 17 per cent of GNP in 1989 to 3.5 per cent in 1993 and the inflation rate from 21.2 per cent to 11.1 per cent in the same period. But this was achieved with high social cost and severely affected the standard of living of the people. The price level was increased almost 300 per cent and the unemployment rate went up to 17.5 per cent[17].

In India the new reforms led to a paradigm shift in economic and social development policies. Liberalisation process led to the removal of import restrictions, reduction of external trade controls, introduction of free markets in food grains and cutting down of subsides[18]. The social welfare subsidies were went down from 2.3 per cent in 1990-91 to 1.3 per cent of the GDP in 1996-97. The fiscal adjustments meant to control balance of payments intrude heavily on public investment and welfare expenditure. The result was the sharp decline in the central government revenue expenditure in rural development projects and food and agriculture subsidies. The prophets of market accused that subsidies only encourage consumption rather than production. If the total subsidy was 2.2 per cent of the GDP in 1988-89, it was only 0.9 per cent of the GDP in the year 2000. During 1995 more restrictions were removed.

Economic liberalization led to greater inequalities in income distribution, unemployment and spread of corruption. Despite the fundamental difference in the state system both states committed to formulating policies to reduce public expenditure especially social service expenditure by way of limiting the budget deficit. Certain institutional changes were also introduced to facilitate market. The political and economic restructuring facilitated by the market economy reversed the populist policies of states[19]. A notable difference between India and Egypt is that it has created certain legitimacy crisis in Egypt due to the specific character of state.

As Asef Bayet observes, "The authoritarian nature of the state in the Middle East restricted meaningful political participation and the development of effective civil society organizations. The regimes etatist ideology and patrimonial tendencies rendered state the main, if not the sole provider of livelihoods for many citizens, in exchange for their loyalty. In etatist models, the state controls the bulk of the economic political and social domains, leaving little space for society to develop itself and for interest groups of surface, compete and act autonomously"[20].

In fact, it was a patron client relationship. Globalisation has changed this from state as the provider of social needs of the people to the facilitator of market economy. But the new policies implemented within the old structure were not competent to question the authority of the authoritarian ruling elite. The deteriorating social conditions created new platforms of mobilization but did not challenge the authority of the regime, any way.

It is observed that modernization process without centralization may eventually lead to the evolution of a democratic system in authoritarian states. The transfer of Egyptian economic system had taken place under a strong centralized regime. This is why the formation of certain representative institutions such as Consultative Council Peoples Assembly and political parties (identified as superstructures of any democratic system) could not make any significant impact on the overall political process[21]. Though some tension was created between state and certain interest groups, especially Islamic groups, especially Islamic groups, it could not undermine the overwhelming influence of the state[22].

In India, the reforms continued within the democratic political setup and the elites and the bourgeoisie substantially gained from the liberalization process. The forces of privatization easily subordinated the marginal opposition from masses with the support of major political organizations. Though the political left mobilized the people that also did not make any substantial influence due to its marginal influence in the country as a whole. At the same time the institutional inability of Indian state prevented it from an effective intervention and regulation of the market system in favour of the large proportion of the population, what China achieved in their economic reform.

Social Capital and Social Development

The concept of social capital refers the networks and relationships, which encourage trust and reciprocity and shape the quality and quantity of the societies' social interactions. It emphasizes on certain features of social organization such as networks, norms and social trust that facilitate coordination and cooperation among people and within societies for mutual benefit. Social capital is the aggregate of actual or potential resources, which are linked to ownership of a durable network of relatively institutionalized relationship of mutual association and recognition.

The concept has been developed through the writings of many social scientists such as Hanifan, Schultz, Coleman, Putnam and Bourdieu[23]. Hanifan emphasized on the importance of committee involvement in education[24], Schultz emphasized on the attributes of human beings such as their education, job, skills and health could be considered as social capital[25]. Coleman emphasized on rational action and relations among individuals and Putman on social organization for the functions of democracy. Pierre Bourdieu the major theorist of capital defined it as, 'the structures and processes that facilitate the power and privilege. It is the aggregate of the actual or potential resources, which are linked to possession of a durable network of more or less institutionalized relationship of mutual social contact and recognition[26]. His studies emphasized on the relations among classes and groups which could enhance social capital in a society. World Bank further popularized the term in the contemporary development/social development debates by emphasizing on the building of social capital as a mechanism to social development and alleviation of poverty. The World Development Reports – 1999-2000 and 2000-2001 have given special emphasis to social capital[27]. The WDR 2000-2001 emphasizes on the importance of building of social institutions in the creation of social capital. It emphasizes on the bonding, bridging and linking of social capital through connecting family members, neighbours, local organization and linking them with formal organizations.

According to World Bank,

Social capital refers the networks and relationships that both encourage trust and reciprocity and shape the quality and quantity of societies' social interactions. The level of social capital has a significant impact on a range of development processes. For example, in education, teachers are more committed, students achieve higher test scores and school facilities are better used in committees where parents and citizens take an action interest in children's educational well-being. In health services, doctors and nurses are more likely to show up for work and to perform their duties alternatively where their actions are supported and monitored by citizen groups. In rural development, villages with higher social capital see greater use of credit and agrochemicals and more village level cooperation in constructing roads. Social capital serves as an insurance mechanism for the poor who are unable to access market based alternatives. It is therefore important to facilitate the creation of new networks in situations where old ones are disintegrating[28].

In fact, the concept social capital sums up the dominant neo-liberal agenda characterized by reduction of state power and a parallel increase in the responsibilities of society itself. It is projected as the mechanism to fill the vacuum, which was created by the withdrawal of state from social sector, or to replace state by strengthening community networks.

Though social capital has attracted much attention in the development debates in the era of globalisation, many scholars criticized the concept and its ineffectiveness in tackling the fundamental issues of social development, especially in the developing countries. Scholars raised serious reservations on the feasibility of social capital as an alternative to state in the social development in such counties. According to John Harris, the exclusion of political parties from the World Bank's list of 'formal organisations', which strengthens social development, is the example of the de-politicisation agenda which is inherent in the social capital debates[29]. By restricting the participation of people in socio-political arena only through 'village committees and development associations' – totally apolitical groups – ultimately de-politicises the fundamental problems of poverty and unequal distribution in Third World countries.

It is pointed out that the depoliticisation of development is aimed at stabilizing the exiting power structure and power relations in those societies. This eventually aims to protect the interests of global capitalism by neglecting the conflict of interests of different classes and groups and power/class relations in the society. The critics of social capital also raised certain legitimate points on the viability of networks (of different groups), which strengthen social development. Once groups start playing the role of interest groups, as it happens in normal cases, the social capital of one become the social exclusion of other. That will automatically lead to conflict rather than co-operation between different apparatus of so-called social capital.

The application of the concept social capital in a wider level in the context of India and Egypt faces many basic problems. The drawbacks of the very concept of social capital in the context of developing countries, which were pointed out by Harris, is clearly reflected in Egyptian and Indian cases. The total neglect of the structural causes, which make deeper the inequality and other social maladies in those societies, remained unaddressed. The so called 'peoples networks and local organisations' which are supposed to improve the socio-economic conditions of the poor was away from the realities of such societies. The inherent structural limits and entrenched contradictions within the society, such as caste, class and ethnicity in India[30] and high regional and economic disparities and class contradictions in Egypt created a situation where the interface between different stake-holders such as workers, local governments, NGOs and the capitalists is unworkable.

The development of community activism and mobilization

through Community Development Associations is pointed out as the major step towards creating social capital. Though the social contribution of such groups is very high, the mobilization impact is very low. The people are not participants, but just beneficiaries. The fact of the matter is that in Egypt, each non-state welfare actor follows the same populist voluntary policies followed by the state where people remains merely a beneficiary, not an active player[31]. The absence of a democratic system prevented the political participation of people in Egypt whereas the immature functional democracy in India prevents the effective popular mobilization[32]. This raises the question whether the development of social capital can tackle the issue of social development through the effective mobilization of people on an apolitical forum remains as the major question of social development in such states.

There is a considerable shift in the character of the groups who participate in socio-political activities. Non-governmental organizations and cultural Islamic groups replaced the former class-based organizations like peasants groups, trade unions and peoples' co-operatives. Their activism is limited only with daycare centers, medical clinics, family planning services, vocational training and loans – the means just related to survival[33]. In short, the new agencies of development such as social capital substantially weakened the possibilities of a political resistance both in Egypt and in India. At the same time they failed to strengthen any effective participatory aspiration of the people in the system.

Social Sector Expenditure in Egypt and India in the Liberalisation Period

A Comparative Perspective: The socioeconomic indicators of Egypt and India show the major trends in the role of state in social sector during the era of globalisation. The gradual withdrawal of state from social sectors is the major policy shift accompanied by liberalization in both states. The major question is as to what was the impact of policy changes in social development was and whether it was uniform in both countries.

There is a gradual decrease in the public expenditure on education in India and in Egypt since globalisation. If the public expenditure on education in Egypt was 6.7 per cent of the GNP in 1990, it went down to 4.8 per cent (14.9 per cent of the total government expenditure) in 1996, which 4.6 per cent in 1998. In India public education expenditure was 3.6 per cent of the GDP in 1990, which went down to 3.1 per cent in 1995 and 3 per cent in 1996. According to World Development Report 2000, public expenditure on education in India was 3.4 per cent in 1994-96 and it went down to 3.2 per cent (11.6 per cent of the total government expenditure) in 1995-97[34].

Adult literacy rate remains almost equal in both Egypt and India, 50 per cent, in the beginning of the 1990s and it reached at 55.3 per cent in Egypt and 57.2 per cent in India by the year 2001. But the primary enrolment rate in Egypt is much higher than that in India, 74 per cent and 54 per cent respectively. Trends show that the number of school dropouts before reaching grade V is increasing in India since the introduction of globalisation. It was 38 per cent during 1990-91 period, increased to 41 per cent in 1992-95 and reached at 48 per cent by 1995-99[35]. Though Egypt gained considerable achievement in female adult literacy during the period it still holds the highest level of gender gaps in education in the Arab world in 1995, the ratio of literacy among males and females was 63.6 per cent and 38.8 per cent respectively[36].

The level of education was very low in India where 125 million males and 196 million females were illiterates in 1991. After 10 years, though the state recorded high rate of growth in education rate (52.21 per cent in 1997 to 65.38 per cent in 2001) the numbers (in absolute terms) remained almost the 296 million[37].

India always spent far less compared to Egypt in health sector before and after the introduction of liberalisation. As the data reveals, the average public expenditure on health during the 1990-97 period was 1.7 per cent of the GDP in Egypt and 0.7 per cent of the GDP in India. In India it was less than 1 per cent of the GDP for the last three decades. When Egypt spent 0.8 per cent of the GDP in 1990-91 and 1.8 per cent in 1996-98 periods in the health sector. It was only 0.2 per cent and 0.6 per cent in India respectively[38].

Owing to the high spending, Egypt has achieved substantial progress in the health sector. The peoples' access to health services in Egypt is almost full both in rural and urban areas. But in India such facilities are still not accessible to a considerable number of the population. Besides, the number of undernourished people is very less in Egypt –only 4 per cent-in 1997-99 compared to 23 per cent in India[39]. Similarly, Infant Mortality Rate was very high in Egypt in 1980-120 per 1000, but it was reduced to 51 per 1000 by 1997 whereas in India, IMR went down from 115 to 71 per 1000 in the same period. By the year 2000 Egypt achieved a great success of IMR of only 37 per 1000[40]. Egypt was always ahead of India as far as life expectancy is concerned. Egypt achieved a notable level of sanitation facility to 94 per cent of the population, fresh water supply to 95 per cent and immunization to 99 per cent by the year 2000. In India, sanitation facilities are available only for 31 per cent.

Health services are more effective in Egypt where it is accessible to 99 per cent of the people against only 70 per cent in India. The situation is more pathetic in villages. While Egypt has successfully eradicated diseases like Malaria and T.B, it is still remaining in India. There is no impact of reform in the grass root level.

India spends lion's share of its health spending for population control measurers. The result, only in the population growth rate India marked better results that Egypt where it is 1.9 and 2.2 respectively during 1975-2000 period[41].

During the 1987-2000 periods the average per cent of the people below poverty line was 22.9 per cent in Egypt and 35 per cent in India. Reduction of poverty was very high in 1970s and 80s in India. Incidence of poverty was reduced from 54.3 per cent of 1972-73 to and 34.1 per cent by 1989-90. The success of India in reducing poverty in 1970s and 1980s halted in 1990s[42]. The reduction of poverty rate has never gone below this level.

In Egypt the rural poverty has increased from 16.11 in 1981 – 82 to 23.3 per cent in 1995-96[43]. The relative neglect of agriculture and the cut in rural development expenditure led a fall in rural income of both states. The notable aspect of poverty in these countries is the high rate of both rural and urban poverty in India compare with Egypt.

The chronic poverty is high among casual agricultural laborers and tribal committees[44]. The National Sample Survey rounds up 1997 shows greater increase in rural poverty in India. Similarly the Report of Indira Gandhi Institute of Development Research 1999-00, shows that in the 1991-94 period-urban poverty declined by 4 per cent and rural poverty increased by 2 per cent in India[45].

The growth promoting polices may not necessarily lead to reduction of poverty because it generally widen the gap between rich and poor within and between states. The unequal growth reflects in the pattern of distribution. Though the data shows an amazing picture of reduction in poverty, the real poverty has not decreased in its real sense because the number of poor does not decrease and the poor became poorer[46]. The suicide of farmers from different parts of India clearly shows this unequal development pattern.

The government subsidies were the major instrument through which the distribution was managed in the pre-globalisation era. There is a massive cut in subsidies since the introduction of globalisation. In Egypt the rate of subsidy as a per cent of GDP went down form an aggregate 13 per cent of GDP in 1980s, to 2 per cent in 1993[47]. The cut in subsidies increased the price of essential commodities in Egypt from 50 to 170 per cent. The subsidy has been distributed as the food subsidy 4.8 per cent of, social assistances 0.15 per cent electricity subsidy 1.7 per cent water subsidy 4.9 per cent and education subsidy 4.9 per cent[48]. According to the World Development Indicators 2000, the total public expenditure in social development during 1990-98 in Egypt was only 1.8 per cent of the GDP. In 1985-90 periods, the social security benefit expenditure alone was around 1.1 per cent of GDP in Egypt. In India, the share of subsidies in the central expenditure of the government went down from 32 per cent in 1980s to 15 per cent in the year 1997[49]. This severely affected the social security programs of the state. Reduction of government expenses in medical care and public health decreased the level of social development. The introduction of certain new security networks/safety nets like JRY, TRYSM, and IRDP had very limited impacts in addressing such issues.

Globalisation has promoted economic openness and growth but it worsened inequality in the global level[50]. The collapse of social safety nets, which were ensuring the distributional management by state, was the major reason of distributional disparities. The studies of Richard Adams shows that in Middle East "the economic growth had no statistical impact on income distribution, inequality may rise or fall with economic growth"[51].

The distribution of income and the social development are two related phenomenon. There is a considerable gap in income distribution between and within the states and this gap is increasing since the introduction of reforms. According to the World Development Report 2002, the income distribution remained unequal in both India and Egypt.

The trends show that the level of income distribution is more equitable in Egypt compared to India. In 1997 the number of the people whose per day income is less than US$ 1 is only 7.6 per cent of the total population in Egypt. But in India it was very high – 44.2 per cent (WDR 2000-01) In Egypt, the poorest 20 per cent of the population possessed only 9.8 per cent of the total income during 1987-98 period and the richest 20 per cent occupied 39 per cent. The distribution was more unequal in India where the poorest 20 per cent obtained only 8.1 per cent of the total income and the richest 20 per cent got 46.1 per cent. This considerable gap in the distribution is the result of the new policies and it remained as the major reason of poverty. In 1991, the poorest 10 per cent got 3.9 per cent of the total income and 20 per cent got

8.7 per cent in Egypt. The richest 10 per cent got 26.7 per cent of the total national income and 20 per cent occupied 41.1 per cent. Similarly, in India the share of the poorest 10 per cent in the national income was 4.1 per cent and the 20 per cent was 9.2 per cent in the year 1994. It was 25 per cent and 39.3 per cent in the richest 10 per cent and 20 per cent respectively[52]. The overall trends in both states show that both in Egypt and India income distribution is becoming more unequal and poverty is not reduced substantially.

Unemployment and decline in the wage were other major fallouts of globalisation process. Both in Egypt and India, rate of unemployment has been increased with the implementation of SAP. According to the ILO Report 1993 unemployment in India as 22 per cent. In Egypt the unemployment rate was 11.1 per cent in 1995. Though there was a marginal increase of 0.86 per cent in the wage in formal sector; there was a 2.53 per cent decrease in wages in the informal sector in India. Moreover, the inflationary pressures lowered the real wages. Institutional policies of multilateral organizations have resulted in more deprivation of the poor by loss of employment opportunities. The neglect of agriculture sector further intensified the unemployment crisis. The withdrawal of employment security provisions and the cutting of labor force in different government sectors have intensified the employment crisis in both states.

Gender Disparities, Development and Globalisation: An Examination

Status of women and their socioeconomic condition are important factors in the measuring social development of any state. It is observed that the forces of globalisation disproportionately affected women at two broad levels (a) the immediate experimental level – lowering of wages, reduction in the access to land and resources, inadequate food, greater work load etc. (b) structural or strategic level – long term disempowerment of women like illiteracy and the feminisation of poverty[53]. Marginalisation, disempowerment and discrimination against women in local, national and global level was a major product of present globalisation based on market. The market system, which is based on the purchase capacity of a person, is inherently against the interests of the weaker sections in the society. It encourages feminisation of labour through underpaid labour in the formal sector, cheap labour in the informal sector and unpaid household labour at the home. The result is the extensive exploitation, economic marginalistation and chronic poverty of women in all sections of the society[54].

The cuts in social spending, hit the women very badly due to the decrease in education and health facilities, rising prices, loss of job security, lack of health care and rising social tensions. According to Heba Nasser 'women are the first victims of economic changes because the structural adjustment program concentrates mainly on the reallocation of resources to achieve stability and growth rather than the micro economic issues of distribution and gender differentiation[55]. These policies are biased which do no consider the specific conditions of woman in labour market.

The HDR 2000 placed Egypt in the 99th position and India in 108th position on the basis of gender related development. However, there is a clear gender gap both in India and Egypt in every sectors of social development. Among the 271.8 million illiterate adults in India a large chunk – 169.3 million – were females in 1992. The gender disparity in adult illiteracy rate was same in Egypt and India during 1992, which was 66 per cent among women. According to the Human Development Report 1998, female literacy rate increased to 41.8 per cent in Egypt and 43.5 per cent in India. But still women were far behind of men in both countries. Egypt has the highest gender gap in the Arab world as far as the literacy rate is concerned.

The average marriage age of women is 21.9 in Egypt and 18.7 in India. But the condition of women in rural areas is no way match with this data in both countries. A study conducted by UNICEF in five Egyptian villages shows that early marriages and the number of girls being married to old man from oil rich West

Asian countries are increasing.

In Egypt the withdrawal of government from public sector/privatization badly affected the employment opportunities of women because maximum number of women were working in service sector[56]. The men women ratio in labour force has decreased to 100: 18.5 during 1995 – 2001. Unemployment rate of women is also very high in Egypt where it is 7.4 per cent among male and 23.8 per cent among female[57]. The female participation in economic activities was very high in Egypt before the introduction of reforms. It had declined from 31 per cent in 1988 to 14.1 per cent in 1998. According to Human Development Report (1998) the strength of women in professional/technical jobs was only 28.4 per cent in Egypt. The participation of woman in labour market decreased from 18.7 per cent in 1984 to 14.1 per cent in 1998. (Source Nasser, p100). The wage discrimination in the manufacturing sector was also very prominent in Egypt and India. If the average wage of men is 64 Egyptian pound per week, for women it was only 48 Egyptian Pound According to Human Development Report (1998) the strength of women in professional/technical jobs was only 20.5 per cent in India.

Most of the women labour is concentrated in agriculture sector in India. The collapse of agriculture has deteriorated the employment crisis in India. It led to limiting of employment opportunities of women labours in Indian villages. The sudden decline in family income also created male biased politics at household level, which discouraged the education and health services for women.

The participation of women in politics is also very less in both the countries. There were 8.9 per cent women in parliament of India and only 2 per cent in Egypt[58]. Globalisation has never done any qualitative change in the participation of women in politics, either in democratic India or in authoritarian Egypt. The representation of women in the government was also merely 6-7 per cent in both states.

The decentralization in India with reservation to women in the local level governing bodies was a revolutionary step. The legislation reserved 33 per cent of total seats for women in the local level governing bodies. But it miserably failed in the functional level. The feudal, patriarchic society successfully blocked the effective participation of women in such bodies. This did not contribute anything substantial for the empowerment of women, especially the village women in India.

An overview of the indicators in the World Development Reports, Human Development Reports and various other reports of Egypt and India give a clear picture of the pattern of social development in India and Egypt after the introduction of globalisation. Generally, there is a clear set back in social development both in Egypt and in India, as far as the indicators – poverty, unemployment and distribution are concerned. But it was more negative in India. The absolute material poverty has remained unchanged and the inequality in the distribution of income is increased. The improvement in the human poverty level is also insignificant because, a 30 per cent of the population remained Below Poverty Line and there is no considerable change in the poor in absolute numbers. It is evident that globalisation has not been accompanied by reduction of poverty and gender disparities. When certain indicators like life expectancy and infant mortality rates show positive trends, the unemployment and poverty remained unchanged and income gap has increased significantly.

Conclusion

The positive effects of globalisation in social development depend on how the process is managed nationally and internationally. The functioning of the system is more important than the structure of state. This is the reason why the local level democratic institutions in India miserably failed to achieve its social development goals. On the other side, the authoritarian Egypt made better results in many fields of social development when compared to India. It was observed that the poor performance of the institutions of governance, both in democratic India and authoritarian Egypt is the major hurdle of social development. It is not the structure but the administrative and institutional capacity of the state that really matters in the question of distribution. Whether social capital weakens or leaves unchanged citizen's participation in a political system would depend on the nature and capacity of the mediating agency – in developing countries the government and political parties. The popular mobilization in India at present is done by political organizations which, but do not have any place in the social capital debates.

The crisis in social development is mainly related to the problems in distribution of resources as well as the poor and inefficient performance of the institutions of governance. The market forces failed to address the underlying structural causes of low social development in such states. So, the question of building capacity of state is very relevant in the ongoing globalisation debates, though the same argument is against the grain of the Washington Consensus that proposes the retreat of the state. Widening of the scope of the apolitical grass-root level organisatons towards generation of social capital, though might be a benevolent objective, the desirability of the same at the neglect of the state led institutions and its democratization is questionable.

The apolitical concept of social capital has same impact in every state, despite the fundamental differences in the political system. The neglect of essentially antagonistic relationship between social classes and other groups in the Third World societies reduced the relevance of the concept in the wider context of Third World. Precisely, the factors such as wealth, status and education or community groups and social networks of social capital was not sufficient to address the social development problems of these societies.

The major problem faced by Egypt and India in the eve of globalisation is the mobility of the state to integrate large sections of the populations into economic process. The class configuration of the state helped the traditional power groups in mounting up wealth in the reform period. The historical absence of masses from political process has deepened this crisis in Egypt. India has failed to continue its ambitions economic liberalization with a human face. The retreat of state from populist policies (subsidy cuts, promotion of private sector etc.) very badly affected the people in the lower strata of the society. The slashing of wages, reduction in social expenditure, public employment and consumer subsidies led to the deterioration of the social conditions of the poor masses. It substantially weakened the poor and unprivileged and strengthened the groups who possessed wealth and power historically. Thus the constant economic growth, which was created by the new policies and reforms, benefited a small group of people who stay at the upper strata of the society. Both Egypt and India failed to maintain any balance between economic and social development policies. Moreover, the growth was achieved largely at the social costs.

The general trend in social development of India and Egypt shows that Egypt had done better performance than India in different sectors of social development. The democratic setup in India where participation of people in the political process did not make any positive impact as far as the conversion of economic growth into social development is concerned. The comparatively complex, but weak and fragmented administration and institutional capacities of the Indian state created hurdles in distributing the results of amazing economic growth with the poor people. Despite its poor performance in economic growth, Egypt has done better in social development and it has shown greater efficiency to facilitate globalisation and also in combine economic growth with redistribution.

Notes

1. Hill, Erind, "First World, Third World, Globalising World: Where is the Middle East" *Arab Studies Quarterly* Vol. 21, no.3, Summer 1999 pp.78-79.

2. See Ankie Hoogvelt, *Globalisation and the Past colonial World* (Basingstoke: Palgrave 2001). See also Augustus Richard Norton "Political Reforms in the Middle East" in Laura Guazzone *The Middle East in Global Change: The Politics and Economics of Interdependence Versus Fragmentation* (London: Mc Millan 1997).

3. Falk, Richard A, "Democratizing Internationalizing and Globalising" in Yoshikazu Sukamoto (ed.) *Global Transformation, Challenges to the State System* (Tokyo: United Nations University Press 1994).

4. World Bank, *World Development Report* 2001 (Washington: World Bank, 2001).

5. Amin Samir "The State and Development" in Held David (ed.) *Political Theory Today* (Cambridge: Polity, 1991) pp-306-302. See also Amin, Samir- *Capitalism in the Age of Globalisation*: The Management of Contemporary Society. (Delhi: Madhyam Books, 1997).

6. Hitti, Nassif, "The Internationalization of the State in the Middle East" in Yoshikazu Sumamoto (ed.) no.3, p93.

7. Robert Springborg "Agrarian Bourgeoisie, Semi proletarians and the Egyptian State: Lessons for Liberalization" *Journal of Middle East Studies*, vol. 22, no.4, 1990 p 447.

8. Kellener, Doughlas "Theorising Globalisation" *International Sociology*, vol.20, no.3, November 2002, pp 285-305.

9. Mark Beeson "Sovereignty Under Siege: Globalisation and the State in South Asia" *Third World Quarterly*, vol.24, no.2, 2003, pp 357-374. See also, Nita Rudra "Globalisation and the Decline of the State in Less Developed Countries", *International Organisation*, vol.52, no.2, Spring 2002.

10. Kellener, no.8.

11. See Dallimayr, Fred R., "Globalisation and Inequality; A Plea for Global Justice" *International Studies Review*, vol.4, no.2, Summer 2002, pp 137-144.

12. Baker, James William, "Egypt in the Time and Space of Globalism" *Arab Studies Quareterly*, vol.21, no.3, Summer 1999, pp1-11.

13. Adams, Richard H., "Evaluating the Process of Development in Egypt 1980-97", *International Journal of Middle Eastern Studies*, vol. 32, no. 2, 2000, pp 255-75.

14. Korany Bahgat, Rex Brynen and Paul Noble, *Political Liberalisation and Democratisation in the Arab World*: Comparative Experiences Volume II (Boulder: Lynne Rienner, 1998 for a detail picture of democratization in the region see also el-Sayyid, Musthafa Kamal "Third Wave of Democratisation in the Middle East", *Arab Studies Quarterly*. P 179.

15. James William Baker-no.12, p-23.

16. World Bank, World Development Indicators 2000 (Washington

DC: World Bank).

17. ibid. See also Adams, Richard H., "Evaluating the Process of Development in Egypt 1980-97", *International Journal of Middle Eastern Studies*, vol.32, no.2, 2000, 99 255-75.

18. Singh, Surendra "Paradigm Shift in Social Development in India: A Critique" *Indian Journal of Social Welfare,* vol. 60, no.1, January 1999.

19. Owen, Roger "State, Power and Politics: The Formation of Modern Middle East" (London, Routledge, 1992). See also Dreze, Jean and Amartya Sen, *India: Economic Development and Social Opportunities.* (New Delhi: Oxford University Press, 1995).

20. Bayat, Asef, "Activism and Social Development in the Middle East", *International Journal of Middle East Studies*, vol. 34, no. 4, February 2002, pp1-28.

21. Kazziha Walid "Egypt in the Balance" in Charles Tripp (ed.) Contemporary Egypt through Egyptian Eyes: Essays in Honor of P.J. Vatikiotis (London: Routledge, 1993) p 128.

22. Ibid, p 129-130. see also Margaret Levi "Social & Unsocial Capital: A Review Essay of Robert Putnam's Making Democracy Work "Politics & Society, vol. 24, 1996. pp 46-58).

23. for a comprehensive picture of social capital debates, see Stephen Samuel Smith & Jessica Kulynych "It May Be Social, But Why Is It Capital? The Social Construction Of Social Capital And The Politics Of Language", *Politics & Society*, vol.30, no.1. March 2002. p 159 and Blakeley, Georgina "Social Capital" in Georgina Blakeley and Valerie Boyson (eds.) *Contemporary Political Concepts: A Critical Introduction* (London: Pluto Press 2002) pp 198-201.

24. Hanifan, Lyda Judson, "Rural Community Center" *Annals of the American Academy of Political and Social Science* no. 67, 1916.

25. Schultz, Theodore W., "Investment in Human Capital" *American Economic Review*, vol.51, no.1, 1961.

26. Pierre Bourdieu, "The Forms of Capital" in John G. Richardson (ed.) Handbook of *Theory and Research for the sociology of Education* (Westfort: Greenwood, 1935) p. 242-243.

27. See World Bank, *World Development Report* 2000/2001 and 2001/2002. (Washington DC: World Bank). P. 128.

28. World Bank, *World Development Report* 1999/2000, (Washington DC: World Bank, 2000).

29. Harris, John, *De-politicising Development: The World Bank and Social Capital*, (New Delhi: Left Word, 2001).

30. Chelliah, R.J. and R. Sundarshan, *Income Poverty and Beyond: Human Development in India.* (New Delhi: Social Science Press, 1999).

31. There is a fundamental difference between Egypt and India that the so called superstructures of democracy such as institutions like parliament and elections are highly developed in India where as in the base level, it is yet to be developed. Both institutions and democratic practices are underdeveloped in Egypt.

32. Bayet, Asef, no. 19.

33. Lofgren, Hans, "Economic Policy in Egypt: A Break Down in Reform Resistance", *International Journal of Middle East Studies*, vol.25, no.3, 1993, pp 407-421.

34. World Bank, *World Development Indicators* 2000 (Washington DC: 2000) p 90 see also World Development Report 1999/2000.

35. *Human Development in South Asia 2001*, (Islamabad: Maqbul Haq Human Development Center). P. 46.

36. *Human Development Report 1999/2000,* (Washington DC: United Nations Development Program, 2000).

37. *Census of India 2001* (Government of India, 2001).

38. *Human Development Report 2000* (Washington DC: United Nations Development Program, 2000).

39. *Human Development Report 2002* (Washington DC: United Nations Development Program, 2002).

40. ibid.

41. ibid.

42. *Human Development in South Asia – 2001*, (Islamabad: Maqbul Haq Human Development Center). P 46.

43. *Central Agency for Public Mobilisation and Statistics 1998*, cited in Richard H. Adams "Evaluating the Process of Development in Egypt – 1980-97", *International Journal of Middle East Studies*, vol.32, no.3, 2000 pp 260.

44. Mehta Asha Kapur and Amita Shah "Chronic Poverty in India, Incidence, Causes and Policies" *World Development*, vol.31, no.3, 2003, pp 493-94.

45. India Development Report 1999-2000 (Bombay: Indira Gandhi Institute of Development Research, 2000.

46. For a detailed picture of the problems in data and measuring poverty see Ravallion Peter "The Debate on Globalisation, Poverty and Inequality" *International Affairs*, vol. 79, no.4, 2003, pp 739-53.).

47. World Bank, *World Development Report 1995* (Washington DC: World Bank 1995).

48. Shafik Nemat (ed.) *Prospects of Middle East and North African Economies from Boom to Bust and Back*, Appendix 9.1. (London: Mac Millan, 1998) p. 254.

49. Human Development in South Asia 2001, (Islamabad: Maqbul Haq Human Development Center) p 46.

50. The studies of World Bank show that the income distribution has worsened in most of the liberal open economies during 1997-2000. For details, see World Bank, *Globalisation, Growth and Poverty: Building an Inclusive World Economy* (Washington DC 2002).

51. Adams, Richard H., and John Page "Poverty, Inequality and Growth in Selected Middle East and north African Countries *World Development*, vol. 31, no.12, 2003 p 2030, and Eric, Thorbecke and Chutatong Charumilind, "Economic Inequality and Its Socio-economic Impact" *World Development* vol.30, no.9, pp-1477-1495, Sen, Amartya, *Economic Development and Social Opportunities* (New Delhi; Oxford University Press, 1995).

52. *Human Development Report 2000* (Washington DC: United Nations Development Program, 2000) see also *Human Development Report 2000* (Washington DC: United Nations Development Program, 2000) pp 237-238.

53. Guttal, Shalimal, *Women and Globalisation: Some Key Issues* 2000.

54. Esther Ngan – ling Chow, "Gender Matters: Studying Globalisation and Social Change in the 21st Century" *International Sociology*, vol. 18, no.3, September 2003, p 452-4.

55. Nasser, Heba, "Egypt Structural Adjustment and Women's Employment" in Eleanor Abdella Daumatol and Marsha Pripstein Posusney (eds.), *Women and Globalisation in the Arab Middle East: Gender, Economics and Society,* (London: Boulder 2002) p 95. For data on Egyptian women, see CAPMAS Census Data (Cairo: CAPMAS 1986, 1996), *Human Development Report of Egypt* (Cairo: UNDP and NIP, 1998), CAPMAS and *Social Fund: Monitoring Social Development in Egypt* (Cairo: CAPMAS, 1995).

56. Asaad, Ragui "Gender and Employment: Egypt in Comparative Perspective" in Eleanor Abdella Daumatol and Marsha Pripsten Posusney (eds.), *Women and Globalisation in the Arab Middle East: Gender, Economics and society,* (London: Boulder 2002) p 139.

57. CAPMAS (Cairo: 2002).

58. *Human Development Report 2002* (Washington DC: United Nations Development Program, 2002).

Part VII: Globalisation, India and Israel-Palestine Conflict

16

Contextualising Israel in India's Middle East Policy

P.R. Kumaraswamy

While the post-Cold War international order brought about far reaching changes in Indian foreign policy, the direct influence of globalisation has not been passive. During the Cold War years, issues like Third World solidarity and anti-imperialism provided a framework for India to perceive the international situation. Events and developments in far off lands were seen and presented through the prism consisting of Afro-Asian solidarity and opposition to colonialism and hegemony. These issues dominated and at times even determined Indian responses to international developments. With regard to the Middle East, the post-Nasser era deprived India of a secular and pan-Arab orientation but compelled its leaders to compete with Pakistan to maintain cordial relations with conservative forces that were on the ascendancy. While friendship with countries such as Ba'athist Iraq remained dominant, India lacked a cohesive regional policy.

The seismic developments of late 1980s and early 1990s fundamentally altered the status quo and India was presented with the freedom to pursuing a foreign policy without any overarching ideological framework or prism. As globalisation took shape, foreign policy became more a function of pursuing national interests. One could even argue that globalisation has not compelled India to evolve a regional policy towards the Middle East or alter its familiar preference for bilateral policy. This was only expected as the end of Cold War meant the end of ideology in International politics as well as East-West rivalry.

India's Israel policy has been the most controversial, contentious and acrimoniously argued issue in its foreign policy.

Initial disagreement over its reluctance to recognize Israel, soon transformed into a debate over the non-relations. For over four decades, the absence of formal ties dominated many foreign policy debates both inside and outside the Indian parliament. Even senior leaders like Jawaharlal Nehru privately admitted that recognition should have been accompanied by normalization of relations.

The belated decision of Prime Minister Narasimha Rao to establish full diplomatic relations with Israel in January 1992 was not universally endorsed. While the support for the move proved many sceptics wrong, normalization at first did not enjoy universal support. For the traditionalists, this move, which took over four decades to materialize, was a hasty, unnecessary and avoidable exercise. Gradually India managed to evolve resemblance of a consensus on this issue, with political parties of different colours playing an active role in promoting bilateral ties with Israel. Even groups, which initially opposed normalization such as the Communist parties and Janata Dal, slowly recognized the need to engage and cooperate with Israel. The visit of veteran Communist leader and the then Chief Minister of West Bengal Jyoti Basu in the summer of 2000 was a highpoint of the bilateral relations. This resemblance of national consensus soon disappeared following the outbreak of the al-Aqsa Intifada.

In other words, while issues such as non-alignment and closer ties with the erstwhile Soviet Union eventually enjoyed national consensus, the Israel policy continues to generate widespread debate within India. Influential segments of the domestic public have not fully accepted that normalization is beneficial to India. While their reasons and motives differed and at times were even questionable, it was essential to recognize that debates on bilateral ties evoke considerable opposition within the country. From politicians to academic to intellectuals many entertain strong reservations towards Israel *per se* which in turn colour their views regarding bilateral relations.

India has normal ties with so many countries and some of them have withstood the test of time and pressures. They however, do not evoke interests, passion and controversy. Many make headlines only when there was a major state visit or a political row. Israel is an exception. Both before and after normalization of ties, Israel has evoked enormous interest in India. Due to emotional admiration, religious animosity or ideological bandwagoning, many Indians have keenly followed the developments surrounding Israel and by extension, the bilateral relations. Relations with Israel attracts interests, debates and hence the need for some serious stocktaking.

How does one contextualize India's Israel policy within its overall policy towards the Middle East?

Bilateral Benefits are Real but Minimal

As with other similar ties, the bilateral relations offer considerable benefits. Israel has emerged as a major destination for scores of Indian officials, businesspersons, artists, academic and students. In the initial years, the central government headed by Rao was rather reluctant to pursue a high-profiled policy towards Israel. This proved useful to a number of state governments who opted to pursue Israel as a major destination for their economic agenda. The economic liberation enabled them to seek and secure a series of agreement with Israel in the field of agriculture.

Since 1992, the trade turnover has gone up many folds; from less than US$ 100 million in 1991-92, it has crossed the two billion dollar mark in 2006. India has emerged as the second largest export destination for Israel in Asia. Israel's trade with India for example, exceeds its trade with China. Likewise, if one excludes energy imports, Israel ranks among the top four trading partners of India in the Middle East. At times, it has even overtaken the much-hyped Indo-Iranian trade. Over the years, the trade has diversified considerably.

Far more serious progress has been made in the military-security arena. Initially India was extremely weary of admitting any military-related relations with Israel and despite pressures from the military establishment delayed the posting of a defence attaché in Israel. Since the late-1990s however, things have improved considerably. By early 21st century Israel had become India's second largest arms supplier and India, the largest export destination for Israeli arms. A host of developments facilitated this turn around and they include, greater Indian confidence in dealing with Israel, marginalization of Palestinian factor in India's relations with the Middle East, Kargil war, professional approach to security decisions, growing Indo-US proximity, ascendance of the BJP known for its traditional support for Israel and growing international concerns over terrorism. Soon areas like counter-terrorism, border management, early warning systems, small arms, ammunition, missiles and missile systems began to dominate the Indo-Israeli security agenda. The military-security ties have emerged as the most prominent and hence widely talked about dimension of the bilateral relations.

At the same time, one cannot ignore the obvious limitations. Unless there is a dramatic transformation, there is little scope for improvement in bilateral trade. In areas like information technology both are competitive players. The bilateral trade continues to be dominated by the diamond trade whose roots can be traced to late 1970s when there were no diplomatic ties. India is yet to benefit from tourism, a major passion for Israelis as India managed to attract only a small number of Israelis who periodically travel worldwide. Opportunities for Israeli investments are rather limited.

On much more serious level, bilateral ties with Israel offers little political capital for India. Unless handled carefully closer ties with Israel could become a serious liability as political parties tended to take anti-Israeli or pro-Arab stand, especially during local or national elections. As highlighted by the Indian stand during the Lebanese crisis in the summer of 2006, even parties like the BJP have been forced to adopt pro-Arab positions.

Israel moreover is not a major player whose friendship would further India's interests. As the result of Arab boycott policies, Israel is not a member of any regional gatherings. The proliferation of political groups since end of the Cold War did not benefit Israel and it was partly due to American arms twisting that Israel has been selectively admitted to the European groupings. Closer ties with Israel would not by itself bestow any political dividends. On the contrary, hostility towards Israel has become a prime focus, if not the rationale for some the regional organizations like the Arab League and the OIC.

Hence the real importance of normalization and need for a closer ties with Israel would have to be understood within the larger Middle Eastern context. A mere bilateral approach towards Israel would prevent India from identifying and benefiting from it.

Regionalizing Israel Policy

So long as an independent state is not established, the Palestinian problem would continue to be a major issue in the Middle East and by extension, in the international arena. Nothing short of a sovereign state with secured and guaranteed boundaries as visualized by UN Resolution 242 would settle the Palestinian longing for self-determination. Despite the obvious limitations and consequences, Israel would have to come to terms with the need for a Palestinian state. Likewise, an unequivocal Palestinian recognition of the Jewish State and their willingness to co-exist irreversibly would resolve the Israeli-Palestinian conflict. Any other attitude on the part of either side would be mere posturing and an unstated wish for the annihilation of the other.

At the same time, however, the Palestinian question has also undergone significant changes. It no longer evokes a near unanimous stand in the Arab world. The heydays of Palestinian issue being the common denominator for the faction ridden and personality oriented Arab League is truly over. Beyond vague verbal assurances and non-acted declarations, the League has not been effective in seeking a solution to the problem.

Furthermore, the attitude of some of the principal countries vis-à-vis the Palestinians underwent radical transformations and this is reflected in the diplomatic fortunes of Israel. Since the late 1970s, the political isolation of Israel in the region and world at large has been crumbling. Even though Arab states did not follow the footsteps of President Anwar Sadat, his visit to Jerusalem in November 1977 marked a new beginning.

The real progress however, had to wait until the Israeli-Palestinian reconciliation at Oslo in 1993. This was followed by Jordanian desire to come out of the closet and the willingness of other Arab countries to seek low-level trade and consular relations with Israel. Moreover, its public rhetoric and hostilities is accompanied by the Syria desire to seek a negotiated peace with Israel and so is Pakistan. Despite its fluctuating fortunes in the region, more countries of the Middle East are not averse to political dealings with Israel. Iran however, remains the lonely exception.

A number of states who were hospitable to the Palestinian people felt led down by the Palestinian leadership. The near civil war situation in Jordan (1970), prolonged civil war in Lebanon (1975-89), Iraqi occupation of Kuwait (1990-91) and the prolonged tension between Yasser Arafat and some of Arab leaders including Hafiz al-Assad, represent the negative picture. By being helpful to the Palestinians, some of these Arab states ended up almost losing their throne and others earned heartburns as their reward. The indifference of the Arab leadership to the prolonged incarceration of Arafat in his Ramallah headquarters towards the end of his life revealed that the Palestinian cause do not evoke universal endorsement, at least in Arab palaces if not in the Arab streets. The post-Arafat uncertainties and the victory of Hamas in the January 2006 elections merely complicated the picture further.

These indicate the limitations of India playing the Palestinian card to further its interests in the Middle East. Unlike the past, India would not be able to further its influence in the region by merely highlighting its support for the Palestinians. The issue is primarily a bilateral issue with the Palestinians and to a lesser extent a trilateral issue with the Israelis. Beyond that, India would not be able to play up the issue to further its interests.

Two, though never explicitly stated by Indian officials normalization brought about a fundamental shift in India's Israel policy. Until 1992, India behaved as if its support for the Palestinians would mean unfriendliness towards Israel. It used and availed every opportunity to highlight its consistent support for the Palestinians and its uncompromising hostility towards Israel. Since the later years of Nehru, New Delhi exploited various developments in the Middle East to underscore this duality and often was in the forefront of various anti-Israeli resolutions in the UN and other international forums.

This ended in January 1992. While the Cold War was not a factor in the prolonged non-relations, the end of the ideological divide smoothened India's desire to move closer to Israel. Without any explicit pronouncements, India recognized that the Israeli-Palestinian conflict was not a zero sum game. That it was possible to maintain close and cordial relations with both the parties to the conflict. That normalization does not dilute its commitments for an independent Palestinian state that co-exists with Israel. That newly found friendship with Israel would not mean India abandoning its traditional support for the rights of the Palestinians. What was different however was the new realization that Israel's 'wrong' policies towards the Palestinians should not be an impediment for India seeking closer ties with the Jewish State. This subtle and nuanced stand however, did not come out clearly in the manner in which India pursued its post-1992 policy towards Israel.

Three, if India were to benefit from its ties with Israel then it would have to develop a clearer policy vis-à-vis the peace process. Here India has two distinct options. One, it could recognize its limitations and choose to stay away from the periodic eruption of violence in the region. The Arab-Israeli conflict has remained elusive to innumerable peace initiatives. When even the US has been unable or unwilling to bring about any improvement, India could aspire to accomplish far less. If this becomes the official posture then India should completely stay away from the peace process except making occasional polite noises of both sides having to return to the negotiating table and resolve their differences politically.

Alternative, if it wishes to play a role even if minor, then India would have to treat all the parties with the same degree of respect. The absence of this principle raise questions about the American role in the peace process. The unwillingness of the Bush administration to treat Palestinian leader Yasser Arafat with respect and formally engage with him was one of the reasons for the failure of the Oslo process. By presenting a picture of too closely aligning with Israel, the US administration has alienated the Palestinians and thereby squandered any chance of influencing the Palestinian leadership.

India should avoid falling into the same trap. Given its past track record of complete identification with the Arabs on their conflict with Israel, New Delhi would have to be more cautious. The recent Lebanese crisis underscored the pitfalls of such a one-sided attitude. Though it initially adopted a balanced position that took into account the kidnapping of the Israeli soldiers, which precipitated the crisis, the Indian government gradually moved more closely to the Hezbollah. The unanimous resolution adopted by the Lok Sabha on July 31, merely talked of the civilian casualties in Lebanon while remaining silent of the civilian deaths caused by Hezbollah rockets in northern Israel.

If such a partisan view of the unfolding developments were not enough Prime Minister Manmohan Singh's special envoy Ambassador Chinmaya Gharekhan went a step further. During his visit to the region following the ceasefire in Lebanon, he was vocal in his criticisms of Israel and its brutalities in targeting civilian population in Lebanon. He conveyed India's sympathy and support during his meeting with the leaders of Lebanon, Syria, Jordan and the Palestinian President Mahmoud Abbas. Israel was notably absent from his itinerary.

Apparently, time and logistical constraints prevented him from going to Israel, the real party to the conflict whose cooperation would be vital if any mediation was to succeed. As happened with the delayed Indian statement on the withdrawal from the Gaza Strip in 2005, the External Affair Ministry has exhibited a lackadaisical approach towards such sensitive issues in the Middle East. Dealing with all the parties to the conflict on an equal footing is first lesson India would have to learn before embarking upon any ambitious moves in the Middle East.

Four, India would have to dispel any notion that closer ties with Israel are part of a larger conspiracy against the Islamic world. For decades, Pakistani commentators have warned of an Indo-Israeli conspiracy against the Muslim world. Some of the Indian critics of Indo-Israeli normalization have also viewed Rao's decision. According to the then Foreign Secretary J.N. Dixit, Human Resources Minister Arjun Singh warned the Prime Minister Rao that normalization would erode Muslim support for the Congress party.

As would be discussed, for long India viewed the problem of Palestinian and the Jewish aspiration for a homeland through an Islamic prism. Likewise, influential segments of the Indian right view the relations through an anti-Islamic prism. This is ably supported by similar views in Israel and other parts of the western world, especially in the US. For ideological, moral and domestic considerations, it would be suicidal for India to present the bilateral relations on an anti-Islamic platform. Such a posture would be morally untenable and political counter-productive.

Domestic Context

If one excludes South Asian region, Middle East remains the only other area, which evokes strong domestic resonance in India. The role of domestic determinants upon foreign policy has always been limited and is confined to a small segment of New Delhi-based intelligentsia. There are however, exceptions. India's policy towards its immediate neighbours does have a strong domestic constituency in the form of ethno-cultural groups. In varying degrees India's policy towards Sri Lanka is influenced by the domestic Tamil population; and the same is true of Bengalis vis-à-vis Bangladesh policy, Kashmiris vis-à-vis Pakistan policy and Hindu right vis-à-vis its Nepalese policy.

Likewise, the Indian Muslim population has taken a keen interest in the Middle East and often been vocal vis-à-vis the

Palestinian issue. As Theodore Wright observed in the early 1980s, the influence of domestic Muslims population upon India's Middle East policy could be compared to the role played by the Jews in shaping American policy towards the region.

Since the days of the Khilafat movement, the Indian nationalists and later on Indian leaders have viewed the problem through an Islamic prism. Mahatma Gandhi's views of Palestine being part of the historic *Jazzirat ul-Arab* symbolized the religious climes to the holy land and their political ramifications.

In the initial years the Congress party was trying to present itself as an *Indian and national* movement. Towards this end, it sought the support of the Muslims and Khilafat movement proved useful. In later years, the Palestinian issue became a bone of contention between the Congress and Muslim League and since 1947, the Indo-Pakistani rivalry in the Middle East has been fought over their respective support for the Palestinian cause.

The issue has also become a domestic issue with Congress party using it as a means of securing the support of the Muslims, especially during elections. A host of issues such as delayed recognition of Israel, absence of normalization, influence of Azad upon India's Israel policy, Rabat fiasco of 1969, Arjun Singh's opposition to normalization in 1992, Foreign Minister Jaswant Singh's admission of domestic factor (summer 2000) and Prime Minister Manmohan Singh's reference to Shia factor in India's Iran vote (September 2005) could be cited as illustrations. Moreover, in their private conversations with foreign leaders, many Indian leaders including Nehru and Morarji Desai referred to Muslim sentiments as a factor in India's Israel policy.

Hence, any meaningful discussion on India's Israel policy would have to consider the domestic dimension. Just as the anti-Muslim bias of the BJP would prevent that party from criticizing Israel, the pro-Muslim bias of the Congress party would result in India intensifying its criticisms of Israel. Since this is a given reality, no government in New Delhi would be able to free itself from the domestic pressures vis-à-vis Israel.

Second and more vocal source of criticism of India's Israel

policy comes from the ideological groups. Even though they were not fully reconciled to normalization in 1992, the disintegration and eventual disappearance of the Soviet Union diminished the ability of the Indian Left to block the move. Having been used to external political support and financial patronage, the Indian Left suddenly found itself orphaned. The willingness of communist China to move closer to Israel literally days before the Indian move meant that ideological rhetoric had few takers. The Indian Left could not ignore the willingness of the entire former eastern bloc countries to normalize ties with Israel. With great reluctance and hesitation, the Indian Left eventually joined the bandwagon when the veteran communist leader Jyoti Basu visited Israel in the summer of 2000. A resemblance of national consensus on Israel was slowly emerging.

This was soon shattered by the onset of the al-Aqsa intifada and the Indian Left reverted back to the Cold War jargons. Soon it made a host of anti-Israeli demands and they include the endorsement of the Arab move in Durban (August 2001) to equate Zionism with racism; opposition to the visit of Israeli Prime Minister Ariel Sharon (September 2003); withdrawal of Indian ambassador from Israel and expelling the Israeli ambassador as a sign of Indian disagreement with Israel's policy towards the Palestinians; suspension of military ties with Israel; and imposition of international sanctions against Israel over the Lebanese conflict.

It is essential to recognize that the Left occupies a pivotal position in India, especially in the present UPA ruling coalition at the Centre. Their support is vital for the survival of the government and as highlighted by the controversy surrounding the Indian vote at the IAEA over Iran's nuclear programme, their vocal opposition could generate unnecessary complications and avoidable tensions for India's foreign policy establishment. With coalition governments becoming the order of the day, the support of the Left is increasingly gaining importance. Hence, any Indian policy towards Israel would have to factor in the ideological dimension.

As highlighted by the visit of Basu, the vocal opposition of the Indian Left is linked to the vagaries of the Middle East peace process. So long as peace remained feasible, the Left was indifferent towards the growing ties with Israel. At the same time, any rapture in the process or return of heightened violence would compel the ideologues to return to their pre-1992 rhetoric, opposition and condemnation. The same is true of the domestic Muslim population. As long as the peace process is smooth and progressing, their criticism of Israel and by extension closer ties with Israel would remain muted. The periodic eruption of violence and counter-violence between Israel and the Palestinians however, compel the masses to join hands with the ideological Left in forming a 'secular coalition' against the Israeli atrocities, as happened in September 2003 when the Left-Muslim combination led the protests against the visit of Sharon.

Prognosis

- The bilateral dividends of Indo-Israeli relations are minimal.
- Domestic factors will continue to play an important role in India's Israel policy.
- Disruption of the peace process would complicate and undermine India's Israel policy.
- The true value of the 1992 decision lays in Indian ability to make Israel an integral part of its Middle East policy.
- Normalization has to be reflected in India's policy towards the peace process as well as its relations with key players in the region, especially Egypt
- Moving away from its tradition policy of merely seeking bilateral ties, India need to evolve an integrative regional policy.
- India needs to avoid presenting itself a partisan player and need to engage with *all* the parties to the Arab-Israeli conflict.
- The existing divisions within the Indian Foreign Office needs to be replaced by a overall Middle East division encompassing the West Asia and North Africa, Gulf and Iran (currently part of Pakistan-Afghan division) Divisions as well

as Hajj and Kuwait cells.

Intellectually Middle East debate in India has to remain free from jargons and name-calling of critics.

17

Globalisation and the Shift in India's Palestine Policy

Bansidhar Pradhan

The year 1991 marked the beginning of a new phase in India's Palestine policy. Towards the later part of that year one witnessed a discernible shift in India's Palestine policy. This paper argues that the significant changes in the international power structure in the post-Cold War era and the compulsions of the current phase of globalisation played key roles in effecting that shift. A corollary of this argument is that while during the Cold War period India's West Asia policy on the whole was articulated more in political, ideological and moral terms, in the post-Cost War period, economic, energy and security related issues have taken precedence over moral and ideological considerations. This is nowhere more evident than in India's Palestine policy. Further, an attempt will be made to show how both the US and Israel played a crucial role in influencing India's Palestine policy.

Cold War Phase

India's Palestine policy during the Cold War period can be divided into two phases: the first covered the period from 1964 – when the Palestine Liberation Organization (PLO) was created – till the June 1967 war and the second started thereafter and continued till mid-1991. During these two phases, India's policy was consistently in conformity with the basic tenets of the country's foreign policy which operated within the Cold War framework. The basic tenets were anti-imperialism, anti-racism, support for the liberation struggle against colonial domination, opposing military occupation of any one's land, solution of any international dispute through negotiation, a relentless struggle against neo-colonialism and, above all, support for the non-alignment movement (NAM) by leading it in every sphere of international politics. Even during these two phases there was a subtle difference in approaches while dealing with the Israel-Palestine conflict.

Till the six-day Arab-Israeli war of June 1967, India's pro-Palestine, anti-Israeli policy operated somewhat at a low key level. The existence of Israel as an established fact, the lack of proper coordination within the Arab world to tackle the Palestine problem and the character of the Palestinian movement and the PLO itself were probably the factors behind such an approach. In this regard, two things must be made clear. First, India became one of the earliest countries to extend formal recognition to Israel (September 17, 1950) despite considerable opposition from the Arab countries. Second, India, at this stage, regarded the problem of displaced Palestinians as a "refugee" problem and therefore directed its efforts to ensure the early return and rehabilitation of the Palestinians who had been uprooted from their ancestral homes.

The consequences of the 1967 war were far-reaching which changed the entire dynamics of West Asian politics. The most important among them was the radicalization of the Palestinian movement which passed into the hands of the leader of al-Fatah faction, Yasser Arafat. India remained in tune with these changes and responded accordingly. Indira Gandhi adopted an activist approach and India's policy became pronouncedly pro-Palestine and anti-Israel. She was often accused of following a pro-Soviet line towards the Israel-Palestine conflict.

Globalisation and the Shift

The coming to power of the Narasimha Rao government roughly coincided with a new era in world politics. At one level, the removal of a countervailing force brought an end to the decades-old bitter, divisive bipolar politics at the global level, but it also ensured the unquestioned supremacy of the only remaining superpower, the US, in international affairs. At another level, the ideas of free market and economic liberalization became a major tendency the world over. Broadly one can identify this trend with the economic dimension of the current phase of globalisation. Each nation had to adjust to this new reality by bringing about suitable changes in its foreign policy, both at the broader as well as specific sectoral levels. India was no exception to this.

Whereas during the Cold War period "divisions were created and alliances formed along ideological lines", during the post-Cold War era "economic competition" drove "international relations" leading to an intensification of competition over access to "vital economic assets" like oil and natural gas[1]. The Rao government faced critical choices. On the one hand, there were the Congress traditions of Nehruvian socialism (mixed economy), non-alignment and anti-imperialist thrust in foreign policy. On the other hand, was the "dramatic worldwide trend towards market reforms" and the necessity to integrate with the world economy[2]. There was also the lurking fear of "Pax American: the eagle spreading its wings" after the 1991 Gulf War[3]. India had to either adapt to the new reality by embarking on the path of economic liberalization and moving closer to the US or risk being isolated. The Rao government preferred the first option. Prime Minister Rao's statement before the Parliament on December 18, 1991 reflected this. While declaring that his government would use foreign policy as a dynamic instrument to further national interest, he listed out the priorities of India's foreign policy in the post-Cold War era. These were preventing any threat to India's unity and territorial integrity; ensuring geopolitical security by creating a durable environment of stability and peace in "our region"; creating a framework conducive to the economic well-being of the people by encouraging a healthy external economic environment; and trying to restore, internationally, the centrality and criticality of development in the evolution of political and economic policies all over the world[4].

The point that needs emphasis here is that the compulsions of globalisation and India's subsequent acceptance of the path of economic liberalization made it more dependent on the US as the latter exercised a decisive say in international financial agencies like the International Monetary Fund (IMF) and the World Bank (WB). In the initial period India needed loans from these institutions. The US went "out of its way" to help India avail US$ 1.8 billion credit from the IMF. Further, India was hoping to receive US$ 400 million from the IMF's Contingency and Compensatory Financial Facility to meet its increasing oil import bill in the wake of the Iraqi invasion of Kuwait. But with the US intervention, India received US$ 1 billion and became the first developing country to avail a loan from this source. Another US$ 777 million standby credit was also given to India, which was negotiated with a record time of six weeks. In November 1991, the IMF approved another US$ 2.2 billion standby loan arrangement. In the following month, a US$ 900 million credit and loan package was cleared by the World Bank[5].

During the last sixteen years, Indo-US relations have undergone a sea-change, thanks to globalisation. This becomes evident from the multi-faceted, ever growing techno-economic cooperation between the two countries. The much-talked about, and somewhat controversial, Indo-US nuclear deal has clearly shown the extent to which both the countries have moved closer in the post-Cold War era. Therefore, it would not be wrong to assume that the US factor has been playing a major role in influencing India's foreign policy orientation in the post-Cold War era. This has been nowhere evident than in India's West Asia policy which witnessed a fundamental shift in more than one way, specially with regard to its Palestine policy. As a result, in terms of pattern, during the post-Cold War era one witnessed the focus shifting away from Palestine, Egypt, and Iraq that formed the core during the major part of the Cold War period. Instead India sought to build a strategic relationship with Israel. Let us discuss the shift in India's Palestine policy.

The first sign of a change in India's anti-Israeli policy appeared in the little known meeting between Prime Minister Rao and Joseph Leibler, a prominent Jewish leader, during the third week of November 1991. The discussion centred around the possibility of establishing diplomatic ties between Israel and India. Rao's response was "positive and pragmatic". Further, the Jewish leader's talks with the Indian Prime Minister was facilitated by the US[6]. The Leibler-Rao meeting was followed by a more visible gesture of India's softened stance towards Israel when India voted for the revocation of the UN Resolution 3379 of November 1975 that had equated Zionism with racism[7]. In this case too, there were reasons to believe that the US factor influenced India's decision. However, the most active US role in facilitating a breakthrough in Indo-Israeli ties came to the fore when an official-level meeting, the highest till then, between the Israeli representative, Joseph Hadass, and India's Deputy Chief of Mission, Lalit Mansingh, took place at the Indian embassy in Washington during the second week of January 1992. Around this time the PLO leader Yasser Arafat who in earlier times visited India more frequently than any other world leader, was having difficulties in getting an audience with Prime Minister Rao[8]. Arafat finally met Rao during the third week of January 1992. During his talks, the PLO leader counseled India to go slow in establishing ties with Israel[9]. However, by then India's course of action had already been decided. Within a few days of Arafat's departure, India announced its decision, on January 29, 1992, to establish full diplomatic relations with Israel[10].

A section advocating normal and friendly relations with Israel had always been there in India from the beginning. This was mostly due to the persistent lobbying by the Zionists in India. India, because of its importance in world politics, never escaped the attention of the Zionists[11]. However, during the Cold War period, the pro-Israeli section in India constituted a microscopic minority in the face of a broad anti-Israeli consensus within the country. With the changing international scenario subsequent to the end of the Cold War, the views of this section gained prominence. Emphasis on pragmatism constituted the basis of the arguments put forward in favour of Israel. There were three main arguments. First, by establishing diplomatic relations with Israel,

India would be in a better position to involve itself in the West Asia peace process and thereby influence the Israeli policy in favour of the Palestinians. Second, it was argued that in concrete terms there were many advantages for India in establishing ties with Israel in specific areas like military modernization, agricultural innovation and global Jewish investment. India could also benefit in combating terrorism in the states of Punjab and Jammu and Kashmir from the Israeli experience and expertise in this regard. Third, the emergence of an Islamic bloc in world politics made it essential that India change its pro-Palestine stance and move closer to Israel. While the first two arguments were nothing new the third one was built upon a threat perception, basically spearheaded by the US in the post-Cold War period[12].

Even though it would be an extreme statement to maintain that India has totally abandoned the Palestine cause subsequent to the high profile and fast developing robust partnership between Israel and India, there has been an evident dilution in India's traditional consistent, unequivocal and strong political support for the Palestinian struggle against Israel. From one of total identification with the Palestinian struggle for their legitimate rights to an independent statehood by unequivocally opposing Israeli policies against the Palestinians at every multilateral for a during the Cold War period, India has come to adopt the so-called policy of equidistance in the Israel-Palestine conflict during the post-Cold War era. Even this policy has often been marked by a subtle tilt towards Israel, specially during the BJP-led NDA regime on the grounds of internal security and anti-terrorism cooperation. In a way the dilution in India's Palestine policy has been built into the very logic of India's growing strategic relationship with both Israel and the US. After the establishment of diplomatic relations with Israel, India's Palestine policy operated at two levels.

One, through public statements issued from time to time, often in a customary and ritualistic manner, it sought to give an impression that the coming closer to Israel has in no way affected India's long-standing commitment to the Palestine cause; there was no dearth of diplomatic niceties and courtesies extended to the Palestinian leader Yasser Arafat and his emissaries at different levels. But in terms of concrete political action, India gave a clear message to the Palestinian leadership that it had little time to adopt an activist policy at the regional or international level in support of the Palestinian struggle, or against the Israeli occupation of the West Bank and Gaza Strip to facilitate the establishment of an independent Palestinian state. Its responses are now measured and nuanced, couched in broad generalities rather than any specific condemnation or even criticism of Israel's brutal policies in the occupied territories. Such a policy has been greatly facilitated by the spate of suicide bombing attacks by the Palestinian militant groups like the *Hamas* and *Islamic Jihad* (IJ) against Israeli civilians. India's muted response to the ongoing Palestinian *intifada* (uprising) against Israeli occupation and the siege of Arafat were some of the instances that reflected a lack of an activist pro-PLO policy in the Israel-Palestine conflict. Two, India sought to help the Palestinians through economic and humanitarian assistance, specially after the establishment of the PNA in pursuance of the Oslo principles. Let us briefly discuss these two facets.

The Rao government was somewhat on the defensive initially, both because of the heated debate within the country on the timing of its decision to establish full diplomatic relations with Israel, as well as the tardy progress on the Israeli-Palestinian peace track. During 1992 the only high-level official contact between India and the PLO was the Rao-Arafat meeting in Tunis on 20 November. This too was a mere courtesy call which Rao paid to the PLO leader during a stopover in Tunis on his way to Dakar for the G-15 Summit. There was no specific agenda even though Arafat was reported to have briefed the Indian Prime Minister about the peace talks in general[13]. However, the September 13, 1993 agreement between the PLO and Israel on their mutual recognition and on Palestinian self-rule provided a good opportunity to the Rao government to justify its decision to establish diplomatic relations with Israel and its balancing act in the Israel-Palestine conflict. This was reflected in a statement issued by the government in response to the agreement[14]. The statement sought to give an impression that India was deeply engaged in the West Asia peace process as a "credible interlocutor" and was in fact somehow expecting the breakthrough; this was an exaggeration. Indeed, India almost forgot to keep itself in tune with what afflicted the Israeli-PLO negotiation subsequent to the euphoria that had been generated with the signing of the September 13 agreement at the White House lawn.

The Hebron massacre, the inordinate delay in starting the autonomy process, the protracted haggling over redeployment of Israeli forces, non-release of Palestinian prisoners, frequent closure of the Israeli borders with the West Bank and Gaza, etc., were all instances of Israeli non-compliance with the letter and spirit of the agreement. India failed to even react properly to these developments, let alone take any political initiative to help the PLO. The assassination of Yitzhak Rabin in November 1995 changed the whole equation in the Israeli-Palestinian peace process. Benjamin Netanyahu, a Likud hardliner opposed to peace with the Palestinians, came into power in 1996. He refused to revive the stalled negotiations and took many unilateral steps that put the peace process virtually in limbo. India merely expressed "deep concern" at the developments "maintaining that unilateral steps not in conformity with the agreements...hinder the peace process"[15]. The signing of the Wye River Memorandum (after a lot of US pressure and personal intervention of President Bill Clinton) on October 23, 1998 provided some relief to India on the vexed issue. While terming the agreement "an important milestone" in the stalled peace process, India argued the "parties concerned to refrain from talking unilateral measures"[16]. The fact was that the Memorandum did not bring any substantial change in the ground realities due to Netanyahu's hostile policies.

The election of Ehud Barak as the Israeli Prime Minister in May 1999 raised hopes and revived the peace talks. Indeed a good beginning was made with the signing of the Sharm el-Sheikh memorandum (on September 4, 1999) which set out a three-phase final status negotiation in very clear terms. Subsequently, however, even Barak failed to make any substantial breakthrough in the peace process as he remained hostage to Israeli coalition politics dictated by the ultra-orthodox Shi'as and other small religious parties. The failure of the Camp David-II talks (in July 2000) almost sounded the death knell of the Oslo process. In the month of August 2000, the Palestinian leader Arafat, as well as Shimon Peres (then as Israel's Minister for Regional Development) visited New Delhi in quick succession. Peres' visit received a better coverage in the media than Arafat's. The ostensible reason behind their visits was to apprise Indian leaders of the developments about the West Asian peace process. But the real issue was the Palestinian ultimatum to unilaterally declare Palestine an independent state on September 13, 2000 if peace talks with Israel continued to remain deadlocked. Arafat sought India's support in favour of such a step while Peres tried to impress upon India about the dangers involved in such a declaration[17]. Israel succeeded in its attempt to prevent the unilateral declaration. In fact, Arafat did not get support from any quarter. This increased the level of frustration and restlessness among the Palestinians and ultimately became of the reasons for the outbreak of the second *intifada* in September 2000, though Ariel Sharon's (then as the leader of Opposition) highly controversial and provocative visit to the Temple Mount/Haram-al-Sharif complex became the catalyst.

During the initial months of the *intifada,* one noticed a peculiar trend. Both the PNA as well as Israel sought India's intervention in ending the escalating Israeli-Palestinian conflict. This was done formally through letters both from Barak and Arafat to Prime Minister Vajpayee. While Israel sought India's intervention in general terms – to exert its influence over the Palestinian leadership to "end violence" – the PNA suggested three specific areas in which India could play a role in resolving the crisis. These areas included India's initiative at the NAM and UN, its influence in the creation of an observer force or protection force under the UN auspices and, finally, India's efforts to ensure the implementation of the UN resolutions on the Israel-Palestine conflict[18]. The Palestinian leadership, thus, genuinely wanted India's intervention on the basis of its past record of total political support for the Palestine cause by firmly opposing Israeli policies. The Israeli move was merely aimed at preventing an outright support to the Palestinians by the Vajpayee government under domestic pressure. The Vajpayee government almost did the same by issuing statements that called for an end to the "cycle of violence" and "avoidance of provocation" and "return to the peace process", etc[19]. It needs to be mentioned that during this period the Vajpayee government was being criticized by the Opposition for not coming out "in clear-cut terms denouncing the Israeli government-sponsored violence". Further, the Arab envoys in New Delhi have also openly expressed their unhappiness over India's "less than whole-hearted condemnation" of Israel[20].

India's policy not to categorically criticize Israeli high-handedness against the Palestinians became more evident with the coming into power of the Sharon government in February 2001 and again in early 2003. The Sharon regime perpetrated the worst forms of violence against the Palestinians, leading to further brutalization and radicalization of the Israeli-Palestinian conflict. It needs to be mentioned that in the aftermath of the September 11, attacks, both the US and Israel very successfully projected the Palestine issue in negative terms globally, at the politico-military level. This was part of a broader strategy of globalizing the so-called war on terror in which those who were not with the US-Israel combine were treated as against it. In the process the Palestinians were portrayed as part of the international terror network. Sharon's preposterous formulation, "Arafat is our bin Laden", was very much in keeping with his post-11 September worldview. What was more important was the fact that the US President fully concurred with the Israeli Prime Minister's viewpoint. Such convergence of perceptions resulted in a methodical attempt by both the US and Israel to isolate Arafat branding him as a "terrorist". India, being a close ally of Israel and more dependant on the US, could not raise its voice against such a trend.

Sharon's policies led to the systematic destruction of the fledgling PNA and with it the marginalization of the moderate sections within the Palestinian movement, led by Arafat, and the ascendancy of extremist forces represented by the *Hamas* and *IJ*. The spate of suicide bombings by these extremist forces and the disproportionately harsh Israeli military responses pushed the region into the brink of a disaster. What surprised the international community most was the treatment meted out to Arafat – the legitimately elected Palestinian President – from March 2002 onwards. India's response to Sharon's policies was marked by a strange ambivalence. Most of the times it remained "gravely concerned" about the deteriorating situation in the region, mildly opposed Arafat's confinement, expressed "concern about" Arafat's "health and well being", etc. This was despite the fact that Arafat had sent a special emissary (Hani-al-Hassan) to Prime Minister Vajpayee seeking India's "good office to restore normalcy in the region"[21]. Indeed, around this time the main Opposition party, the Congress, became critical of the Vajpayee government's tendency to depart from the "consensus" in India's foreign policy, particularly with regard to the Palestine issue[22]. A few months before Arafat was besieged in his Ramallah headquarters, India had given a clear indication of its subtle tilt towards Israel on the ideological plane when it refused to heed the Arab and Palestinian request to equate Zionism with racism in the "World Conference against Racism, Racial Discrimination, Xenophobia and Related Intolerance" in Durban (September 2001). Israel too had lobbied with India in this regard[23].

It was these factors which made Sharon's visit to India in September 2003 so controversial. The very fact that India could invite Sharon to pay a state visit spoke enough about India's commitment to the Palestine issue under the pressure of globalisation. India's gesture to Israel was a clear message to the Palestinians. During Sharon's visit, India's stand on the Palestine issue was marked by a certain degree of ambiguity. While Prime

Minister Vajpayee, in his press statements, maintained that there was no change in India's "principled stand" on the issue, neither his banquet speech (in honour of Sharon) nor the joint statement (the Delhi Statement on Friendship and Cooperation between India and Israel) mentioned India's support for the establishment of an independent Palestinian state. In both the cases, the government sought to take refuge in broad generalities like an end to "violence and restoration of peace", establishment of a "just and durable peace" in West Asia, etc. In fact Vajpayee adopted the same evasive tactic in an interview to the Israeli daily, *Ha'aretz,* on the eve of Sharon's visit. When confronted with a direct question about India's response to the Israeli policy of assassinating Palestinian leaders (particularly to kill the *Hamas* spiritual leader Sheikh Ahmed Yassin), he stated: "Violence does not contribute to anything".

However, on the issue of the relevance of Arafat in the peace process both the countries differed with India maintaining that it still considered him a "symbol" of Palestinian nationalism[24]. India reiterated its support for Arafat by "disapproving" the Israeli cabinet decision (taken a couple of days after Sharon returned to Tel Aviv) to "remove" the Palestinian president from his headquarters. Again in this case too, the government did not refer to the government of Israel directly and spoke in general terms[25]. The Congress and Left parties, however, condemned the Israeli government directly for its threat to expel or even kill Arafat[26]. The present Congress-led United Progressive Alliance Government, headed by Prime Minister Manmohan Singh, has taken no such steps to indicate that its Palestine policy is in anyway fundamentally different from the previous government. For instance, while participating in the Arab League Summit (Khartoum) in March 2006, the government made a broad, general and implied reference about the Palestine issue. The Prime Minister's message to the Summit read: "Arab issues occupy a prominent place in India's foreign policy priorities and India has extended principled and consistent support to causes dear to the Arab people"[27]. However, on the issue of the refusal by

Israel and Western governments to deal with the elected *Hamas* government, India became slightly forthright in finding fault with the approach. While urging Israel and other countries to deal with the *Hamas* government, it made a comparison between the Likud and *Hamas* before they came to power[28].

At the second level, India made conscious efforts to increase economic and commercial cooperation with the Palestinians since the establishment of the PNA in 1994. It needs to be mentioned that India had recognized the State of Palestine symbolically in response to the declaration of Independence by the PLO issued after the Algiers Palestine National Council (PNC) meet in 1988. In 1995 India first recognized the passport travel documents issued by the PNA. A year later (on June 24, 1996) India's representative office in the PNA administered area (Gaza city) was opened. The office was aimed at "further strengthening the close friendly relations" between India and the Palestinian people and to "promote, expand, and diversify these relations in economic, commercial, cultural, and other fields"[29]. On its part, the PNA sought India's help and cooperation in the fields of infrastructure and technology. In 1997, during President Arafat's visit to India, an MoU was signed between the two sided. It provided a "structured framework for bilateral cooperation" in various areas like commerce, trade, culture, science and technology, including collaboration, information and broadcasting, etc[30].

The following year in June 1998 two MoUs and Agreed Minutes for the implementation of two Indian-aided projects in Gaza Strip were signed. Further, India also pledged US$ 1 million at the International Donors Conference (held in Washington, D.C. on November 30, 1998) to help the Palestinian people[31]. In 2001, India gifted medicines and food supplies worth Rs. 75 lakh and hospital equipment worth Rs 1.40 crore approximately[32]. As regards bilateral trade it is estimated to be around US$ 18 to 20 million consisting primarily of one-way Indian exports[33]. Thus, subsequent to the establishment of the PNA, India conducted its relationship with it as between two governments. But the interaction remained at a low-key level. Arafat as president continued to visit India at regular intervals. From the Indian side so far there have been two high-level visits which included the then Home Minister Advani and External Affairs Minister Singh. They visited Gaza on June 17 and June 30, 2000, respectively. However, these visits were basically symbolic ones aimed at sending a message that India still valued its traditional ties with the Palestinians. It needs to be remembered that both the leaders had paid their high-profile visits to Israel during the same period. Most of the substantive transactions mentioned above were conducted during the visits of the external affairs ministry officials like Secretary (East) and Joint Secretary (West Asia and North Africa) from the Indian side to Gaza. This is not to deny the occasional visits of Ministers of State.

Thus, in the post-Cold War period, the compulsions of globalisation and the predominant role that the US plays in the process have probably forced India to dilute its earlier pronouncedly pro-Palestine policy. It needs to be emphasized that the Palestinians want India's political support more than anything else. That is not coming as forcefully and pro-actively as it used to be during the Cold-War period. Its policy of equidistance in the Israel-Palestine conflict has in no way resolved the Palestine issue. In fact, one would argue that now that India has a growing and deepening relationship with Israel, it should seek to impress upon the Israeli political class about the necessity of resolving the Palestine issue peacefully through negotiations. *Hamas* is merely an excuse, not the reason, for not resuming the peace talks. Peace and stability in the region, which is very crucial for India's own national interests, cannot be achieved without a just resolution of the Palestine issue.

Notes

1. Michael T. Klare, "The New Geography of Conflict", *Foreign Affairs,* vol. 80, no. 3, May-June 2001, p. 50.

2. Ramesh Thakur, "India after Nonalignment", *Foreign Affairs,* vol. 72, no. 3 (Spring) 1992, p. 167.

3. Ibid., p. 178.

4. Rao's Statement in the Parliament on 18 December 1991. See Lok Sabha Debates.

5. Thakur, "India after Nonalignment", p. 180.

6. Leibler openly admitted this in the press conference. See Bansidhar Pradhan, "Establishing Ties with Israel: Prudence or Pressure?", *Link*, vol. 34, no. 23, January 19, 1992, pp. 29-31. Also see *The Times of India,* 22 November 1991.

7. The Resolution was revoked on December 16, 1991. The fact remained that the mere revocation of Resolution 3379 had not changed the basic character of the State of Israel at that time. It would be interesting to note the observation of India's permanent representative at the UN, Rikhi Jaipal, in his statement explaining India's vote in favour of Resolution 3379 in 1975. He had stated then: "Zionism had deprived the Arab people of their national rights and of the right to self-determination. It is surely understandable that the victims of Zionism should regard it as a form of racial discrimination".

8. See *The Hindu*, January 22, 1992.

9. See Bansidhar Pradhan, "seeking Clarity in Arafat's Message", *Link*, vol. 34, no. 25, 02 February 1992, pp. 30-31. Also see the *Times of India*, 22 January 1992; *The Hindu*, January 22, 1992.

10. It is interesting to note that the announcement was made on the eve of Prime Minister Rao's departure for the UN Security Council Summit.

11. On the Zionist attempt to influence Nehru and Gandhi see G.H. Jansen, *Zionism, Israel and Asian Nationalism* (Beirut: The Institute for Palestine Studies, 1971). As regards the Zionist pressure on Mrs. Indira Gandhi and Rajiv Gandhi, it was one Greville Jannr who happened to be the President of the commonwealth Jewish Council. See *Patriot*, August 15, 1987.

12. For a detailed and critical assessment of these arguments see Bansidhar Pradhan, "India's Policy towards the PLO", in Riyaz Punjabi and A.K. Pasha, eds., *India and the Islamic World* (New Delhi: Radiant Publishers, 1998), pp. 75-83.

13. *The National Herald*, November 21, 1992.

14. See *Foreign Affairs Record* (Hereafter *FAR*), no. 9, September 1993, pp. 267-68.

15. This statement was issued during the visit of Arafat to New Delhi on 5 April 1997 to attend the NAM meet; see *FAR*, no. 4 (April) 1997, p. 59.

16. *FAR*, no. 10 (October) 1998, p. 150.

17. See *The Hindu*, August 25, 2000.

18. See *The Hindu*, December 23, 2000, p. 11; 14 October 2000; and 16 November 2000.

19. See *The Hindu*, November 30, 2000.

20. See *The Hindu*, October 15, 2000; and *The Times of India*, October 17, 2000 (Q and A with the Israeli Ambassador to India, David Aphek).

21. *FAR*, no. 4 (April) 2002, p. 60 and p. 64. Also see *The Hindu*, 4 April 2002, p. 1; Inder Malhotra, "Palestine: India Must Speak out", April 3, 2002, p. 12; Mushrul Hassan, "To Arafat, in anguish", April 9, 2002, p. 10.

22. With regard to the Arab-Israel conflict the AICC Resolution on foreign policy adopted in the third week of May 2002 stated: "Improvement in our relations with Israel cannot be at the cost of our traditional support for the legitimate rights of the people of Palestine.... India's growing relationship with Israel consciously nurtured by the NDA has unfortunately betrayed its conceptual and ideological inadequacy in the wake of the latest (second) *intifada*", cited in *The Hindu*, 27 May 2002, p. 12.

23. For details see *the Hindustan Times*, August 23, 2001; *The Hindu*, August 24, 2001; August 27, 2001; August 28, 2001; September 4, 2001; and September 9, 2001.

24. *The Times of India*, September 9, 2003, p. 9; *The Hindustan Times*, September 9, 2003 (p. 1 and p. 13); *The Hindustan times*, September 10, 2003, p. 1; *The Indian Express*, September 10, 2003; *The Hindu*, September 11, 2003, p. 1 and p. 11. For excerpts of Vajpayee's interview see *The Hindu*, September 10, 2003, p. 11.

25. See *The Hindu*, 14 September 2003, p. 9.

26. See *The Hindu*, 16 September 2003, p. 11.

27. *The Hindu*, 30 March 2006, p. 13.

28. *The Hindu*, 27 March 2006, p. 14.

29. See *FAR*, no. 6 (June) 1996, pp. 108-9. Sri T.S. Tirumurti, First Secretary, was appointed as the Acting Representative to the PNA. While welcoming the Indian decision, the PNA expressed the hope that India's support and solidarity to the peace process world finally lead to a comprehensive, just, and lasting peace. On the recognition of passport travel documents issued by the PNA, see *FAR*, no. 7 (July) 1995, p. 176.

30. See *Ministry of External Affairs Annual- Report*(Hereafter *MEA-AR*), 1997-98, p. 55.

31. See *MEA-AR*, 1998-99, p. 46. The two projects in Gaza related

to the construction of a Library at Al Azhar University and construction of a Library-cum-Activity Centre at Palestinian Technical College al-Deir El Balah. These were inaugurated by Jaswant Singh during his visit to Gaza on 30 June 2000.

32. *MEA-AR*, 2001-2002, p. 43.

33. *The Hindu*, 8 May 2000.

18

Palestinian-Israeli Peace Process in the 'New Middle East': Can India Have a Role to Play?

Sujata Ashwarya Cheema

Introduction

The Palestinian-Israeli conflict is one of the major issues of regional and international concern in contemporary times. Numerous attempts have been to find a viable and lasting solution to the conflict in particular and in the broader context of Arab-Israeli conflict. The peace process, or the efforts by concerned parties and external actors involved in the region, to achieve a lasting solution to this protracted conflict, has been a feature of international politics since the 1970s. The peace process, which received a strong impetus with the Oslo Accords, signed between the Palestinians and the Israelis in 1993, has collapsed for all practical purposes. Given the persistence and the intensification of violence and counter-violence between the parties and the failure of the parties to engage in a dialogue on contentious issues[1], chances of a lasting and viable peace is nowhere in the offing. The involvement of external players with divergent interests has further complicated the situation. The role of the United States, the sole superpower and one of the dominant players in region, has been central to the success and failure of the peace process. It is, in this context, that the American idea of the New Middle East, which was voiced by Secretary of State Condoleezza Rice, in the wake of the Israeli invasion of Lebanon in July 2006[2], acquires significance. This essay analyses the future of the peace process in the context of the New Middle East, as understood by the current US administration, and seeks to investigate India's role therein.

At the outset, it must be stated that the interests of the United States in the West Asian affairs in general and the Palestinian/Arab-Israeli issue in particular began since the aftermath of the World War II, when it emerged as the dominant global player in world politics with unprecedented wealth and power[3]. Oil was a commodity that the US needed to continue fuelling the exceptional growth of its economy and emerging global supremacy and hegemony. The US understood that "Whatever power controls the region has not only access to enormous wealth but also a very powerful global influence because control of energy resources is an extremely powerful lever in world affairs[4]." Hence West Asia became a realm of immense importance for the US. Ever since, "A high priority has been to assure that control over the world's cheapest and most abundant energy reserves is in US hands[5]." The basic principle of oil policy enunciated during World War II was that the United States, while maintaining its "absolute position" in the Western Hemisphere, must insists "upon the Open Door principle of equal opportunity for United States companies in new areas[6]." The deep involvement of the US in the region thus emerged from the core national interest of securing the oil realm[7]. This has remained the basic premise of the involvement of the United States in West Asia throughout the Cold War and in the post-Cold War periods.

In the post-cold war period, the hegemony of the US in the region has been threatened by growing indigenous nationalistic groups, imbued with Islamic principles. These groups have questioned its presence in the region, primarily, the control over oil resources, and support for Israel against the Palestinians. They also have the support of the Arab street and are in a position to threaten pro-American regimes in the region. The term, New Middle East, acquires pertinence in this context. President George Bush and the neoconservatives in the US administration have invoked this term in recent times in the context of creating a 'new' order in the West Asia deriving substance from the larger project of the New American Century, essentially based on the idea of extending American hegemony by force of arms across the globe, to safeguard pivotal economic and strategic interests. Therefore, regimes and groups hostile to the American interest have to be confronted and vanquished. The current US policy of "war against terrorism", which euphemistically means a strategy to silence those who question American dominance in the Arab-Islamic world is based on this crucial premise.

New American Century and New Middle East

. New American Century is an idea propagated by a Washington-based neo-conservative or neocon think tank, Project for the New American Century (PNAC), founded by William Kristol and Robert Kagan in 1997. PNAC was launched shortly after the publication of their article in Foreign Affairs journal entitled, *Toward a Neo-Reaganite Foreign Policy*[8], in which they called for Washington to exercise "benevolent global hegemony" to be sustained "as far into the future as possible". While critical of then President Bill Clinton's pacifist foreign policy, the article was directed more against a Republican Congress which, in their view, had grown increasingly isolationist, particularly after the US withdrawal from Somalia in 1994 and strong Republican opposition to intervention in the Balkans. It was in this spirit that the two co-founded PNAC, whose charter was signed by leading neo-conservatives, including Dick Cheney, Donald Rumsfeld, I. Lewis Libby, Paul Wolfowitz, Elliott Abrams, Zalmay Khalilzad, Peter Rodman, Richard Perle and others, who would later go on to chair significant posts in the Bush administration.

In its statement of principles posted on its website[9], the stated goal of PNAC is to "promote American global leadership" premised on the assumption that the "American leadership is both good for America and good for the world" and "a Reaganite policy of military strength and moral clarity" is imperative for safeguarding America's interests in the far off domains. The document begins by framing a series of questions, which the rest of the document proposes to answer: "As the 20th century draws close, the United States stands the world's pre-eminent power. Having led the West to victory in the Cold War, America faces an opportunity and a challenge: Does the United States have the wisdom to build upon the achievement of the past decades? Does the United States have the resolve to shape a new century favourable to American principles and interests? In response to these questions, the PNAC states its aim to "remind America" of "lessons" learned from American history, drawing the following "four consequences" for their country: "we need to increase defense spending significantly if we are to carry out our global responsibilities today and modernize our armed forces for the future; we need to strengthen our ties to democratic allies and to challenge regimes hostile to our interests and values; we need to promote the cause of political and economic freedom abroad; we need to accept responsibility for America's unique role in preserving and extending an international order friendly to our security, our prosperity, and our principles[10]."

A closer look at the stated aims and objectives of the PNAC reveals the idea that the United States, the last remaining superpower, by way of economic and military force, must to bring the rest of the world under the umbrella of a new socio-economic Pax Americana. The fundamental essence of PNAC's ideology can be found in a White Paper produced in September of 2000 entitled, *Rebuilding America's Defenses: Strategy, Forces and Resources for a New Century*[11]. Amongst other things, this paper said, the USA must rearm and build a missile shield in order to put itself in a position to fight numerous wars simultaneously and chart its own course. Whatever happened, the Gulf would have to be in US control: "The US has sought for years to play an ongoing role in the security architecture of the Gulf. The unresolved conflict with Iraq provides a clear basis for our presence, but quite independent of the issue of the Iraqi regime, a substantial US presence in the Gulf is needed[12]." The paper describes these US forces stationed overseas the "the Cavalry on the New American Frontier". Even peace efforts, the paper continues, should have the stamp of the USA rather than the UN.

Two events brought PNAC into the mainstream of American government: the election of George W. Bush, and attacks of

September 11, 2001. With Bush's presidency, the neoconservatives, who created and nurtured the imperial dreams of PNAC, became key figures in the Pentagon, the Defence Department and the White House. When the twin-tower was attacked, they found a chance to turn their White Papers into substantive policy. In a letter[13] sent to Bush on September 20, 2001, just nine days after the 9/11 attacks, the PNAC called for the ouster of the Taliban and war on al Qaeda. The letter also called for waging a broader and more ambitious "war on terrorism" that would include cutting off the Palestinian Authority under Yassir Arafat, taking on Hezbollah, threatening Syria and Iran and, most importantly, ousting Saddam Hussein regardless of his relationship to the attacks or al Qaeda. Seven months later, the PNAC issued another letter signed by many of the same people urging Bush to step up preparations for war with Iraq, sever all ties to the Palestinian Authority under Arafat and give full backing to Israeli Prime Minister Ariel Sharon's efforts to crush the Palestinian intifada. "Israel's fight against terrorism is our fight. Israel's victory is an important part of our victory," the letter noted. "For reasons both moral and strategic, we need to stand with Israel in its fight against terrorism[14]." Bush acted in accordance with the terms of the letter two months later.

The neocons along with the Israel lobby, whose vast influence in the US administration, has been brought out eloquently by professors John Mearsheimer and Stephen Walt, advanced the idea of conjunction between American and Israeli interests[15]. Israel had to be armed and protected, its strategic situation improved, to be able to advance war on 'terror'. After 9/11, "US support has been justified by the claim that both states are threatened by terrorist groups originating in the Arab and Muslim world, and by 'rogue states' that back these groups and seek weapons of mass destruction. This is taken to mean not only that Washington should give Israel a free hand in dealing with the Palestinians and not press it to make concessions until all Palestinian terrorists are imprisoned or dead, but that the US should go after countries like Iran and Syria. Israel is thus seen as a crucial ally in the war on terror, because its enemies are America's enemies[16]." Thus, Washington's gave Israel unequivocal support, when the latter attacked Lebanon in July 2006. In fact, reports say that the war was the result of the pressure exerted on Olmert by the Bush administration (staffed by the neocons and the influenced by the Lobby), which had long been pushing the Israelis to launch a war on Lebanon to cripple Hezbollah[17].

However, the Hizbullah was neither destroyed nor crippled after the Lebanon War; it emerged even more confident enjoying greater support from the Lebanese people. Iran and Syria are far from being cowed down by threats emanating from Washington or Tel Aviv. The neocons' war in Iraq has gone awry with the country in the vortex of a civil war. Because of these reasons, Richard Haass write that the American era in the West Asia is over. "It was the Iraq war – the enormous military, economic and diplomatic costs, the shifting internal balances in the region – that brought to an end. Other factors contributed: the demise of the 'peace process,' the rise of Hamas and Hizbullah, the Israeli embrace of unilateralism and the disinclination of George W. Bush and his administration to undertake active diplomacy[18]." The New Middle East, then, is a region of considerable but diminished US influence, rise of Iran, proliferation of militias, Islamic assertion, and terrorism among others, according to Haass. It can be surmised that the New Middle East is a region in flux, where America's hegemony has been challenged by regional players. It is not region of absolute dominance of the United States which the neocons had imagined in their PNAC.

Peace Process in the New Middle East

The first Bush administration, with neocons at the helm of affairs[19], was preoccupied with Iraq. The administration was beset by a number of public disagreements over such issues as whether to strengthen sanctions against Iraq or whether to take a more aggressive military stance against Iraq. In addition the Bush administration had to deal with a significant degree of optimism in the Arab world, and especially among Palestinians, that Bush, following the steps of his father, who had then clashed openly with then Israeli Prime Minister Yitzhak Shamir, as well as Sharon, would take a much tougher stance toward Israel than Clinton had done. In this they were greatly mistaken. The neoconservative nature of the Bush administration ensured that the Israeli actions in the Occupied Territories and towards the Palestinian population were condoned.

To begin with Bush followed essentially 'hands off' policy and refused to get involved in trying to settle the conflict. Secretary of State Colin Powell repeatedly emphasized the primary responsibility of the parties themselves to resolve the conflict. "We will facilitate, but at the end of the day, it will have to be the parties in the region who will find the solution[20]." This was the reason why, when the special envoy to West Asia, Dennis Ross, retired in January 2001, no replacement was named, and it was not until late May, with the Israeli-Palestinian conflict rapidly escalating that a 'Special Assistant' William Burns was appointed. Secondly, Bush did not send a representative to the Israeli-Palestinian negotiations at Taba which took place at the end of January, just before the February 7, 2001 elections. Finally, Bush supported the Israeli position that the offers made by Israel at Camp David II and Taba, were "off the table" once the new Israeli government headed by Likud leader Ariel Sharon, was elected on February 7, 2001.

Despite the efforts made by the US administration to dissociate itself from the Arab-Israeli conflict, in his first official visit to the West Asia, Colin Powell, called for a renewal of peace talks after a reduction in violence – not the total cessation of violence – demanded by Sharon. However, Powell moved closer to the Israeli position soon after. On the eve of the Sharon visit to Washington in mid-March, Powell gave a major speech on the West Asia to a conference AIPAC, the most important Jewish lobby. Here, he supported Sharon's position on the violence, noting that the starting point for talks had to be the end of violence. In a clear indictment of Arafat, Powell stated that "leaders have the responsibility to denounce violence, strip it of legitimacy and stop it[21]." When Sharon met with Bush several days later, he was again reassured that the US would facilitate, not force the peace process. Sharon, for his part pressed Bush not to invite Arafat to the White House unless he publicly called for an end to the violence, a request endorsed by nearly 300 members of Republican Congress under the influence of the neocons and the Lobby. It is important to note that on the eve of the visit, Sharon had authorized the construction of more Jewish housing in the East Jerusalem suburb of Har Homa, near Bethlehem, a development that was termed by the State Department spokesman, Richard Boucher, merely as a unilateral act "not contributing to peace and stability"[22].

At the end of March, the US vetoed a UN Security Council resolution calling for an UN Observer force on the West Bank and Gaza as unbalanced and unworkable. Following Sharon's visit to Washington, the intifada escalated. Israeli forces invaded Gaza and captured it. Powell mildly reprimanded Israeli for "excessive and disproportionate" use of force and at the same time he also blamed the Palestinians for precipitating the Israeli attack with "provocative" mortar attacks on Israeli territory. As the fighting escalated further, mortar attacks by Palestinians was met with increasingly severe Israeli reprisals, including the use, for the first time, of Israeli jet fighters to bombard Palestinian positions, and targeted killing of Palestinian leaders. In the meanwhile, Sharon also pressed ahead with expansion of settlements, claiming that the West Bank and Gaza were not "occupied" but "disputed territory". While during their visits to Washington in late March and early April, the Egyptian President, Hosni Mubarak, and the Jordanian King, Abdallah ibn Hussein, called for a more active US role, the Bush Administration continued to insist that the Israelis and Palestinians had to bear the primary responsibility for coming to an agreement. This was to change after the attacks on the World Trade Centre and the Pentagon on September 11, 2001.

In the five weeks since the terrorist attacks on the World Trade Centre and the Pentagon, the U.S. changed its 'hands off' policy toward the Israeli-Palestinian conflict and sought to build Arab support against Arab states against Osama Bin Laden and al-Qaeda. Thus the Bush administration announced its support for a Palestinian state and exercised pressure on Sharon to agree to a meeting between Israeli Foreign Minister Shimon Peres and Arafat to establish yet another cease-fire. This development was not to the Lobby's liking; it immediately jumped into the fray to persuade the administration that the United States and the only democracy in the region, Israel, faced a common threat from terrorism. The Israeli officials and the Lobby painted Arafat and Osama bin Laden with the same brush, asserting that they were both terrorists. They insisted that the United States and Israel should isolate the Palestinian leader and should not negotiate with him on any account.

By the year's end, the efforts of the Lobby and change in international situation had an effect on Washington's attitude toward the Palestinians. America's war in Afghanistan against the Taliban and al-Qaida was bearing fruit; the NATO forces were able to wrest significant victories. This reduced the perceived need for a coalition of Arab support in dealing with the terrorist threat. Sharon again visited the White House in early December and he was assured to US support. When the IDF launched Operation Defensive Shield in April 2002 and captured the Palestinian areas in the West Bank, the Bush administration was in a quandary. Since 9/11, America had been trying to build a positive image in the Islamic world. Given the sensitive nature of the Palestinian issue, the Israeli action could damage America's image and undermine the war on terrorism. Therefore, President Bush demanded that Sharon "halt the incursions and begin withdrawal". He underscored this message two days later, saying he wanted Israel to "withdraw without delay". On 7 April, Condoleezza Rice, then Bush's national security adviser, told reporters: "Without delay" means without delay, It means now[23]." That same day Colin Powell set out for West Asia to persuade all sides to stop fighting and start negotiating. The Israel lobby along with the neocons in the vice-president's office and the Pentagon, as well as neo-conservative authorities like Robert Kagan and William Kristol, turned the heat on President Bush, and he gave in. A week later, the White House press secretary said that the president believed Sharon was 'a man of peace', a statement Bush repeated on Powell's return from his failed mission.

The Bush administration, henceforth, refused to deal with Arafat. After his death, it supported Mahmoud Abbas, but this did not translate in terms of meeting the Palestinian demand for a state in West Bank and Gaza. The US administration supported the Sharon's plan of imposing a unilateral settlement on the Palestinians, based on 'disengagement' from Gaza coupled with continued expansion on the West Bank. By refusing to negotiate with Abbas on the status of the West Bank and other core issues leading to Palestinian statehood, Sharon's strategy contributed directly to Hamas's electoral victory in the legislative election in January 2006. With Hamas at the helm of affairs on the Palestinian side, Israel had another pretext not entering into any negotiation. The US administration supported Sharon's actions and went on to approve those of his successor, Ehud Olmert. Bush has even endorsed unilateral Israeli annexations in the Occupied Territories, calling settlements as "facts on ground[24]" reversing the stated US policy since 1967.

The noecon and Lobby have effectively sabotaged all efforts towards Palestinian-Israeli peace, but this is not all that they want. Their larger aim is to maintain Israel's dominance in the region and have worked towards shaping the administration's policy towards Iraq, Syria and Iran, as a grand scheme for reordering the region. Extending American hegemony by force of arms across the globe and ensuring Israel supremacy are pivotal to their agenda in West Asia. Within this imperial agenda, the demands and plight of the Palestinians are insignificant. The Palestinians, shorn of wealth and power are "insignificant people" experiencing "delusion of significance",[25] to paraphrase influential neoconservative intellectual Irving Kristol. Palestinians are not only "insignificant people" but are much worse, because they get in the way of the arrangements devised by world's most "significant people": Americans and Israeli Jews. The Israeli Arabists had predicted in 1948 that the Palestinians would either assimilate in other countries or "would be crushed" and "die[26]." If current American-Israeli plans succeed, these predictions may be fulfilled soon.

Does India have a Role to Play?

India has extended strong political and moral support to the Palestinian cause at international and bilateral levels, since 1948. In post-1947 period, independent India took a principled stand on Palestine. While she recognised Israel as a state in the comity of nations, India also recognised the rights of Palestinians to self-determination, as of other peoples struggling against imperialism and for freedom. This was also the reason why India refused to develop full-fledged diplomatic relations with Israel. It was part of anti-colonial, anti-imperialist vision of India's first Prime Minister Jawaharlal Nehru's foreign policy. With the inauguration of the Oslo process, New Delhi established diplomatic relations with Israel without abandoning support for Palestinian statehood.

Despite its consistent support for the Palestinian cause and later normalization of relations with Israel, India has not been able to play any role in the peace process. This is a reflection of the international balance of power. During the Cold War years, the West Asia was the arena of superpower politics, of political alignments and realignments, being played out by the United States and the then Soviet Union. The Arab-Israeli conflict and the peace initiatives too were mired by superpower competition, though a stalemate in the October 1973 war, paved the way for "ambitious diplomacy, including the Egyptian-Israeli peace accord"[27]. During this period, India still emerging from her colonial past and saddled with the task of development remained at the diplomatic margins as far as the peace initiatives were concerned. However, India was an active player in the United Nations voicing support for the recognition of Palestinian rights. During the Arab-Israeli War of 1973, India supported the Arabs and blamed the Israel for the existence of conflict in the region.

India endorsed the PLO'S bid for observer status to the UN in 1974 and became the first Arab country to extend formal diplomatic accreditation to the PLO representative. India joined the Arab countries in cosponsoring the UN General Assembly Resolution 3379, which equated Zionism with racism. The basic reason behind India's support for the cause of Palestinian Arabs has been the anti-colonial character of the movement, which had been the principle of India's own struggle for independence.

The Oslo accords gave many governments, including India, the necessary 'rationale' to establish full diplomatic relations with Israel[28]. At this time, India too, wanted to be involved in the peace process. India believed that "using quiet and unobtrusive diplomacy" she could, "smoothen the bumpy and halting transition of the occupied West Bank and Gaza to full Palestinian statehood[29]." However, India remained a marginal player, as the peace agreements were implemented and later when they fell through. This, of course, was not a reflection of the inability of India to play a role at a decisive moment in the region. It were the parties, who considered United States as the sole guarantor of the peace process, and therefore, even the European countries, with significant economic ties with the countries of the region, were marginalised when the Accords were signed and implemented. With the neocon agenda of establishing total hegemony in the region and the Lobby working overtime to ensure that Israel is not pressurised to negotiate with the Palestinians, the fate of peace process itself, is under question. In this scenario, the role of India in the peace process in the New Middle East is insignificant.

Further, over the last two years, India has sought close relations with the United States, especially in the area of nuclear cooperation. Therefore, India is hardly in a position to deviate from the line of the US in West Asia. "Neocons do no see a role for India in their plan of the New American Century and the New Middle East... [they] would like India to fall in line and not obstruct their agenda in West Asia; the attitude of linking up civilian nuclear deal with vote on Iran is suggestive of this intent. The invitation to India to join the main table emanates out of it[30]."

Unlike the Cold War, when India could freely voice her opinion on the Palestinian-Israeli issue, the recent years have evoked little response from her. "India in the post Cold War order is looking for a place in the global hierarchy by incrementally endorsing the dynamics of a unipolar world...Its emerging relation with the USA ... is certainly pointer to the fact that the Indian state has recognised and accepted the necessity of sharing the global and regional concern as perceived and articulated by the American state[31]."

Conclusion

The neocon project of the New Middle East is based on military power projection to establish the supreme dominance of the United States. It is a project to build an empire, comprising of regional client states who service the empire with local resources. The actions of the neocons and the Lobby have ensured that Israel continues to grab Palestinian territories by direct aggression or through settlements. It is no coincidence that official peace talks between Palestinians and Israelis have been virtually non-existent. The future of the peace process is bleak, indeed, given the nature of forces at work. The Palestinian people continue to suffer, their chances of statehood, in good measure, been retarded by forces beyond their control. India's moral and political support had once been a recognised as a great source of strength for the Palestinians. This is not the case anymore. India has accepted the junior position for herself in the unipolar world order, under the rhetoric of national self-interest. Thus, her ability to act autonomously on issues of regional and international concern has been greatly reduced.

Notes

1. The Declaration of Principles (DOP) or the Oslo Accords signed by Israeli Prime Minister Yitzhak Rabin and Palestine Liberation Organisation (PLO) Chairman Yasir Arafat on September 13, 1993, consisted of a two-phase timetable. First was a five-year 'interim' or 'transitional' period during which time Israel would incrementally withdraw from Palestinian areas in the West Bank and Gaza Strip,

transferring administrative powers to a soon-to-be elected Palestinian Authority. Second was the 'permanent' or 'final status' negotiations, to begin at the start of the third year of the interim period. As written in the text of the DOP, it was understood that these negotiations shall cover remaining issues, including: the status of Jerusalem, the right to return of Palestinian refugees, Israeli settlements in West Bank and Gaza, security arrangements, final borders of the two resultant states, relations and cooperation with other neighbours, and other issues of common interest. See the text of the Oslo Declaration of Principles on website http://www.mideastweb.org/meoslodop.htm (Accessed 12 May 2007).

2. The U.S. State Department; Secretary of State Condoleezza Rice; Special Briefing on the Travel to the Middle East and Europe of Secretary Condoleezza Rice, Washington, DC. July 21, 2006. Retrieved from http://www.state.gov/secretary/rm/2006/69331.htm (Accessed on 12 May 2007)

3. Abbas Amanat (ed.), *The United-States and the Middle East: Diplomatic and Economic Relations in Historical Perspective* (New-Haven: The Yale Center for International and Area Studies, 1999)

4. See Noam Chomsky, "The Peace Process in Global Strategy" in *Middle East Illusions* (New Delhi: Penguin, 2003), p. 164.

5. Ibid, p. 168

6. US Department of State, "Petroleum Policy of the United States (1944)", quoted in ibid., 160.

7. See Edward W. Chester, *United States Oil Policy and Diplomacy: A Twentieth-Century Overview* (Oxford: Greenwood Press, 1983).

8. William Kristol and Robert Kagan, "Towards a Neo-Raeganite Foreign Policy", *Foreign Affairs*, July/August 1996. Reprinted on website http://www.carnegieendowment.org/publications/index.cfm?fa=view&id=276 (Accessed on 14 May 2007)

9. Project for the New American Century, "Statement of Principles", retrieved from website http://www.newamericancentury.org/statementofprinciples.htm 3 June 1997. (Accessed on 14 May 2007)

10. Ibid.

11. *Rebuilding America's Defenses: Strategy, Forces and Resources for a New Century, A Report of the Project of the New American Century.* http://www.newamericancentury.org/RebuildingAmericasDefenses.pdf (Undated). (Accessed on 14 May 2007)

12. Ibid.

13. Full text of the letter is available on the website http://www.newamericancentury.org/Bushletter.htm Dated 20 September 2001 (Accessed on 14 May 2007)

14. See full text of the letter on website http://www.newamericancentury.org/Bushletter-040302.htm (3 April, 2002) (Accessed on 14 May 2007).

15. John Mearsheimer, political science professor at the University of Chicago, and Stephen Walt, academic dean of the Kennedy School of Government at Harvard University, in a working paper, *The Israel Lobby and U.S. Foreign Policy* written by in 2006, state that that the United States has been willing to set aside its own security in order to advance the interests of another state (Israel). Further, U.S. Middle East policy is driven primarily by the "Israel Lobby", defined as a "loose coalition of individuals and organizations who actively work to steer US foreign policy in a pro-Israel direction." The core of the Lobby is the American Israel Public Affairs Committee (AIPAC). The Lobby also includes prominent Christian evangelicals like Gary Bauer, Jerry Falwell, Ralph Reed and Pat Robertson. In addition, the Lobby's membership includes neoconservative such as John Bolton, Robert Bartley, former Secretary of Education William Bennett, former U.N. Ambassador Jeanne Kirkpatrick, and columnist George Will. AIPAC and the Conference of Presidents of Major American Jewish Organizations, are run by hardliners who generally support the Likud Party's expansionist policies, including its hostility to the Oslo Peace Process. The Lobby consults Israel on policy issues. The Lobby also has significant leverage over the Executive branch. That power derives in part from the influence Jewish voters have on presidential elections. See For full text of the article see website ksgnotes1.harvard.edu/Research/wpaper.nsf/rwp/RWP06-011 - 13k (13 March 2006). Accessed on 14 May 2007.

16. Ibid.

17. Stephen Zunes, "U.S. Role in Lebanon Debacle" on website http://www.worldpress.org/Mideast/2802.cfm (25 May 2007). Accessed on 14 May 2007

18. Richard Haass, "The New Middle East," on website http://www.msnbc.msn.com/id/16408291/site/newsweek/ (8 January 2007). Accessed on 14 May 2007

19. The situation is even more pronounced in the Bush administration, whose ranks have included such fervent advocates of the

Israeli cause as Elliot Abrams, John Bolton, Douglas Feith, I. Lewis ('Scooter') Libby, Richard Perle, Paul Wolfowitz and David Wurmser. Op. cit Mearsheimer and Walt.

20. Dana Milbank, "Powell vows US will match foes," *Washington Post*, 17 December 2000. Quoted on http://www.jcpa.org/jl/vp516.htm

21. Roula Khalaf, "Powell sets out Bush line on Middle East", *Financial Times*, 20 March 2001. Quoted on http://www.jcpa.org/jl/vp516.htm

22. Alan Sipress, "Bush assures Sharon on US role in talks", *Washington Post*, 21 March, 2001. Quoted on http://meria.idc.ac.il/journal/2005/issue1/jv9no1a4.html

23. Paul d'Amato and Anthony Arnove, "Lies, Damned Lies and Israeli Propaganda," *International Socialist Review* Issue 23, May-June 2002.

Quoted on

http://www.isreview.org/issues/23/lies_damned_lies.shtml (Accessed on 14 May 2007)

24. "Bush Letter to Sharon Recognizes 'Facts on the Ground' ", Settlement Report, Vol. 14, No. 3, May-June 2004. Retrieved from website http://www.fmep.org/reports/vol14/no3/04-bush_letter.html (14 April 2004). Accessed on 14 May 2007

25. Irving Kristol, *Wall Street Journal*, 13 December 1973. Quoted in op. cit. Chomsky, p. 171

26. Avi Shlaim, *Collusion across Jordan* (New York: Columbia University Press, 1988), p. 491. Quoted in ibid., p. 197.

27. Richard Haass, "The New Middle East", *Foreign Affairs*, November/December 2006. Retrieved from Website http://www.foreignaffairs.org/20061101faessay85601/richard-n-haass/the-new-middle-east.html?mode=... Accessed on 4 May 2007.

28. John Cherian, "A Breach of Trust", *Frontline*, vol. 21, issue 25, Dec 04-15, 2004. Retrieved from website http://www.hinduonnet.com/fline/fl2125/stories/20041217000405900.htm Accessed on 4 May 2007.

29. M.S. Agwani, "India and West Asia," *World Focus*, vol. 15, nos. 11&12, Nov-Dec 1994, p. 65.

30. Girijesh Pant, "Imagining West Asia Beyond Neocon Construct", in the paper presented at the national Seminar on West Asia

31. Ibid.

Index

Index

A
Abbasids in Baghdad (1258), 133
Abdel Aziz Bouteflika, 235
Abdullah Madani, 78
Abu Bakr, 147
Abu Zohra, 129
Afro-Arab and Asian Cooperation, 224
Ahmed Aboul Gheit, 149
Al Qalqashandi, 129
Algiers Palestine National Council (PNC), 298
Ali Abdel Gadir Ali, 5
Al-Rajhi Bank, Oman Polypropylene, 63
Amnesty International Report of June 2001, 96
Amre Moussa, 149
Anti-Colonial Movement, 220
Anwer Sadaat, 112
Arab Fund for Economic Development Abdlatif Al-Hamad, 5
Arab Maghreb Union (AMU), 231
Arab-Africa of Post-Cold War, 222
Asia Energy Grid, 34
Asia Security Summit Singapore, 821
Asian Development Bank, 37
Asian Oil Market Conference 67

B
Babri Masjid's demolition in 1992, 206
Baghdad Pact, 110
Baker Plan, 233
Baku-Tblisi-Ceyhan (BTC) pipeline, 34
Bengalis vis-à-vis Bangladesh policy, 281
Bill Clinton, 39
Black Sea Fleet, 35
Boutros Boutros Ghali, 149

C
C.D. Deshmukh, 147
Community Development Associations, 255
Concentrates on Capturing Neo-Liberal Mechanisms, 26
Condoleezza Rice, 40
Conference for Cooperation, 140
Congressional Research Services on Western Sahara, 234
Congress-led Progressive Alliance Government, 297

Contemporary structural constraints for foreign policy, 25
Crown Prince Abdullah, 80
Cultural Exchange Program [CEP], 148

D
D'Arcy Exploration Company, 167
Department of Economic Analysis, 173
Dubai Chamber of Commerce and Industry (DCCI), 59, 66
Dubai Holding, 63
Dubai Internet City (DIC), 65

E
El Gran Gasoducto del Sur, 35, 36
Emaar Properties PJSC, 64
Emaar-MGF Land Private Limited, 64
Energy Information Administration, 34
Energy Information Administration's, International Energy Outlook 2006, (EIA IEO 2006), 43
European Union and the NATO alliance, 101
Exclusive Economic Zone (EEZ), 37

F
Federation of Indian Chambers of Commerce and Industry (FICCI), 66
Foreign Affairs Committee, 40
Foreign Operations Appropriation Act, 2006, 236
Free Trade Agreement (FTA), 59, 60, 118
Future of Culture in Egypt, 147

G
Gamaal Abdul Nasser, 112
Geopolitics of Transnational Gas Pipelines, 41
George W Bush, 34
Girijesh Pant, 30
Global Indian Diaspora, 163
Great Gas Pipeline of the South, 36
Gujarat State Petroleum Corporation (GSPC), 224
Gulf Cooperation Council (GCC), 71, 117

H
Hamas and Islamic Jihad (IJ), 292
HAMAS victory in the elections held in the Palestinian Area, 103
High Level Committee

Report on the Indian Diaspora (2001), 181
Hindu right vis-à-vis its Nepalese policy, 281
Hu Jintao, 85
Hugo Chavez, 36
Human Development Report 1998, 261
Human Development Reports, 263

I

ILO Report 1993, 260
India Friendship Association (EIFA), 151
India's anti-Israeli policy, 289
India's Arab-African foreign policy, 223
India's foreign policy, 29, 208
India's Palestine policy, 109
India's policy towards West Asia, 25
India's Ties with Arab-Africa, 222
India's Withdrawal of Recognition of SADR, 234
Indian and National Movement, 282
Indian Council of Social Science Research, 152
Indian External Affairs Ministry, 231
Indian Foreign Policy towards West Asia, 23
Indian Foreign Policy, 108
Indian Institute of Management-Ahmedabad (IIM-A), 63
Indian International Film Academy (IIIFA), 66
Indian National Congress [INC], 139
Indian occupied territory, 114
Indian Oil Corporation Ltd. and Bharat Petroleum Corporation Ltd., 69
Indian Technical and Economic Cooperation (ITEC), 150
India-West Asia relations, 30
Indo-Iran and Indo-Turkmenistan gas pipelines projects, 119
Indo-Yemeni trade, 166
Infant Mortality Rate, 257
International Atomic Energy Agency, 41
International Islamic Finance Corporation (IIFC), 56
International Monetary Fund (IMF), 289
International Oil Companies (IOC), 68
Internationalisation and Domestic Politics, 3

Iran and Libya Sanctions Act (ILSA), 39
Iran Counter-Proliferation Act, 40
Iran-Pakistan-India Gas Pipeline, 37
Iran-Pakistan-India pipeline, 35
Islamic Chambers of Commerce and Industry, 56
Islamic Development Bank (IBD), 56
Islamic Salvation Front (FIS), 228
Israeli-Anglo-French aggression on Egypt, 193

J

Jamaat-e-Islami and Jamiat Ulema-e Islam, 113
Jaswant Singh, 37
Joint Counter-terrorism, 205

K

K Natwar Singh, 38
K.N. Chaudhri, 131
K.N. Raj, 147
K.R. Singh, 29
Kashmiris vis-à-vis Pakistan Policy, 281
Kenneth Waltz, 15
Kofi Annan, 221

L

Larsen & Toubro Limited (L&T), 62
Legitimation or Justification, 11
Liberation of Saqiat al Hamra and Rio de Oro (Polisario), 227
Liquefied Natural Gas (LNG), 68
Look East Policy, 120

M

M. H. Al-Shaya, 63
M.K. Narayanan, 81
Madhvendra Singh, 83
Mahmud Fawzy, 148
Mani Shankar Aiyar, 40
Manmohan Singh, 81
Maqbool Ali Sultan, 64
Middle East Defence Organization, 141
Miler Commission, 145
Ministry of External Affairs, 29
Ministry of Overseas Indian Affairs (MOIA), 182
Mohaderat Fi Muqarinat al Adyan, 134
Mohammed Hussein Heykal, 147
Multi-Partyism (1976), 248

N

Nabila Al-Bassam, 66
National Democratic Party,

249
National Liberation Front (FLN), 229
National Sample Survey, 258
Neo-Conservative Foreign Policy, 101
Neo-liberal Globalism and India's Foreign Policy, 28
Neo-liberal Globalist Transformations and Nation-State, 26
Neo-liberal globalization, 27
Non-Alignment Movement (NAM), 193, 228, 287
Non-Resident Indian Deposits (NRDs), 173

O

Oil & Gas Journal, 43
Oman-India Fertiliser Company (Omifco), 64
ONGC Videsh Limited (OVL), 38
Open Door policy, 93
Orange Revolution, 36
Organisation of Petroleum Exporting Countries (OPEC), 34
Organization of African Unity (OAU), 231
Organization of Islamic Conference (OIC), 56, 232
Osama bin Laden, 46

P

P.V. Narasimha Rao, 232
Pakistani Exclusive Economic Zone, 37
Palestine Liberation Organization (PLO), 286
Pan-Arab Nationalist Leaders, 109
Pan-Arab nationalist Movement, 111
Policy of the Reserve Bank of India, 173
Polisario Front of Western Saharawi, 221
Pressler Amendment, 95
Price Waterhouse Coopers and the Dubai-based Moutamarat group, 55
Pro-Israeli Lobby, 66
Project for the New American Century (PNAC), 305
Pro-Palestinian policy, 105
Prophet Mohammad, 56
Public Relations Campaign (PRC), 189

R

Realism and National Interest, 10
Rebuilding America's Defenses: Strategy, Forces and Resources for a New Century, 306
Report of Indira Gandhi Institute of Development

Research 1999-00, 258
Roots of Muslim Rage, 101
Royal Commissions, 145

S
S. Radhakrishnan, 146
S.M.H. Adeli, 38
Sahrawi Arab Democratic Republic (SADR), 227, 230
Samuel Bodman, 40
Sardar Swaran Singh, 143
Saud Al-Faisal, 80
Second World War, 140
Shimla and Lahore Agreements, 76
Shyam Saran, 38
Simon Commission in India, 145
Social Capital and Social Development, 252
Special Commonwealth African Assistance Programme (SCAAP), 222
Stephen G Rademaker, 40
Structural Adjustment Programme (SAP) Agreement, 243

T
The Shield of Achilles, 4
The Two Key Aims of Indian Foreign Policy since 1991, 19
Third World solidarity and anti-imperialism, 2273
Thomas Barnett, 3
Toward a Neo-Reaganite Foreign Policy, 305
Trans-Afghan Gas Pipeline (TAGP), 34
Turkmenistan-Russia-Ukraine Gasgrid, 35
Turkmenistan-Russia-Ukraine pipeline, 35
Twin-Pillar Policy, 79

U
Ukraine-Russia-Turkmen Gas pipeline, 35
UN General Assembly Resolution 3379, 314
UN Security Council Resolution 1675 of April, 2006, 233
UN Security Council Resolution 690 (April 29, 1991), 233
UN Security Council Resolution, 238, 310
UN Transition Assistance Group in Namibia, 225
United Nations Emergency Force (UNEF), 207
United Nations Mission for the Organization of a Referendum in the Western Sahara (MINURSO), 233
UNSC Resolution, 238
US Hegemony in WANA

Region, 98

W

Wafd Party Mustafa El-Nahhas, 191
Wahabite Islamic rule in Arabia, 113
Wataniya Telecom, 63
West Asian and North African Region, (WANA), 60
Western Defense System, 109
Westerns Nations interests, 107
William Kristol and Robert Kagan, 305
William R. Thompson, 98
World Conference against Racism, Racial Discrimination, Xenophobia and Related Intolerance, 296
World Development Report 2000, 256
World Development Report 2002, 259
World Economic Forum, 59
World Food Programme (WFP), 227
World Trade Organisation, 27

Z

Zionist demand for Jewish National Home in Palestine, 109